$3
Make-and-Take
Meals

$3
Make-and-Take
Meals

Delicious, Low-Cost Dishes for Picnics,
Potlucks, and Brown-Bagging It

Ellen Brown

LYONS PRESS
Guilford, Connecticut
An imprint of Globe Pequot Press

Lyons Press is an imprint of Globe Pequot Press.

Text design: Sheryl P. Kober
Project editor: Julie Marsh
Layout artist: Melissa Evarts

Library of Congress Cataloging-in-Publication Data

Brown, Ellen.
  $3 make-and-take meals : delicious, low-cost dishes for picnics, potlucks, and brown-bagging it / Ellen Brown.
      p. cm.
  ISBN 978-1-59921-931-8
  1. Quick and easy cookery. 2. Low budget cookery. I. Title. II. Title: Three dollar make-and-take meals.
  TX833.5.B737 2010
  641.5'52—dc22

2009048850

Printed in the United States of America

10 9 8 7 6 5 4 3 2 1

Contents

This chapter is your recipe to eating better for less money. Here are all the tips you need to stretch your food budget, such as using coupons, shopping sales, and shopping your own pantry.

Food safety is a reason for concern when foods are transported farther than from the kitchen stove to the dining room table. You'll learn how to prevent food-borne illness, plus get some basic recipes for stocks and roasts that are used in other chapters.

Finger foods can be as simple as a homey deviled egg or as exotic as innovative variations on sushi, but finger foods of all categories are great for picnics, lunches, and parties. And all these treats are less than $1 per serving.

Millions more Americans are toting lunch to the office these days, both to save money and to control what they eat. The recipes in this chapter will add some light and hearty soups, delicate Asian summer rolls, and sturdy wrap sandwiches to your repertoire.

The recipes in this chapter—drawn from many of the world's great cuisines—are all intended for al fresco dining. While most are chilled, there are also some entree salads and other dishes that can be brought hot to the picnic site or served at room temperature.

Chapter 6: Supporting Players   122

Here is a cornucopia of wonderful and varied side dishes to bring to either a picnic or a potluck meal. Some are simple and others are more complex, but they're all easy to make and delicious.

Chapter 7: The Casserole Connection   151

The hot "covered dish" is traditionally the centerpiece for a potluck meal, and this chapter contains a wide array of options, from some American classics to international favorites. All of the dishes can be doubled for a big group, too.

Chapter 8: Exciting Hot Hors d'Oeuvres   179

It's common for hosts to ask their guests to bring pre-dinner snacks, lumped under the term *hors d'oeuvres,* to a meal because that portion of the evening is separate from the meal that follows. Here are inexpensive recipes that will wow.

Chapter 9: Desserts for Delivery   204

Diners always look forward to the sweet finale to a meal. This chapter offers tantalizing cake and cookie recipes, specifically chosen to transport beautifully and easily. Many include healthful fresh fruits, too.

Chapter 10: Putting It All Together   237

There are no recipes in this chapter, but it's one you may consult many more times than you'll cook an individual dish. It gives you pointers on menu planning, as well as specific menus created from the dishes in this book.

Preface

What would the Fourth of July be without a picnic? Or a gridiron rivalry without some tailgate revelry? And what about the festive potluck suppers that have spawned hearty meals in church basements and neighborhood centers for generations? Traditionally Americans have brought food to special gatherings to share with others, to raise money for an honored cause, or to celebrate and sanctify their meetings.

But today new occasions are joining this time-honored mix of cookahead and bring-along meals, and on a daily basis at that. The skyrocketing cost of food, when joined with Americans' desire to exercise control over what they eat as well as to save money, has increased the numbers of people toting lunch into the millions. Many of these meals can go beyond the "brown bag" because offices now supply both refrigerators to preserve food and microwave ovens to heat it.

Added to the number of people packing lunches for work are the many thousands more who anticipate food needs while traveling. After decades of criticism of the quality of the offerings served thousands of feet aloft, it's now all but disappeared, and "airline food" is now culled from fast-food kiosks while racing through an airport—and those are only options if time permits. So savvy travelers now bring their own picnic fare in their carry-on bags, and the same is true for travelers in railroad coaches or on long-distance buses who can bring beverages as well.

The same expansion of summer country picnics to include food for traveling is occurring in the realm of communal and participatory cooking. What used to be called *potluck* is becoming a way of life for entertaining at home, as few hosts have the time or the money to prepare a full dinner party from soup to nuts—or hors d'oeuvres to dessert. So it's becoming increasingly common for guests to participate in meal preparation and augment the hosts' efforts. The potluck concept of everyone bringing a contribution is also extending to office parties and replacing catered events as companies need to tighten their financial waistlines.

If *$3 Make-and-Take Meals* was not part of the $3 Meals series of cookbooks, all of which are dedicated to helping you produce delicious meals that hide the fact that they're created on a strict food budget, it could have been titled *Car Cuisine.* Cooking food that must be moved farther than from the stove to the kitchen table can present problems for many cooks. A dish might look scrumptious and elegant when it emerges from the oven but break apart when jostled in the car, or it has a tantalizing taste that fades when it's reheated.

But you don't have to worry when cooking the disparate recipes from this book. Some are cold and some are hot. Some are totally finished in your kitchen, while others have their final assembly just before they go onto the picnic blanket or the buffet table. The common denominator is that all these foods are sturdy as well as delicious, and I'll tell you with each dish what can be done when and where.

But don't picture yourself spending hours in the kitchen to make these meals. None requires more than 25 minutes of your time—so the whole working time can be spent listening to the evening news. While many dishes need additional cooking time, you can be doing something else.

Here's the predicament in which we find ourselves. On one side there's the skyrocketing cost of food that challenges all of us shopping with a limited food budget. Even if the cost of gasoline drops back, prices at the supermarket will barely change, because the reasons for increasingly expensive food are global and not national. The era when Americans spent less of a percentage of income on food than citizens in other industrialized countries is disappearing as rapidly as drive-in theaters.

For example, the conversion of wheat fields in Umbria to produce sunflowers for ethanol led to a great surge in the price of pasta—a food to which we've always turned for the foundation for a low-cost meal—because there's a scarcity of durum wheat. And halfway around the world from this sun-drenched region of Italy, the long-awaited growth of a middle class in both India and China has given Western countries competition for the world's meat supply—and increased the cost of all meats we find in the supermarket.

Even if the cost of food stabilizes in the years to come, it remains one area of our budgets that we can control to compensate for those increases forced upon us which we cannot. While I can't help you to reduce your electric bill, I can teach you that you'll save money by covering a pot of water as it heats to a boil. And while I'm powerless to keep your son's college tuition from rising, I can help you to prepare meals that will always make you feel that you're eating like a prince on a peon's budget.

With today's economy, gathering a group for a communal meal is becoming more of a way of life. Taking time off from work, but not leaving home, is now dubbed a "stay-cation" by trend watchers.

Travel, even by car as gas prices rise, is the first notch on the belt to be tightened. But we don't have to make simple foods for these scaled-back times. Every cuisine and culture around the world has some form of picnic or potluck, and cooking that exotic fare makes an event feel more like a foreign vacation. So stick with me and the recipes in *$3 Make-and-Take Meals,* and not only will your family be praising your cooking, your friends will be too.

This is the moment to make these changes in your life. As you have noticed, the pace of life in America seems only to get faster. And, as with evolution, it seems that nothing ever goes backward. We now all have cell phones and all of us have too much to do in too few hours every day.

So this is the time to take stock and see how a new style of cooking and sharing can enhance your life and make it possible to visit with friends and family in a new way. All of us need it, but only some of us have discovered this trick: Make and Take is a new way to live—embrace it!

Happy eating!

—Ellen Brown
Providence, Rhode Island

Acknowledgments

While writing a book is a solitary endeavor, its publication is a team effort. My thanks go to:

Mary Norris, editorial director at Globe Pequot Press, for serving as captain on this ship crewed by able production people.

Julie Marsh, project editor at Globe Pequot Press, for her guidance and help all through the production process, and Jessie Shiers for her eagle-eyed copy editing.

Diana Nuhn, senior designer at Globe Pequot Press, for her inspired covers.

Ed Claflin, my agent, for his constant support and great sense of humor.

My many friends with whom I picnic and potluck on a regular basis for their favorite recipes and their tips for saving money. Special thanks to Fox Wetle, Suzanne Cavedon, Kenn Speiser, Pam Parmal, Bill Van Siclen, Jan Mariani, Beth Kinder, Vicki Veh, and my dear sister, Nancy Dubler.

Tigger and Patches, my furry companions, whose time romping in my office always cheers up my day.

Introduction

Food writer MFK Fisher once wrote that "there is a communion of more than our bodies when bread is broken and wine drunk." Sharing a picnic lunch or a potluck supper with friends and family, or sharing time with coworkers at the office over a scrumptious lunch that you made and brought, is more important than the caloric content of the food. We know that food is more important than the fuel to power our bodies; it's the cement for personal relationships.

What you'll learn reading—and cooking from—this book is how far your limited food budget can stretch. The goal of *$3 Make-and-Take Meals,* as well as other books in the $3 Meals series, is an ambitious one; this small amount of money—less than the cost of a large fast-food burger or a slice of gourmet pizza—is for your whole meal!

That includes the greens for your tossed salad, and the pasta or rice you cook to enjoy all sauce placed on top of it. And it includes a sweet treat for dessert. So unlike many books that promise cost-conscious cooking, this book really means it.

These recipes are made with foods that are ingredients; at one time they grew from the earth, walked upon it, or swam in its waters. The most processing that has taken place is the milk of animals having been transformed into natural cheeses. So when you're cooking from *$3 Make-and-Take Meals,* you're satisfying your body as well as your budget.

Not only for your body, but also for the planet, it is beneficial to use organic ingredients whenever possible. While organics used to be priced higher than conventional products, that is no longer the case. Most major supermarket chains, and mass retailers such as Wal-Mart, now carry extensive lines of organic ingredients, both fresh and shelf-stable. So buying organic is now a choice open to all—regardless of food budget.

The term was vague until 2001, when the U.S. Department of Agriculture set standards that clearly defined the meaning of *organic* both in terms of the food and the farming practices.

Organic agriculture prohibits the use of most synthetic fertilizers and pesticides, sewer sludge fertilizers, genetic engineering, growth hormones, irradiation, antibiotics, and artificial ingredients. In modern times antioxidants in our bodies have had to work even harder to combat the ravages of environmental pollutants, and organic farming does not add to those factors.

When organic is used in relation to meats, eggs, and dairy products, it means that the animals have not been given drugs or growth hormones, and they have been kept in conditions that allow for regular exercise and humane treatment.

In terms of saving the earth, the agricultural practices used for organic farming are environmentally friendly. Soil fertility and crop nutrients must be managed to improve soil conditions, minimize erosion, and prevent contamination of crops. Farmers must use crop rotation methods and fertilize with composted animal manure and plant materials rather than chemicals. Pests are controlled by traps rather than chemical sprays, and plastic mulches are forbidden.

In these recipes there are a few ingredient compromises taken to trim costs; however, these shortcuts trim preparation time, too. For my series of $3 Meals books I've used bottled lemon and lime juice in recipe development rather than freshly squeezed juices from the fruits themselves; I discovered it took a bit more juice to achieve the flavor I was after, but with the escalated cost of citrus fruits this was a sacrifice that I chose to make.

The same is true with vegetables; many of these recipes call for cost-effective frozen vegetables rather than fresh. For vegetables such as the chopped spinach added to a soup or casserole, or the peas added to many dishes, it really doesn't matter. Unlike canned vegetables, which are high in sodium and devoid of taste and texture, frozen vegetables are just like fresh vegetables, and they can save considerable money as well as time.

I've also limited the range of herbs and spices specified to a core group of less than a dozen. There's no need to purchase an expensive dried herb that you may never use again. If you grow fresh herbs, please feel free to substitute them at the rate of 1 tablespoon of a chopped fresh herb for each 1 teaspoon of a dried herb. While I adore fresh herbs, a small bunch in most supermarkets is double the cost of a dozen eggs—and that can serve as the protein for six people's dinner.

On the other hand, there are standards I will never bend. I truly believe that unsalted butter is so far superior to margarine that any minimal cost savings or savings of saturated fat grams from using margarine is not worth the trade-down in flavor.

Chapter 1:
Saving Money at the Supermarket

Learning how to trim your grocery bill is one of the reasons you bought this book, and that starts immediately with this chapter. By following the recipes in this book, you'll be eating delicious healthful meals both at home and in a variety of fun settings—from beach picnics to neighborhood potluck dinners. In fact, you can save more than the cost of this book in one week once you adopt some hints you don't know to implement more savings.

As you can well imagine, as a cookbook author I spend a lot of time in supermarkets, as well as other venues that sell food—from picturesque farmers' markets to the food aisles of chain drugstores. One thing is certain—every other customer I talk to is as interested as you and I are to eat better on a limited food budget. Those are the strategies you'll learn in this chapter.

Think of plotting and planning your supermarket trips as if you were planning to take the kids on a vacation. Your first step is to decide on your "vehicle"—what supermarket or other stores you'll use to reach your destination. After that you buy some guidebooks (in this case the Sunday newspaper) and do other research online (like print out coupons), and then you start looking for the good deals to get you to where you want to go.

In this case, where you want to go is a great vacation, and the way you're going to afford it in these challenging economic times is by savvy shopping. At any given moment there are billions of dollars of grocery coupons in the world waiting to be redeemed. Unfortunately, a large percentage of coupons are for processed foods that are high in sodium, so won't be part of your list. But if you really don't care that much about the brand of toothpaste, laundry detergent, or yogurt you eat, there are ways to save money every week.

In addition to coupons, there are rebates; if you spend a few cents on a stamp, it could reap many dollars coming back from manufacturers. They usually throw in some extra coupons, too.

Most of the tips here are specific to food shopping; this is a cookbook. But there are also hints for saving money in other segments of your budget. It all comes out of the same wallet.

I wish I could promise you a clear and uncluttered path. But every rule has an exception, as you'll see. You're now turning shopping from a simple task into a complex ritual. But the results are worth the effort you'll be putting in.

PLAN BEFORE YOU SHOP

The most important step to cost-effective cooking is to decide logically and intelligently what you're going to cook for the week. That may sound simple, but if you're in the habit of deciding when you're leaving work at the end of the day, chances are you've ended up with a lot of frozen pizza or Chinese carry-out. And if those are your contributions to a communal dinner, the cost is even more.

The first step is to "shop" in a place you know well; it's your own kitchen. Look and see what's still in the refrigerator, and how that food—which you've already purchased and perhaps also cooked—can be utilized. In some cases, the leftovers from a dinner can be used as part of the next day's lunch. In fact, I encourage you to cook all six servings of a recipe, even if there are only three or four members in your family, if it's a dish that can be "nuked" at the office for your lunch.

Now look at what foods you have in the freezer. Part of savvy shopping is stocking up on foods when they're on sale; in fact, sales of free-standing freezers have grown by more than 10 percent during the past few years, while sales of all other major appliances have gone down. And with good reason—a free-standing freezer allows you to take advantage of sales. Especially foods like boneless, skinless chicken breasts—the time-crunched cook's best friend—that go on sale frequently and are almost prohibitive in price when they're not on sale.

But preparing food for the freezer to ensure its future quality is important. Never freeze meats, poultry, or seafood in the supermarket wrapping alone. To guard against freezer burn, double wrap food in freezer paper or place it in a heavy resealable plastic bag. Mark the purchase date on raw food, and the date the food was frozen on cooked items, and use them within three months.

Most supermarkets have a lower cost for buying larger quantities, and by freezing part of a package you can take advantage of that savings. Scan recipes and look at the amount of the particular meat specified; that's what size your packages destined for the freezer should be.

A good investment is a kitchen scale to weigh portions, if you don't feel comfortable judging weight freestyle.

Keep a list taped to the front of your freezer. It should list the contents and date when each item was frozen. Mark off foods as you take them out and add foods as you put them in.

Also, part of your strategy as a cook is actually to cook only a few nights a week or on one day of a weekend; that means when you're making recipes that can be doubled—like soups and stews—you make larger batches and freeze a portion. Those meals are "dinner insurance" for nights you don't want to cook. Those are the nights that you previously would have brought in the bucket of chicken or the high-priced rotisserie chicken, and spent far more money.

The other factor that enters into the initial planning is looking at your depletion list to see what foods and other products need to be purchased. A jar of peanut butter or a bottle of dishwashing liquid might not factor into meal plans, but it does cost money—so these items have to be factored into your budget. Some weeks you might not need many supplies, but it always seems to me that all the cleaning supplies deplete the same week.

Now you've got the "raw data" to look at the weekly sales circulars from your newspaper or delivered with your mail. Those sales, along with online research to accrue even more money-saving coupons, should form the core for your menu planning.

COUPON CLIPPING 101

It's part art, it's part science, and it all leads to more money in your wallet. Consider this portion of the chapter your Guerilla Guide to Coupons. There's more to it than just clipping them. Of course, unless you clip them or glean them from other channels (see ideas to follow), then you can't save money. So that's where you're going to start—but, trust me, it's just the beginning.

Clipping coupons—in case you haven't heard—is cool. And it should be. At any given moment there are billions of dollars of coupons floating around out there, according to the folks at www.grocerycoupon guide.com, one of the growing list of similar sites dedicated to helping you save money.

Not only is it becoming easier to access these savings, you're a Neanderthal if you don't. The fact that you're reading this book—and

Sometimes coupons expire *before* their stated expiration date because retailers allot so many dollars per promotion. If, for example, a retailer is offering a free widget if you buy a widget holder, and the widgets run out, there's probably a way to justify turning you away. Read the fine print.

will be cooking from it—shows that you care about trimming the size of your grocery bill. So it's time to get with the program.

Coupon usage grew by a whopping 192 percent in the year between March 2008 and March 2009, according to Coupons.com, which has seen an increase in traffic to its site of 25 percent per month since the current recession began.

Every Sunday newspaper (as long as they still exist) is a treasure-trove of coupons. I found a $5-off coupon for a premium cat food my finicky cats like in a local paper, which cost 50 cents. It was worth it to buy four copies of the paper; I spent $2, but I then netted an $18 savings on the cat food.

The Internet is increasingly a place to turn for coupons, both for a few dollars here and there on groceries and many dollars off for major purchases like computers or televisions. Stores like Target frequently have coupons for up to 10 percent off an order, too.

Here are some good sites to browse. For many coupons you have to download some free software to print them off; it's worth the few minutes of your time:

- www.GroceryCoupons.com

- www.CouponMom.com

- www.GroceryGuide.com

- www.PPGazette.com

- www.GroceryCoupons4U.com

LEARN THE LINGO

Coupons are printed on very small pieces of paper, and even with 20/20 eyesight or reading glasses, many people—including me—need to use a magnifying glass to read all the fine print. There are many legal phrases that have to be part of every coupon, too.

In the same way that baseball fans know that RBI means "runs batted in," coupon collectors know that WSL means "while supplies last." Here's a list of many abbreviations found on coupons:

AR. After rebate.

B1G1 or BOGO. Buy one, get one free.

CRT. Cash register tape, also called your receipt.

DC. Double coupon, which is a coupon the store—not the manufacturer—doubles in value.

DCRT. Dated cash register receipt, which proves you purchased the item during the right time period.

FAR. Free after rebate.

IP. Internet printed coupons.

ISO. In-store only.

IVC. Instant value coupon, which are the pull offs found on products in the supermarket that are redeemed as you pay.

MIR. Mail-in rebate.

NED. No expiration date.

OAS. On any size, which means the coupon is good for any size package of that particular product.

OYNSO. On your next shopping order, which means that you must return to the same store; the coupon will not be good at another store.

POP. Proof of purchase, which is the little panel found on a package that you cut out and send in to receive a rebate.

WSL. While supplies last, which means you can't demand a "rain

While you just may be becoming more aware of them, coupons are nothing new. They began in the late 1800s when Coca-Cola and Grape-Nuts offered coupons to consumers. Currently more than 3,000 companies use coupons as part of their marketing plans, and shoppers save more than $5 billion a year by redeeming the coupons.

check" to use the coupon at a later date when the product is once again in stock.

GET ORGANIZED!

So you now have a fistful of coupons with which you're going to save money at the supermarket. That's a start; if you don't have the coupons you can't use them.

The first decision you have to make is how you're going to organize your coupons. There are myriad ways and each has its fans. It's up to you to decide which is right for you, your family, and the way you shop:

- **Arrange the coupons by aisle in the supermarket.** This is only good if you shop in one store consistently.

- **Arrange the coupons by category of product.** Dairy products, cleaning supplies, paper disposables, and cereals are all categories with many weekly coupons, so arrange your coupons accordingly.

- **Arrange the coupons alphabetically.** This system works well if you redeem coupons in various types of stores beyond the grocery store.

- **Arrange the coupons by expiration date.** Coupons are only valid for a certain time period; it can be a few weeks or a few months. And part of the strategy of coupon clipping is to maximize the value, which frequently comes close to the expiration date. Some of the best coupons are those for "buy one, get one free." However, when the coupon first appears the item is at full price. But what about two weeks later, when the item is on sale at your store? Then the "buy one, get one free" can mean you're actually getting four cans for the price of one at the original retail price.

Storage systems for arranging coupons are as varied as methods of organizing them. I personally use envelopes, and keep the stack held together with a low-tech paper clip. I've also seen people with whole wallets and tiny accordion binders dedicated to coupons. If you don't have a small child riding on the top of the cart, another alternative is to get a loose-leaf notebook with clear envelopes instead of pages.

BARGAIN SHOPPING 2.0

Every grocery store has weekly sales, and those foods are the place to start your planning for new purchases; that's how you're saving money beyond using coupons. And almost every town has competing supermarket chains that offer different products on sale. It's worth your time to shop in a few venues, because comparison shopping will generate the most savings. That way you can also determine which chain offers the best store brands, and purchase them while you're there for the weekly bargains. As I said before, your options are more limited because you won't be buying any high-sodium processed foods, but it's more than worth your time to use every trick in the book to trim that grocery budget. Here are other ways to save:

Shuffle those cards. Even if I can't convince you to clip coupons, the least you can do for yourself to save money is take the five minutes required to sign up for store loyalty cards; many national brands as well as store brands are on sale only when using the card. While the current system has you hand the card to the cashier at the checkout, that will be changing in the near future. Shopping carts will be equipped with card readers that will generate instant coupons according to your purchasing habits. I keep my stack of loyalty cards in the glove box of my car; that way they don't clutter my purse, but I always have them when shopping.

Segregate items not on your list. Some of these might be marked-down meats or vegetables, and some might be impulse buys that end up in the cart despite your pledge to keep to the list. Place these items in the "baby rack" rather than in the cart; you'll have a good visual sense of how much money is represented.

"Junk mail" may contain more than junk. Don't toss those Valpak and other coupon envelopes that arrive in the mail. Look through them carefully, and you'll find not only coupons for food products, but for many services, too.

Look for blanket discounts. While it does take time to cull coupons, many supermarket chains send flyers in the mail that offer a set amount off the total; for example, $10 off a total of $50. These are the easiest way to save money, and many national drugstore chains, such as CVS, do the same. Just remember that you may need a loyalty card for those stores to take advantage of the savings.

Spend a stamp to get a rebate. Despite the current cost of a first-class postage stamp, sending in for rebates is still worth your trouble. Many large manufacturers are now sending out coupon books or cash vouchers usable in many stores to customers who mail in receipts demonstrating that they have purchased about $50 of products. For example, Procter & Gamble, the country's largest advertiser and the company for which the term "soap opera" was invented, is switching millions of dollars from the airwaves to these sorts of promotions.

Find bargains online. There are some specific coupon sites listed on page 4, but there are other places to look, too. Go to specific manufacturers of foods you like, even high-end organic foods. You'll find coupons as well as redemption offers. I also look for the coupon offers on such culinary sites as www.epicurious.com and www.foodnetwork.com. You will find coupons there, some tied to actual recipes.

Find coupons in the store. Look for those little machines projecting out from the shelves; they usually contain coupons that can be used instantly when you check out. Also, don't throw out your receipt until you've looked at it carefully. There are frequently coupons printed on the back. The cashier may also hand you other small slips of paper with your cash register receipt; most of them are coupons for future purchases of items you just bought. They may be from the same brand or they may be from a competing brand. Either way, they offer savings.

Stock up on cans. The same plastic containers that fit under your bed to hold out-of-season clothing can also become a pantry for canned goods. It's not worth the space and investment to buy canned beans, or other canned goods that are always inexpensive. But when the $1.49 can of tuna is on sale for 88 cents, jump on it.

Get a bargain buddy. There's no question that supermarkets try to lure customers with "buy one, get one free" promotions, and sometimes one is all you really want. And those massive cases of paper towels at the warehouse clubs are also a good deal—if you have unlimited storage space. The answer? Find a bargain buddy with whom you can split large purchases. My friends and I also swap coupons we won't use but the other person will. Going back to my example of the cat food savings, there were dog food coupons on the same page, so I turned them over to a canine-owning friend.

PUSHING THE CART WITH PURPOSE

So it's a "new you" entering the supermarket. First of all, you have a list, and it's for more than a few days. And you're going to buy what's on your list. Here's the first rule: Stick to that list. Never go shopping when you're hungry; that's when non-essential treats high in sodium wind up in your basket.

Always go shopping alone; unwanted items end up in the cart to keep peace in the family. And—here's an idea that might seem counter-intuitive—go shopping when you're in a hurry. It's those occasions when you have the time to dawdle that the shortcakes end up coming home when all you really wanted were the strawberries.

But, as promised, here are some exceptions to the rule of keeping to your list. You've got to be flexible enough to take advantage of some unexpected great sales. Next to frugality, flexibility is the key to saving money on groceries.

It's easy if the sale is a markdown on meat; you see the $2-off coupon and put it in the cart, with the intention of either cooking it that night or freezing it. All supermarkets mark down meat on the day before the expiration date. The meat is still perfectly fine, and should it turn out not to be, you can take it back for a refund. So go ahead and take advantage of the markdown.

Then you notice a small oval sticker with the word *Save*. Is turkey breast at $1.09 a real bargain? You'll know it is if you keep track of prices, and know that a few weeks ago it was $3.99 per pound.

You now have two options. Buy the off-list bargains and freeze them, or use them this week. In place of what? And what effect will that have on the rest of your list?

That's why I suggest freezing bargains, assuming you can absorb the extra cost on this week's grocery bill. If not, then look at what produce and dairy items on the list were tied to a protein you're now crossing off, and delete them too.

But meat isn't the only department of the supermarket that has "remainder bins." Look for produce too. I've gotten some perfectly ripe bananas with black spots—just the way they should be—for pennies a pound, while the ones that are bright yellow (and still tasteless) are five times the cost.

Almost all supermarkets are designed to funnel traffic first into the produce section; that is the last place you want to start shopping. Begin with the proteins, since many items in other sections of your list relate to the entrees of the dinners you have planned. Once they are gathered, go through and get the pasta, rice, or other shelf-stable items, then the dairy products (so they will not be in the cart for too long), and end with the produce. Using this method, the fragile produce is on the top of the basket, not crushed by the gallons of milk.

The last step is packing the groceries. If you live in an area where you have the option of packing them yourself, place items stored together in the same bag. That way all of your produce can go directly into the refrigerator, and canned goods destined for the basement will be stored in one trip.

LEARNING THE ROPES

The well-informed shopper is the shopper who is saving money, and the information you need to make the best purchasing decisions is right there on the supermarket shelves. It's the shelf tag that gives you the cost per unit of measurement. The units can be quarts for salad dressing, ounces for dry cereal, or pounds for canned goods. All you have to do is look carefully.

But you do have to make sure you're comparing apples to apples and oranges to oranges—or in this example, stocks to stocks. Some can be priced by the quart, while others are by the pound.

Check out store brands. Store brands and generics have improved in quality over the past few years, and according to *Consumer Reports,* buying them can save anywhere from 15 to 50 percent. Moving from a national brand to a store brand is a personal decision, and sometimes money is not the only factor. For example, I have used many store brands of chlorine bleach, and have returned to Clorox time and again. But I find no difference between generic shredded wheat and those from the market leaders. Store brands can also be less expensive than national brands on sale—and with coupons.

Compare prices within the store. Many foods—such as cold cuts and cheeses—are sold in multiple areas of the store, so check out those alternate locations. Sliced ham may be less expensive in a cellophane package shelved with the refrigerated foods than at the deli counter, but if you only need a few slices of ham, you're better off getting it at the deli than wasting the remainder of a half-pound package.

Avoid single-serving packages. It's another example of paying for convenience. Those little packs of cookies and chips are far more expensive per ounce than larger sizes. Reuse some resealable plastic bags, and buy bigger.

Look high and low. Manufacturers pay a premium price to shelve products at eye level, and you're paying for that placement when you're paying their prices. Look at the top and bottom shelves in aisles like cleaning products and pasta. That's where you'll find the lower prices.

Buy the basics. Remember that any time a person other than you is working on food, you're paying for that labor cost. You'll learn how to cut up your own chickens in Chapter 2, and maybe it takes a few minutes to turn those carrots into carrot sticks, but it's a lot cheaper than buying baby carrots, and you'll have leftover peels that can flavor your stocks.

Watch the scanner. I know it's tempting to catch up on pop culture by leafing through the tabloids at the checkout, but that's the last thing you should be doing—and that's another reason to go shopping without the kids, because they will be a distraction. Watching the clerk scan your order usually saves you money. For example, make sure all the instant-savings coupons are peeled off; this includes marked-down meats and coupons on boxes and bags. Then, make sure sale items are ringing up at the right price.

WASTE NOT, WANT NOT

We're now going to start listing exceptions to all the rules you just read, because a bargain isn't a bargain if you end up throwing some of it away. Remember that the goal is to waste nothing. Start by annotating your shopping list with quantities for the recipes you'll be cooking. That way you can begin to gauge when a bargain is a bargain. Here are other ways to buy only what you need:

Don't overbuy. Sure, the large can of diced tomatoes is less per pound than the smaller can. But what will you do with the remainder of the can if all you need is a small amount? The same is true for dairy products. A half-pint of heavy cream always costs much more per ounce than a quart, but if the remaining three cups of cream will end up in the sink in a few weeks, go with the smaller size.

Know the rules about sales. Most weekly supermarket sales encourage a larger purchase, like "six cans for $3." There are times that you do have to buy all six to get the savings, but most of the time you don't. You can buy one can and pay 50 cents for it. If it's a discount for bulk purchase only, then there should be a sign that says: "six cans for $3, 79 cents a can if bought individually."

Use the scale in the produce department. There's an appendix at the back of this book that gives you the volume and weight equivalencies of many commonly used ingredients, from apples to zucchini. In general, people overbuy rather than underbuy foods—especially produce. Use the scale if you're buying an ingredient listed by weight in a recipe.

Buy what you'll eat, not what you should eat. Ah, this is where parental guilt comes into play. You've just read an article on the wonders of broccoli, and there it is on sale. But if your family hates broccoli, the low sale cost doesn't matter; you'll end up throwing it away. We all think about healthful eating when we're in the supermarket, but if you know that the contents of your cart are good thoughts rather than realistic choices, you're wasting money.

Just because you have a coupon doesn't mean you should buy something. We all love bargains, but if you're putting an item into your cart for the first time, you must decide if it's because you really want it and haven't bought it before because of its cost, or because you're getting $1.50 off of the price. This is a subset of buying what you eat, and not what you should eat.

Avoid high-priced cleaning gizmos. A can of furniture polish and some old rags do an even better job than those disposable dusters that are now filling the cleaning products aisle. And a bottle of chlorine bleach disinfects surfaces at a fraction of the cost of bubbling cleaners. Use a bit of elbow grease, and keep cleaning supplies basic.

Sometimes bigger isn't better. If you're shopping for snacks for your kids, look for the *small* apples rather than the giant ones. Most kids take a few bites and then toss the rest, so evaluate any purchases you're making by the pound.

Ring that bell! You know the one; it's always in the meat department of the supermarket. It might take you a few extra minutes, but ask the real live human who will appear for exactly what you want; many of the recipes in *$3 Make-and-Take Meals* specify less than the weight of packages you find in the meat case. Many supermarkets do not have personnel readily available in departments like the cheese counter, but if there are wedges of cheeses labeled and priced, then someone is in charge. It might be the deli department or the produce department, but find out who it is and ask for a small wedge of cheese if you can't find one that's cut to the correct size.

Check out the bulk bins. Begin buying from the bulk bins for shelf-stable items, like various types of rice, beans, dried fruits, and nuts. Each of these departments has scales so you can weigh ingredients like dried mushrooms or pasta. If a recipe calls for a quantity rather than a weight, you can usually "eyeball" the quantity. If you're unsure of amounts, start by bringing a 1-cup measuring cup with you to the market. Empty the contents of the bin into the measuring cup rather than directly into the bag. One problem with bulk food bags is that they are difficult to store in the pantry; shelves were made for sturdier materials. Wash out plastic deli containers or even plastic containers that you bought containing yogurt or sour cream. Use those for storage once the bulk bags arrive in the kitchen. Make sure you label your containers of bulk foods both at the supermarket and at home (if you're transferring the foods to other containers) so you know what they are, especially if you're buying similar foods. Arborio and basmati rice look very similar in a plastic bag, but they are totally different grains and shouldn't be substituted for each other.

Shop from the salad bar for tiny quantities. There's no question that supermarkets charge a premium price for items in those chilled bins in the salad bar, but you get exactly what you need. When to shop there depends on the cost of the item in a larger quantity. If you don't see how you're going to finish the $4 pint of cherry tomatoes, then spend $1 at the salad bar for the handful you need to garnish a salad. And if you're not crazy about celery, get the 1/2 cup you need from the salad bar rather than buying a whole stalk for a few dollars.

SUPERMARKET ALTERNATIVES

All the hints in this chapter thus far have been geared to pushing a cart around a supermarket. Here are some other ways to save money:

Shop at farmers' markets. I admit it: I need a 12-step program to help me cure my addiction to local farmers' markets. Shopping al fresco on warm summer days turns picking out fruits and vegetables into a truly sensual experience. Also, you buy only what you want. There are no bunches of carrots; there are individual carrots sold by the pound. The U.S. Department of Agriculture began publishing the *National Directory of Farmers' Markets* in 1994, and at that time the number was fewer than 2,000. That figure has now doubled. To find a farmers' market near you, go to www.ams .usda.gov/farmersmarkets. The first cousins of farmers' markets for small quantities of fruits are the sidewalk vendors in many cities. One great advantage to buying from them is that their fruit is always ripe and ready to eat or cook.

Shop at ethnic markets. If you live in a rural area this may not be possible, but even moderately small cities have a range of ethnic markets, and that's where you should buy ingredients to cook those cuisines. The vegetables are frequently less expensive. Even small cities and many towns have ethnic enclaves, such as a "Little Italy"; each neighborhood has some grocery stores with great prices for those ingredients and the fresh produce used to make the dishes, too.

Shop alternative stores. Groceries aren't only at grocery stores; many "dollar stores" and other discount venues stock herbs and spices as well as pasta and rice. If you live in New England, Ocean State Job Lot should be on your weekly circuit; this discount store chain is loaded with food bargains.

Shop for food in drugstores. Every national brand of drugstore— including CVS and Walgreen's—carries grocery products, and usually has great bargains each week. In the same way that food markets now carry much more than foods, drugstores stock thousands of items that have no connection to medicine. Those chains also have circulars in Sunday newspapers, so check them out—even if you're feeling very healthy.

Shop online. In recent years it's become possible to do all your grocery shopping online through such services as Peapod and Fresh Direct. While there is frequently a delivery charge involved, for housebound people this is a true boon. If you really hate the thought of pushing the cart, you should explore it; it's impossible to make impulse buys. There are also a large number of online retailers for ethnic foods, dried herbs and spices, premium baking chocolate, and other shelf-stable items. Letting your cursor do the shopping for these items saves you time, and many of them offer free shipping at certain times of the year.

TIME FOR MENTAL CALISTHENICS

Just as an athlete goes through mental preparation before a big game, getting yourself "psyched" to save money is the first step toward accomplishing that goal. You've got to get into a frugal frame of mind. You're out to save money on your food budget, but not feel deprived. You're going to be eating the delicious dishes in this book.

Think about where your food budget goes other than the grocery store. The cost of a few "designer coffee" treats at the local coffee shop is equal to a few dinners at home. Couldn't you brew coffee and take it to work rather than spend $10 a week at the coffee cart? And those cans of soft drinks in the vending machine are four times the cost of bringing a can from home. But do you really need soft drinks at all? For mere pennies you can brew a few quarts of iced tea, which has delicious flavor without chemicals.

Planning ahead is important, too. Rather than springing for a chilled bottle of spring water because you're thirsty in the supermarket, keep a few empty plastic bottles in your car and fill one from the water fountain. That water is free.

Until frugality comes naturally, do what diet counselors suggest, and keep a log of every penny spent on food. Just as the empty calories add up, so do the meaningless noshes.

Part of *$3 Make-and-Take Meals* is devoted to recipes that help you become one of the growing number of people who "brown-bag it" at work. Bringing your lunch to work does increase your weekly supermarket tab, but it accomplishes a few good goals. It adds funds to the bottom line of your total budget, and it allows you to control what you're eating—and when. If you have a pressured job, chances are there are days that you end up eating from snack-food vending machines or eating fast food at your desk.

Almost every office has both a refrigerator and a microwave oven, so lunch can frequently be a leftover from a dinner the night or two before, so the extra cost and cooking time are minimal.

So now that you're becoming a grocery guru, you can move on to find myriad ways to save money on your grocery bill while eating wonderfully. That's what *$3 Make-and-Take Meals,* and the other books in the $3 Meals series, is all about.

Chapter 2

Basics of the Carry-Off Kitchen

The tips and tricks you'll learn in this chapter will make you a smarter cook and a safer cook. When playing jazz you can't learn to improvise until you master the fundamentals, and there are some basics in cooking, too.

The first, and most important, are the rules of food safety. If you know all of these by rote, feel free to skip a few pages.

Then I'll give you my basic recipes for stocks and some roasted meats. These foods are the building blocks for numerous meals, and making them at home and keeping them handy will help you to save countless dollars down the road.

SAFETY FIRST

The biggest nuisance at a picnic or potluck isn't the flies or even the uninvited guests; it's a case of food-borne illness.

The first—and most important—requirement for good cooking is knowing the basic rules of food safety. This begins with trips to the supermarket and ends after leftovers are refrigerated or frozen at the end of a meal. The sections that follow may seem like common sense, but after many decades as a food writer who has heard horror stories about very sick people, please believe me, they're not.

Safe Shopping

Most supermarkets are designed to funnel you into the produce section first. But that's not the best place to start. Begin your shopping with the proteins, because they determine the choice of ancillary ingredients, then go to produce, and end with the refrigerated and frozen sections.

Never buy meat or poultry in a package that is torn and leaking, and it's a good idea to place all meats and poultry in the disposable plastic bags available in the produce department if they don't have them in the meat department. Check the "sell-by" and "use-by" dates, and never purchase food that exceeds them.

For the trip home, it's a good idea to carry an insulated cooler in the back of your car if it's hot outside or if the perishable items will be out of refrigeration for more than 1 hour. In hot weather, many seafood departments will provide some crushed ice in a separate bag for the fish.

Banishing Bacteria

Fruits and vegetables can contain some bacteria, but it's far more likely that the culprits will grow on meat, poultry, and seafood. Store these foods on the bottom shelves of your refrigerator so their juices cannot accidentally drip on other foods. And keep these foods refrigerated until just before they go into the dish.

Bacteria multiply at room temperature. The so-called "danger zone" is between 40°F and 140°F. As food cooks, it's important for it to pass through this zone as quickly as possible.

If you want to get a jump start on dinner by cutting up meats and vegetables in advance, that's fine. Just refrigerate all foods separately until it's time to combine them and cook the finished dish. Like all rules, this one has exceptions; for example, raw eggs can come into contact with other foods.

Don't Cross-Contaminate

Cleanliness is not only next to godliness, it's also the key to food safety. Wash your hands often while you're cooking, and never touch cooked food if you haven't washed your hands after handling raw food.

The precept that cooked food and raw food shall never meet extends beyond the cook's hands. Clean cutting boards, knives, and kitchen counters often. Or if you have the space, section off your countertops for raw foods and cooked foods, as many restaurant kitchens do. Don't place cooked foods or raw foods that will remain uncooked (such as salad) on

A good way to prevent food-borne illness is by selecting the right cutting board. Wooden boards might be attractive, but you can never get them as clean as plastic boards that can be run through the dishwasher. Even with plastic boards, it's best to use one for only cooked food and foods such as vegetables that are not prone to contain bacteria, and another one devoted to raw meats, poultry, and fish.

cutting boards that have been used to cut raw meat, poultry, or fish. Bacteria from raw animal proteins can contaminate the other foods.

CHICKEN 101

Just look at the range of prices for chicken in the supermarket! They can range from less than $1 per pound for whole birds and leg/thigh quarters to $5 or $6 per pound for coveted boneless, skinless breasts. Always keep in mind that you're paying for someone else's labor.

It is far more economical to purchase a whole chicken, and cut it up yourself, rather than buy one already cut. Another benefit is that you can save the scraps and freeze them to keep you "stocked up" for soups and sauces. Here are some methods of chicken cutting you should know:

Cutting up a whole chicken: Start by breaking back the wings until the joints snap. Then use a boning knife to cut through the ball joints and detach the wings; cut off the wing tips and save them for stock. When holding the chicken on its side, you will see a natural curve outlining the boundary between the breast and the leg/thigh quarters. Use sharp kitchen shears and cut along this line. Cut the breast in half by scraping away the meat from the breastbone and using a small paring knife to remove the wishbone. Cut away the breastbone using the shears and save it for stock. Divide the leg/ thigh quarters by turning the pieces over and finding the joint joining them. Cut through the joint and sever the leg from the thigh.

Boning chicken breasts: If possible, buy the chicken breasts whole rather than split. Pull the skin off with your fingers, and then make an incision on either side of the breastbone, cutting down until you feel the bone resisting the knife. Treating one side at a time, place the blade of your boning knife against the carcass and scrape away the meat. You will then have two pieces—the large fillet and the small tenderloin. To trim the fillet, cut away any fat. Some recipes will tell you to pound the breast to an even thickness so it will cook evenly and quickly. Place the breast between 2 sheets of plastic wrap or waxed paper and pound with the smooth side of a meat mallet or the bottom of a small, heavy skillet or saucepan. If you have a favorite veal scallopini recipe and want to substitute chicken or turkey, pound it very thin—to a thickness of ¼ inch. Otherwise, what you are after is to pound the thicker portion so that it lays and cooks evenly. To trim the tenderloin, secure the tip of the tendon that will be visible with your free hand. Using a paring knife, scrape down the tendon, and the meat will push away.

Cooking Chicken Correctly

The rules changed for cooking poultry a few years ago, and the revision means that you can avoid overcooked, dry chicken and turkey. The minimum temperature is now 165°F for both white and dark meat. At that temperature there's no chance for microorganisms to survive.

The best way to test this is to use an instant-read meat thermometer. When the thickest part of the chicken is probed, the reading should be 165°F. If you do not want to take the temperature of every piece of chicken, recognize these visual signals: The chicken should be tender when poked with the tip of a paring knife, there should not be a hint of pink even near the bones, and the juices should run clear. Always test the dark meat before the white meat. Dark meat takes slightly longer to cook, so if the thighs are the proper temperature, you know the breasts will be fine.

Cutting the Calories

If you say "wow" at the number of calories contained in some of these chicken recipes, it's because the recipes were calculated with the assumption that you're going to eat the chicken skin, which is where more than half the fat on a chicken is located.

According to the U.S. Department of Agriculture, it makes no difference in the fat content if the skin is discarded before or after the chicken is cooked. From the culinary perspective, chicken remains far moister and more tender if cooked with the skin. The exceptions are recipes formulated for quick-cooking boneless, skinless breasts and thighs.

It's also easier to discard the skin after the chicken is cooked. So cook the chicken pieces or whole chicken with the skin attached, and then decide after it is cooked if you want to enjoy the crispy skin or save those calories and discard it.

STOCKING UP

A category of essential foods is stocks—from a few tablespoons to moisten food to cups and quarts to serve as the basis for soups and the gravy for stews. It's the long-simmered homemade stocks that add the depth of flavor to the soups and sauces enjoyed at fine restaurants. Classically trained chefs have known for centuries what you're about to learn in this chapter—making stocks is as easy as boiling water and, if you're judicious and save bits and pieces destined for the garbage when prepping foods to be cooked, they're free.

Cans and cartons of stocks are priced in many supermarkets in a way that's confusing; some are calculated by the pound while others are by the ounce. Looking at a range of costs as well as flavors at a recent taste testing, a generic stock that tasted like salted water with some chemical chicken flavor was still a whopping $2 per quart, while one that actually had some flavor was almost $5 per quart.

Here's how I navigate the process of stock-making: I keep a few heavy resealable gallon bags in my freezer. Into one go all appropriate vegetable and herb trimmings. Three others are designated for poultry, beef, and fish or seafood trimmings. When one protein bag gets full, I join it with the contents of the vegetable bag, and it's time to make stock.

Once you've made the stock, the next step is to freeze it in convenient forms. Use a measuring tablespoon to calculate the capacity of your ice-cube trays; if you have an automatic ice-cube maker, then it's worth the few cents to buy a plastic tray too. Freeze some of your stock in the ice-cube tray; that's for the times you see "$1/4$ cup chicken stock" in a recipe. Then freeze the remainder in 1-quart plastic bags. Plastic bags take up less room in the freezer than plastic containers. You can freeze the bags flat on a baking sheet, and then stack them.

Chicken Stock

Richly flavored, homemade chicken stock is as important as good olive oil in my kitchen. Once you've gotten into the habit of "keeping stocked," you'll appreciate the difference that it makes in all soups and sauces. And making it is as easy as boiling water.

Yield: 4 quarts | **Active time:** 10 minutes | **Start to finish:** 4 hours

> 6 quarts water
> 5 pounds chicken bones, skin, and trimmings
> 4 celery ribs, rinsed and cut into thick slices
> 2 onions, trimmed and quartered
> 2 carrots, trimmed, scrubbed, and cut into thick slices
> 2 tablespoons whole black peppercorns
> 6 garlic cloves, peeled
> 4 sprigs parsley
> 2 teaspoons dried thyme
> 2 bay leaves

1. Place water and chicken in a large stockpot, and bring to a boil over high heat. Reduce the heat to low, and skim off foam that rises during the first 10–15 minutes of simmering. Simmer stock, uncovered, for 1 hour, then add celery, onions, carrots, peppercorns, garlic, parsley, thyme, and bay leaves. Simmer for 2½ hours.

2. Strain stock through a fine-meshed sieve, pushing with the back of a spoon to extract as much liquid as possible. Discard solids, spoon stock into smaller containers, and refrigerate. Remove and discard fat from surface of stock, then transfer stock to a variety of container sizes.

Note: The stock can be refrigerated and used within 3 days, or it can be frozen for up to 6 months.

Each ½-cup serving contains:

6 calories | 0 calories from fat | 0 g fat | 0 g saturated fat | 0 mg cholesterol | 0 g protein | 1 g carbohydrates | 12 mg sodium

Variation:
• Substitute turkey giblets and necks for the chicken pieces.

Vegetable Stock

You may think it's not necessary to use vegetable stock for a vegetarian dish that includes the same vegetables, but that's not the case. Using stock creates a much more richly flavored dish that can't be replicated by increasing the quantity of vegetables cooked in it.

Yield: 2 quarts | **Active time:** 10 minutes | **Start to finish:** 1 hour

> 2½ quarts water
> 2 carrots, scrubbed, trimmed, and thinly sliced
> 2 celery ribs, trimmed and sliced
> 1 large onion, peeled and thinly sliced
> 1 tablespoon whole black peppercorns
> 3 sprigs fresh parsley
> 2 teaspoons dried thyme
> 4 garlic cloves, peeled
> 2 bay leaves

1. Pour water into a stockpot, and add carrots, celery, onion, peppercorns, parsley, thyme, garlic, and bay leaves. Bring to a boil over high heat, then reduce the heat to low and simmer stock, uncovered, for 1 hour.

2. Strain stock through a fine-meshed sieve, pushing with the back of a spoon to extract as much liquid as possible. Discard solids, and allow stock to cool to room temperature. Spoon stock into smaller containers, and refrigerate.

Note: The stock can be refrigerated and used within 3 days, or it can be frozen for up to 6 months.

Each ½-cup serving contains:

8 calories | 0 calories from fat | 0 g fat | 0 g saturated fat | 0 mg cholesterol | 0 g protein | 2 g carbohydrates | 14 mg sodium

Beef Stock

While beef stock is not specified as often as chicken stock in recipes, it is the backbone to certain soups and the gravy for stews and roasts.

Yield: 2 quarts | **Active time:** 15 minutes | **Start to finish:** 4½ hours

2 pounds beef trimmings (bones, fat) or inexpensive beef shank
3 quarts water
1 carrot, trimmed, scrubbed, and cut into thick slices
1 medium onion, peeled and sliced
1 celery rib, trimmed and sliced
1 tablespoon whole black peppercorns
3 sprigs fresh parsley
1 teaspoon dried thyme
2 garlic cloves, peeled
2 bay leaves

1. Preheat the oven broiler, and line a broiler pan with heavy-duty aluminum foil. Broil beef for 3 minutes per side, or until browned. Transfer beef to a large stockpot, and add water. Bring to a boil over high heat. Reduce the heat to low, and skim off foam that rises during the first 10–15 minutes of simmering. Simmer for 1 hour, uncovered, then add carrot, onion, celery, peppercorns, parsley, thyme, garlic, and bay leaves. Simmer for 3 hours.
2. Strain stock through a fine-meshed sieve, pushing with the back of a spoon to extract as much liquid as possible. Discard solids, and spoon stock into smaller containers. Refrigerate; remove and discard fat from surface of stock.

Note: The stock can be refrigerated and used within 3 days, or it can be frozen for up to 6 months.

Each ½-cup serving contains:

11 calories | 2 calories from fat | 0 g fat | 0 g saturated fat | 1 mg cholesterol | 1 g protein | 2 g carbohydrates | 15 mg sodium

Variation:
- Substitute ham bones and trimmings for the beef.

BUILDING BLOCKS

Many great dishes for picnics and potlucks, not to mention super sandwiches for daily lunches for you and your kids, begin with roast meats. Ham, chicken, and turkey are perennial favorites, and they're specified in many recipes in *$3 Make-and-Take Meals.*

These foods are also on sale quite often, especially around the holidays. It only makes sense to buy them on sale, and cook at least one right away. Once cooked, the meat can be frozen so any number of dishes can be cooked in the months that follow.

Basic Baked Ham

Not only does this recipe render the ham succulent and moist, it also creates some wonderful stock to use for your next batch of bean soup! This is a master recipe and creates enough meat for a lavish Sunday dinner plus leftovers for myriad recipes located in other chapters of this book. Plus, always save the ham bone for making soups.

Yield: 10–12 servings | **Active time:** 10 minutes | **Start to finish:** 3½ hours

HAM

1 (8-pound) fully cooked ham (not spiral-sliced)
1½ cups Chicken Stock (recipe on page 22) or purchased stock
1 small onion, peeled and diced
1 small carrot, peeled and sliced
3 parsley sprigs

GLAZE (OPTIONAL)

½ cup apricot preserves
3 tablespoons grainy mustard
2 tablespoons grated fresh ginger

1. Preheat the oven to 325°F, and grease a large roasting pan.
2. Remove ham from plastic, if necessary, and rinse well under cold water. Cut away and discard any thick skin with a sharp knife, and trim all fat to an even ¼-inch layer.
3. Place ham, cut side down, in the prepared pan, and add stock, onion, carrot, and parsley. Cover the pan with heavy-duty aluminum foil, and bake ham for 1¾ hours. Remove ham from the oven, discard foil, and remove pan juices; save juices and freeze for soups and stews. Turn ham over, and bake for an additional 1½ hours, or until an instant-read thermometer registers 145°F.
4. While ham bakes, make glaze, if using. Combine apricot preserves, mustard, and ginger in a small mixing bowl, and stir well. Increase oven temperature to 400°F, if serving glazed ham. Remove ham from the oven. Cut off all ham to be used for future dishes, and apply glaze to remaining ham.

5. Return ham to the oven and bake for an additional 15 minutes, basting with glaze every 5 minutes.

Note: The ham can be prepared up to 3 days in advance and refrigerated, tightly covered. Serve it cold, or slice and reheat it in a 350°F oven for 5–10 minutes, or until warm.

Each 4-ounce serving of meat contains:

128 calories | 36 calories from fat | 4 g fat | 1 g saturated fat | 54 mg cholesterol | 19 g protein | 4 g carbohydrates | 1,416 mg sodium

Variations:
- Substitute ¾ cup dry sherry or white wine for ¾ cup of stock.
- Substitute ½ cup orange marmalade or red currant jelly for the apricot preserves.
- Glaze alternative: Reduce 3 cups pineapple juice to ¾ cup, and add ¼ cup Dijon mustard, ¼ cup firmly packed dark brown sugar, and ¼ teaspoon ground cloves.
- Glaze alternative: Substitute prepared horseradish for the mustard.

I have no idea why spiral-sliced hams have become the norm rather than the exception; they are always more expensive than ham that is not sliced, and it's nearly impossible to cook one without having dried-out slices. Also, because the slices are so thin, you are severely limited as to the recipes you can make with the leftovers.

Basic Roast Chicken

While we credit President Herbert Hoover with the expression "a chicken in every pot," the phrase praising this luxury actually dates back to the kings of seventeenth-century France. There are few foods as wonderful, and there's so much you can do with the leftovers.

Yield: 8 servings | **Active time:** 15 minutes | **Start to finish:** 2 hours

1 (5–7-pound) roasting chicken
4 sprigs fresh parsley, divided
4 sprigs fresh rosemary, divided
6 garlic cloves, peeled and minced, divided
2 sprigs fresh thyme
1 teaspoon salt or to taste
Freshly ground black pepper to taste
4 tablespoons (½ stick) unsalted butter, softened
1 large onion, peeled and roughly chopped
1 carrot, peeled and thickly sliced
1 celery rib, rinsed, trimmed, and sliced
1 cup Chicken Stock (recipe on page 22) or purchased stock

1. Preheat the oven to 425°F. Rinse chicken, and pat dry with paper towels. Place 2 sprigs parsley, 2 sprigs rosemary, 4 garlic cloves, and thyme in cavity of chicken. Sprinkle salt and pepper inside cavity, and close it with skewers and string.
2. Chop remaining parsley, rosemary, and garlic. Mix with butter, salt, and pepper. Gently stuff mixture under the skin of breast meat. Place chicken on a rack in a roasting pan, breast side up.
3. Bake for 30 minutes, reduce the oven temperature to 350°F, and add onion, carrot, and celery to the roasting pan. Cook an additional 1–1½ hours, or until chicken is cooked through and no longer pink, and registers 165°F on an instant-read thermometer. Remove chicken from the oven, and allow it to rest on a heated platter for 10 minutes.
4. Spoon grease out of the pan, and add chicken stock. Stir over medium-high heat until the liquid is reduced to a syrupy consistency. Strain sauce into a sauce boat, and add to it any liquid that accumulates on the platter when the chicken is carved. Serve immediately.

Note: The chicken can be roasted up to 3 hours in advance and kept at room temperature, covered with aluminum foil.

Each 4-ounce serving of meat contains:

312 calories | 207 calories from fat | 23 g fat | 9 g saturated fat | 100 mg cholesterol | 22 g protein | 4 g carbohydrates | 124 mg sodium

Variations:

- Replace the seasonings with 3 tablespoons smoked Spanish paprika, 1 tablespoon ground cumin, 1 tablespoon dried thyme, and 3 minced garlic cloves.
- Use 3 tablespoons Italian seasoning, 3 tablespoons chopped fresh parsley, and 3 garlic cloves in place of the seasonings listed.
- Use 3 tablespoons dried oregano and 5 garlic cloves instead of the seasonings listed, and add 1 sliced lemon to the cavity.
- Rather than chicken stock, deglaze the pan with white wine.

Here's how to carve a roast chicken or turkey: To add a flourish to carving that also assures crisp skin for all, first "unwrap" the breast. Use a well-sharpened knife and fork. Carve and serve one side at a time. From the neck, cut just through the skin down the middle of the breast and around the side. Hook the fork on the skin at the tail and roll the skin back to the neck. Holding the bird with the fork, remove the leg by severing the hip joint. Separate the drumstick from the thigh and serve. Cut thin slices of the breast at a slight angle and add a small piece of rolled skin to each serving. Repeat all steps for the other side. Remove the wings last.

Basic Roast Turkey

There are two schools of thought to roasting a turkey—either relatively low heat or high heat—and I prefer the latter. Using this roasting method, the turkey basically steams; the meat remains moist since it is being cooked by a moist rather than dry heat method.

Yield: 10 servings, plus enough for leftovers | **Active time:** 15 minutes |
Start to finish: at least 2¼ hours, but varies by the weight of the turkey

> 1 (12–16-pound) turkey
> 6 tablespoons (¾ stick) unsalted butter, softened and divided
> 3 garlic cloves, peeled and minced
> 3 tablespoons smoked Spanish paprika
> 1 tablespoon dried thyme
> 1 teaspoon salt or to taste
> Freshly ground black pepper to taste
> 1 large onion, peeled and diced
> 1½ cups Chicken Stock (recipe on page 22) or purchased stock
> 1 tablespoon cornstarch
> 2 tablespoons cold water

1. Preheat the oven to 450°F. Rinse turkey inside and out under cold running water, and place it in a large roasting pan.
2. Combine 3 tablespoons butter, garlic, paprika, thyme, salt, and pepper in a small bowl, and mix well. Rub mixture over skin of turkey and inside cavity. Place onion and stock in the roasting pan, and place turkey on top of it. Create a tent with two sheets of heavy-duty aluminum foil, crimping foil around the edges of the roasting pan, and joining the two sheets in the center by crimping.
3. Place turkey in the oven, and roast for 12–15 minutes per pound. After 2 hours, remove the foil, and remove liquid from the roasting pan with a bulb baster. Return turkey to the oven, covered as before.
4. Reduce the oven temperature to 350°F, and uncover turkey for the last 1 hour of roasting so skin browns. Rub skin with remaining butter after removing the foil. Turkey is done when it is cooked through and no longer pink, and dark meat registers 165°F on an instant-read thermometer. Remove turkey from the oven, and allow it to rest on a heated platter for 10–15 minutes, lightly covered with foil.

5. While turkey rests, prepare gravy. Pour all juices and flavoring ingredients from the roasting pan into a saucepan. If there are any brown bits clinging to the bottom of the pan, add 1 cup chicken stock or purchased stock. Stir over medium heat, scraping brown bits from bottom of pan. In a small bowl, mix cornstarch and water, and set aside. Remove as much fat as possible from the surface of juices with a soup ladle, and then reduce liquid by at least $1/4$ to concentrate flavor. Stir cornstarch mixture into the pan, and cook for 1–2 minutes, or until liquid boils and slightly thickens. Season gravy with salt and pepper.

6. To serve, carve turkey, and pass gravy separately.

Note: The turkey can be left at room temperature for up to 1 hour after removing it from the oven; keep it lightly tented with aluminum foil.

Each 4-ounce serving of meat contains:

258 calories | 144 calories from fat | 16 g fat | 7 g saturated fat | 95 mg cholesterol | 24 g protein | 4 g carbohydrates | 312 mg sodium

Variations:
- Replace the seasonings with 2 tablespoons herbes de Provence or Italian seasoning along with 3 garlic cloves.
- Use $1/4$ cup chopped fresh rosemary, 1 tablespoon grated lemon zest, and 3 garlic cloves instead of the seasonings listed.

Chapter 3:
Chilled $1 Finger Foods

Versatile, easy-to-eat, and inexpensive finger foods are a stalwart for so many occasions. You can take them to the office for lunch, make them part of a picnic, or serve them as hors d'oeuvres before a dinner. Those are the recipes you'll find in this chapter, and none costs more than $1 per serving.

When we think of finger foods, categories like dips and traditional favorites like deviled eggs come to mind. But finger foods exist as part of all cuisines and cultures. Sushi is a finger food; in fact, there's a whole category called finger sushi. And bowls of smooth mixtures into which you dip a carrot stick or tortilla chip are now being augmented in popularity by chunky toppings placed on top of slices of toast. Called bruschetta in Italy, these topped toasts now include many non-traditional variations.

BRUSCHETTA BASICS
If you know how to preheat your oven broiler, you can make bruschetta. Traditionally bruschetta is grilled, and grilling does enhance the flavor, but the oven broiler works just as well. While you can use a toaster, I'm assuming you're making a whole loaf of bread at a time, and it's really more efficient to grill or broil it all at once rather than a few slices at a time.

Day-old bread is not only better for creating crisp toast slices, it's also less expensive. Dishes like bruschetta—along with bread puddings, French toast, and strata—are perfect candidates for the contents of the half-price bakery bin at the supermarket.

While traditionally bruschetta is made with a plain French baguette or Italian bread, there's no reason that you can't substitute an herb bread, whole-wheat loaf, or olive bread.

Bruschetta is easy to transport, because the toasts can be packed in one container and the topping in another; the only utensil you'll need is a spoon with which to scoop the topping. There are specific bruschetta combinations in this chapter, but you can also use Tapenade (recipe on page 53) or any of the bean salads in Chapter 6 as alternatives.

Toast Alternatives

A small slice of toast is the way bruschetta is supposed to be served, but there are alternatives to consider too. While crackers are always appropriate, it takes very little effort to create more interesting and inexpensive carbohydrates for dipping. Here are some ideas:

- Pita toasts are easy to make. Separate pita breads into their two natural layers and spread each layer with melted butter. Sprinkle the pieces with salt, pepper, and any herbs you like—anything from oregano to chili powder. Bake the bread at 375°F for 10–15 minutes, or until browned and crisp. Then break into dipping-size pieces.

- Fried wonton skins are excellent with any Asian dip. Heat oil in a saucepan over medium-high heat to a temperature of 375°F, and cut wonton wrappers into quarters. Fry them for 45–55 seconds, or until brown and crisp. Drain well on paper towels.

The Crudité Collection

What differentiates a dip from a bruschetta topping is the consistency. Dips are smooth and bruschetta toppings are chunky. But many of the recipes in this chapter can be used interchangeably with vegetables or bread. Slices of cucumber or small cups made from leaves of iceberg or leaf lettuce are great additions if people are on low-calorie or gluten-free diets.

A basket of vegetables served with dips—often called crudités—can be as simple as carrots and celery, but whatever the contents, the key is to arrange it artistically. I line a low basket with plastic wrap, and then cover the plastic with lettuce leaves.

Vegetables such as cauliflower, string beans, and broccoli should be blanched before serving. But rather than dirty a pot, it's more efficient to accomplish this in a microwave. Steam the vegetables for 1–2 minutes, then plunge them into ice water to stop the cooking action. Drain, and you're ready to arrange.

If you're serving crudités at a large party, prepare them in advance with this trick learned from my catering business. Cut up and/or steam your vegetables and wrap them in damp paper towels. Then wrap the packets in plastic wrap and refrigerate them for up to one day.

SUSHI SAVVY

Sushi is not only chic, it's also healthy. And while it's expensive even at supermarkets, let alone at sushi restaurants, it's extremely inexpensive to make at home. It's also a perfect food to take to the office for lunch, to take on a picnic, or to offer as an hors d'oeuvre in the evening.

There are all sorts of rituals that go along with making sushi, and myriad pieces of specialized equipment you can buy that are harmonious with the Japanese minimalist aesthetic. But you don't have to buy a thing to make sushi at home.

Contrary to popular belief, sushi has nothing to do with fish; it literally means "vinegared rice." And about 75 percent of what you eat with any bite of sushi is the seasoned rice, which can be prepared in a matter of minutes, and then formed or rolled with other ingredients to form sushi.

Anyone can boil rice and water, but to create seasoned rice with the proper flavor and texture is a bit more complicated—but it is not much more complicated. To begin with, you have to start with the correct rice, which is commonly called sushi rice both in Asian markets and supermarkets. It's occasionally just called short-grain rice, but there are other species that also fit that description, so take the time to find sushi rice.

The first recipe in the sushi section of this chapter gives you the method for making the rice. Here's a rundown on the various types of rolls or other forms you can make:

Finger sushi. This is the easiest of all forms to make because you do it right in the palm of your hand. For each individual piece, you start by using a piece of topping—a small slice of fish or a vegetable—and then you smear a bit of wasabi on what will be the bottom of the topping. Then you take about 1 tablespoon of seasoned rice, and build a "finger" above the topping. The last step is to turn it over to serve.

Molded sushi. Here's where mass production enters the equation to make many pieces of sushi at one time. Cut a sheet of plastic wrap and push it into the indentations in an ice-cube tray. Place a bit of topping in the bottom of each indentation, rub it with wasabi, and then fill the remainder with the seasoned rice. Invert it onto a serving platter, remove the tray, pull off the plastic wrap, and it's done.

Ball sushi. For this variation, cut squares of plastic wrap, and place a piece of topping in the center. Rub the topping with wasabi, and place a heaping tablespoon of seasoned rice on top of it. Pull up the corners of the plastic wrap, and form the rice into a ball. Then unwrap the ball and discard the plastic wrap. Both ball sushi and molded sushi are best transported before being unmolded if you're taking them to someone else's house.

Maki rolls. While all forms of finger sushi are just rice and some other ingredient or ingredients, what unites the family of maki rolls is that there's a sheet of nori, a shiny dehydrated seaweed, somewhere in the equation. The rolls can be thin or thick, and the nori can be showing or hidden under a layer of rice. These rolls are the assembly line of sushi-making. Thin rolls are made with ½ cup of seasoned rice and a half sheet of nori, and usually contain just one ingredient. Thick rolls and inside-out rolls use 1 cup of seasoned rice and a whole sheet, and the combinations of flavors and textures can include up to five or six other ingredients.

Merrily We Roll Along

All rolls are basically made the same way. Your key piece of equipment is an inexpensive bamboo sushi mat, called a *makisu,* although you can improvise one from a plastic placemat too. The bamboo mat is a good choice, however, because its slats work as a guide to keep the nori straight and the roll even.

Place the bamboo mat on the counter in front of you with the slats going horizontally; you will be rolling the roll away from you. Then place the nori with its shiny side down on the mat, leaving three slats uncovered to use as your guiding edge.

The first step to rolls is patting the rice onto the nori, which is done with a technique I call the "patchwork approach." Keeping your hands moist—but not dripping wet—dot the surface of the section of nori to be covered with a few teaspoons of rice placed at ½-inch intervals. Then pat the rice down so that it forms an even layer. By using this method there is very little chance of ripping the nori, and it is possible to keep the rice layer thin.

For thin rolls, leave a ½-inch border on the far side of the nori, and for a thick roll, leave a 2-inch border. If using wasabi, spread a thin line down the middle of the rice, and then arrange your filling in the center of the rice; it should go the length of the nori, so join a few pieces if necessary. If using more than one strip, push them as close together as possible, and angle cut the ends so that they join smoothly.

When assembling the ingredients to place in the center of the roll, place them in the center of the rice rather than in the center of the sheet of nori. This will keep them centered once the maki is rolled.

Lift the mat with your thumbs while pressing the filling into the rice with the rest of your fingers. Roll the mat over the filling, stopping when the mat reaches the far side of the roll. Work as quickly as possible so that the filling does not slide out, and keep even pressure on the roll between your hands.

The next part of the procedure is what tightens the roll. Pull the partially completed roll toward you with one hand while the other hand holds the mat taut. Then open the mat, and move the roll back to the edge in front of you, leaving three slats uncovered by the roll.

Now finish the roll by rolling it again until the free edge of the nori is covered and adheres. Take the roll out of the mat, and place it seam side down on a plate; if the nori has not completely adhered, it will after sitting for a few minutes from the inherent moisture in the rice. If you are not thrilled with the shape of the roll, now is the time to act. Use the bamboo mat and adjust the shape from the top to make it rounder or more square, depending on your preference.

Cut each roll into eight pieces with a very sharp serrated knife. First trim the ends, and cut the roll in half. Then cut each half into four slices. Wipe your knife with a damp cloth between slices to keep the knife from getting sticky and crushing the roll.

Drama without Fuss

It's always showy to serve inside-out rolls, which means the rice is on the outside rather than the inside. Once rolled, you can coat the rolls with toasted sesame seeds or a finely chopped herb such as cilantro or chives. The good news is that these rolls are no more difficult to make than any other—perhaps even easier because the rice naturally holds them together.

Cover your bamboo mat with plastic wrap to keep the sticky rice from adhering to the mat instead of itself. Place the bamboo mat on the counter in front of you with the slats going horizontally; you will be rolling the roll away from you. Place a full sheet of nori with its shiny side down on the mat, leaving three slats uncovered to use as your guiding edge. Spread about 1 cup of sushi rice on top, using the patchwork approach described above. If the rice starts to cling to your fingertips, moisten your hands again.

Then rinse your fingers again and turn over the sheet so that the rice is facedown on the plastic-covered mat. Rub a line of wasabi down the center of the nori, and place your chosen fillings on top of the nori, about a third of the way up from the bottom edge. Lift the mat with your thumbs while holding the filling with the rest of your fingers. Roll the mat over the filling, stopping when the mat reaches the far side of the roll. Work as quickly as possible so that the filling does not slide out, and keep even pressure on the roll between your hands.

The next part of the procedure is what tightens the roll. Pull the partially completed roll toward you with one hand while the other hand holds the mat taut. Then open the mat, and move the roll back to the edge in front of you, leaving three slats uncovered by the roll.

Take the roll out of the mat, and place it on a plate; make sure that the rolls do not touch or they may stick together. Wrap the roll in plastic wrap to facilitate slicing, and cut the roll into eight pieces with a very sharp knife; cut it first in half, and then cut each half into four equal slices. Wipe your knife with a damp cloth between slices to keep the knife from getting sticky and crushing the roll. Remove the plastic wrap from each piece, and serve.

Serving Sushi

Sushi should be eaten in one bite, although some restaurants make this difficult by "super-sizing" their pieces. The topping or nori is what should be dipped into soy sauce, *not* the rice. It is considered very bad form to have grains of rice floating in your soy sauce saucer. If a piece of sushi is too large to eat in one bite, feel free to eat it in two, but don't set it back down on your plate once you have taken the first bite; it is considered rude.

Also considered bad form, especially in restaurants, is stirring wasabi into the soy sauce dish. Chefs season sushi with the amount of fiery flavor they deem proper, and if you want more, rub some on the sushi itself. The other traditional condiment, pickled ginger (*gari*), is supposed to be eaten between pieces of sushi as a palate cleanser. It is never eaten piled on top of the sushi itself, nor is it eaten as a random snack.

Seasoned Sushi Rice

Here's your master recipe that forms the basis for all the sushi recipes that follow. Once you've made it a few times, it will become second nature, so don't be scared by the length of the recipe for a dish that is basically rice.

Yield: 3 cups rice | **Active time:** 10 minutes | **Start to finish:** 1½ hours

> 1 cup short-grain sushi rice
> 1¼ cups water
> 3 tablespoons unseasoned rice wine vinegar
> 1 tablespoon granulated sugar
> ½ teaspoon salt

1. Place rice in a sieve under cold running water, and rinse until water runs clear. Place rice in rice cooker or heavy saucepan, and cover with cold water. Allow rice to soak for 30 minutes, then drain. Return rice to the rice cooker or saucepan, and add 1¼ cups fresh water.

2. If using a rice cooker, cook according to manufacturer's instructions. If cooking on top of the stove, bring rice to a boil, covered, over medium heat. Reduce the heat to low without removing the lid, and cook for 15–17 minutes, or until water is absorbed. Turn off heat, and allow rice to sit undisturbed for 15 minutes. While rice sits, prepare seasoning liquid by stirring vinegar, sugar, and salt together.

3. Turn rice out into a mixing bowl by running a wooden paddle or spatula around the rim of the pan in which rice cooked to loosen it, and then invert it. Sprinkle vinegar mixture all over the rice by pouring it onto the back of the paddle. Then wait about 10 seconds to allow the liquid to be absorbed by the hot rice. Use the paddle in an up-and-down cutting motion to spread rice into a thin even layer; do not stir rice to avoid breaking the grains. After the rice is spread into an even layer, turn over small portions gently to allow steam to escape. When rice is cool enough to handle, it is ready to form sushi.

Note: To keep rice ready to use for up to 6 hours, dip a clean lint-free dish towel into cold water, and wring it out well. Totally cover the mixing bowl with the cloth, and check the towel every hour or so to ensure that it has not dried out.

Each ¼-cup serving contains:

64 calories | 1 calorie from fat | 0 g fat | 0 g saturated fat | 0 mg cholesterol | 1 g protein | 14.5 g carbohydrates | 105 mg sodium

> If you don't have a rice cooker, you can also cook sushi rice in a slow cooker. Because there is very little evaporation, use equal amounts of rice and water. If using a slow cooker, set it on High, and use these times as a guide:
>
> 1 cup rice for 1½ hours
>
> 2 cups rice for 2 hours
>
> 3 cups rice for 2¼ hours

Grilled Sesame Eggplant Finger Sushi

Japanese eggplants are light, almost amethyst purple, and they're long and thin. When treated simply and broiled, they are a great treat to have as a topping for sushi.

Yield: 24 pieces | **Active time:** 15 minutes | **Start to finish:** 25 minutes

> 2 tablespoons reduced-sodium soy sauce
> 2 teaspoons toasted sesame oil
> 2 Japanese eggplants*, sliced on the diagonal into ¼-inch slices
> 2½ cups Seasoned Sushi Rice (recipe on page 38)
> Wasabi* to taste
> 3 tablespoons toasted sesame seeds

1. Preheat a grill or oven broiler. In a small mixing bowl, combine soy sauce and sesame oil, and stir well. Brush mixture on both sides of eggplant slices, and grill for 2 minutes per side, or until eggplant softens.
2. To make sushi, follow the method on page 35, and then sprinkle completed pieces with sesame seeds.

Note: The fingers can be prepared up to 6 hours in advance and refrigerated, tightly covered with plastic wrap.

Each 3-piece serving contains:

146 calories | 29 calories from fat | 3 g fat | 0.5 g saturated fat | 0 mg cholesterol | 4 g protein | 27 g carbohydrates | 267 mg sodium

---

Wasabi, pronounced *wah-sah-bee,* is a Japanese form of horseradish that's light green and has a sharp, fiery flavor. It's sold both as a paste and powder, and the powder is mixed with water like dry mustard to make a paste. In a pinch you can use bottled Western horseradish.

---

*Available in the Asian aisle of most supermarkets and in specialty markets.

Vegetarian California Rolls

Sushi became popular in California a few decades ago, and both this vegetarian mélange and one containing crab sticks are the result. This is a very pretty roll to serve; it contains a number of colors and textures.

Yield: 24 pieces | **Active time:** 20 minutes | **Start to finish:** 20 minutes

3 sheets nori*
3 cups Seasoned Sushi Rice (recipe on page 38)
Wasabi* to taste
1 small cucumber, peeled, halved lengthwise, and seeded, with
  each half cut into 3 long strips
1 ripe avocado, peeled and thinly sliced
1 carrot, peeled and cut into fine julienne
3 tablespoons black or toasted white sesame seeds, optional
For serving: Pickled ginger, additional wasabi, and reduced-
  sodium soy sauce

1. Gather all ingredients, and make 1 roll at a time. Treat each sheet of nori with 1 cup seasoned rice as detailed on page 35, and spread a line of wasabi on top of rice. Divide cucumber, avocado, and carrot on top of rice and sprinkle with sesame seeds, if using.
2. Roll according to the method on page 36.
3. Cut each roll into 8 pieces with a very sharp serrated knife. First trim the ends, and cut it in half. Then cut each half into 4 slices. Wipe your knife with a damp cloth between slices to keep the knife from getting sticky and crushing the roll.

Note: The rolls can be prepared up to 6 hours in advance and refrigerated, tightly covered with plastic wrap. Do not slice them until just prior to serving.

Each 3-piece serving contains:

135 calories | 25 calories from fat | 3 g fat | 0 g saturated fat | 0 mg cholesterol | 3 g protein | 25 g carbohydrates | 167 mg sodium

Variation:
- Substitute fennel for the cucumber.

*Available in the Asian aisle of most supermarkets and in specialty markets.

California Rolls

I introduce friends to sushi with this popular American form. The combination of the buttery avocado and crunchy cucumber with the delicate crab sticks, which are far less expensive than crab meat, is always a winner.

Yield: 24 pieces | **Active time:** 15 minutes | **Start to finish:** 15 minutes

> 3 sheets nori*
> 3 cups Seasoned Sushi Rice (recipe on page 38)
> Wasabi* to taste
> 1 Japanese or Kirby cucumber or ¼ English cucumber, cut into
>   ¼-inch batons
> 1 ripe avocado, peeled and thinly sliced
> 6 crab sticks

1. To make rolls, treat each sheet of nori with 1 cup seasoned rice, and reverse onto plastic-covered bamboo mat as described on page 37.
2. Spread a thin line of wasabi on top of nori, and divide cucumber and avocado onto the 3 rolls. Place 2 crab sticks on each roll, and roll according to the method on page 37.
3. Cut each roll into 8 pieces with a very sharp serrated knife. First trim the ends, and cut it in half. Then cut each half into 4 slices. Wipe your knife with a damp cloth between slices to keep the knife from getting sticky and crushing the roll.

Note: The rolls can be prepared up to 6 hours in advance and refrigerated, tightly covered with plastic wrap. Do not slice them until just prior to serving.

Each 3-piece serving contains:

147 calories | 25 calories from fat | 3 g fat | 0 g saturated fat | 3.5 mg cholesterol | 4 g protein | 27 g carbohydrates | 311 mg sodium

Variation:
 • Substitute cooked shrimp for the crab sticks.

*Available in the Asian aisle of most supermarkets and in specialty markets.

Steamed Salmon and Scallion Rolls

While fresh salmon is a pricey food, there's so little of it used in making these colorful sushi rolls that you can splurge and treat yourself and your friends. Because the salmon is cooked, even folks who shy away from sushi made with raw fish will enjoy them.

Yield: 24 pieces | **Active time:** 15 minutes | **Start to finish:** 35 minutes

> ¼ pound salmon fillet, skinned
> 1 tablespoon soy sauce
> 1 tablespoon mirin* or sweet sherry
> 3 sheets nori*
> 3 cups Seasoned Sushi Rice (recipe on page 38)
> Wasabi* to taste
> 3 scallions, green tops only

1. Rinse salmon, and cut into 3 long pieces. Sprinkle salmon with soy sauce and mirin. Place salmon on a microwave-safe dish, and cover the dish with plastic wrap. Cook salmon on High (100 percent power) for 1½–2 minutes, or until strips are cooked through. Allow salmon to cool to room temperature for at least 15 minutes before rolling.

2. Gather all ingredients, and make 1 roll at a time. Treat each sheet of nori with 1 cup seasoned rice as detailed on page 35, and spread a line of wasabi on top of rice. Place 1 salmon strip and ⅓ of the green scallion tops on each sheet on top of rice and roll according to the method on page 37.

3. Cut each roll into 8 pieces with a very sharp serrated knife. First trim the ends, and cut it in half. Then cut each half into 4 slices. Wipe your knife with a damp cloth between slices to keep the knife from getting sticky and crushing the roll.

Note: The rolls can be prepared up to 6 hours in advance and refrigerated, tightly covered with plastic wrap. Do not slice them until just prior to serving.

Each 3-piece serving contains:

137 calories | 18 calories from fat | 2 g fat | 0.5 g saturated fat | 8 mg cholesterol | 5 g protein | 24 g carbohydrates | 328 mg sodium

*Available in the Asian aisle of most supermarkets and in specialty markets.

Chicken Teriyaki Rolls

Chicken teriyaki, marinated in a sweet and salty marinade and then grilled, is joined with colorful scallion greens in this family-pleasing roll. **Yield:** 24 pieces | **Active time:** 20 minutes | **Start to finish:** 4³/₄ hours, including 4 hours for marinating

CHICKEN

1 (4-ounce) boneless, skinless chicken breast half
¹/₂ cup reduced-sodium soy sauce
2 tablespoons mirin* or sweet sherry
1 tablespoon firmly packed light brown sugar
1 tablespoon Asian sesame oil*
2 garlic cloves, peeled and crushed
2 teaspoons grated fresh ginger

ROLL

3 sheets nori*
3 cups Seasoned Sushi Rice (recipe on page 38)
Wasabi* to taste
9 scallions, green parts only

1. Rinse chicken and pat dry with paper towels. Trim off all visible fat, and place between 2 sheets of plastic wrap. Pound chicken with the flat side of a meat mallet or the bottom of a small heavy skillet to an even thickness of ¹/₂ inch.
2. Combine soy sauce, mirin, brown sugar, sesame oil, garlic, and ginger in a 1-quart resealable plastic bag. Mix well, and add chicken. Marinate for 4 hours, refrigerated, turning the bag occasionally.
3. Preheat an oven broiler or grill. Remove chicken from marinade, and discard marinade. Grill chicken for 4 minutes per side or until chicken is cooked through and no longer pink. Allow chicken to cool, and cut it into 6 strips.

*Available in the Asian aisle of most supermarkets and in specialty markets.

4. Gather all ingredients, and make 1 roll at a time. Treat each sheet of nori with 1 cup seasoned rice as detailed on page 35, and spread a line of wasabi on top of rice. Place 2 chicken strips and ⅓ of the green scallion tops on each sheet on top of rice and roll according to the method on page 36.
5. Cut each roll into 8 pieces with a very sharp serrated knife. First trim the ends, and cut it in half. Then cut each half into 4 slices. Wipe your knife with a damp cloth between slices to keep the knife from getting sticky and crushing the roll.

Note: The rolls can be prepared up to 6 hours in advance and refrigerated, tightly covered with plastic wrap. Do not slice them until just prior to serving.

Each 3-piece serving contains:

139 calories | 11 calories from fat | 1 g fat | 0 g saturated fat | 8 mg cholesterol | 6 g protein | 26 g carbohydrates | 320 mg sodium

BLT Rolls

I invented this totally unorthodox recipe three years ago, and these rolls are always the biggest hit at any of my parties. Crunchy bacon, ribs of romaine, and tomatoes are all moistened with mayonnaise mixed with wasabi for a variation on the beloved American sandwich.

Yield: 24 pieces | **Active time:** 15 minutes | **Start to finish:** 25 minutes

> 9 strips bacon
> 1/3 cup mayonnaise
> 1 tablespoon wasabi*
> 6 leaves romaine
> 3 ripe plum tomatoes
> 3 sheets nori*
> 3 cups Seasoned Sushi Rice (recipe on page 38)

1. Cook bacon in a heavy skillet over medium-high heat for 5–7 minutes, or until crisp. Remove bacon from the pan with tongs, drain on paper towels, and set aside.

2. In a small mixing bowl, stir together mayonnaise and wasabi; set aside. Cut thick rib out of each lettuce leaf. Discard core and cut each tomato in half lengthwise. Squeeze seeds out, and slice each half into 1/4-inch slices.

3. Gather all ingredients, and make 1 roll at a time. Treat each sheet of nori with 1 cup seasoned rice as detailed on page 35, and spread a line of wasabi-mayonaise mixture on top of rice. Place 3 bacon strips, 2 lettuce ribs, and 1/3 tomato slices on top of rice and roll according to the method on page 36.

4. Cut each roll into 8 pieces with a very sharp serrated knife. First trim the ends, and cut it in half. Then cut each half into 4 slices. Wipe your knife with a damp cloth between slices to keep the knife from getting sticky and crushing the roll.

Note: The rolls can be prepared up to 6 hours in advance and refrigerated, tightly covered with plastic wrap. Do not slice them until just prior to serving.

*Available in the Asian aisle of most supermarkets and in specialty markets.

Each 3-piece serving contains:

372 calories | 241 calories from fat | 27 g fat | 8 g saturated fat | 32 mg cholesterol | 7.5 g protein | 25 g carbohydrates | 568.5 mg sodium

An alternative to frying bacon is to bake it in a 375°F oven until crisp. The length of time will depend on the thickness of the bacon, but count on at least 20 minutes.

Basic Bruschetta

Bruschetta (pronounced *brew-SKEH-tah*) is just a fancy word for toast that's rubbed with a garlic clove while still hot.

Yield: 18 slices | **Active time:** 10 minutes | **Start to finish:** 15 minutes

> 1 thin French baguette
> 3 tablespoons olive oil
> 1 large garlic clove, peeled and halved lengthwise

1. Light a charcoal or gas grill, or preheat the oven broiler.
2. Slice bread into slices $3/4$ inch thick. Brush bread lightly with oil. Grill or broil bread slices for 1–1$1/2$ minutes per side, or until toasted. Rub cut side of garlic clove on 1 side of toast.

Note: The slices can be toasted up to 2 days in advance and kept at room temperature in an airtight container.

Each 3-slice serving contains:

215 calories | 51 calories from fat | 6 g fat | 1 g saturated fat | 0 mg cholesterol | 7 g protein | 35 g carbohydrates | 385 mg sodium

Curried Tomato Bruschetta

A hint of aromatic curry and some sautéed vegetables blend with the luscious ripe tomatoes in this cooked topping for the toasts.

Yield: 6 servings | **Active time:** 20 minutes | **Start to finish:** 40 minutes

> 3 tablespoons olive oil
> 1 small onion, peeled and chopped
> 1 celery rib, rinsed, trimmed, and chopped
> ½ small green bell pepper, seeds and ribs removed, and chopped
> 2 garlic cloves, peeled and minced
> 1 tablespoon curry powder, or to taste
> 1 pound ripe plum tomatoes, rinsed, cored, seeded, and chopped
> ½ teaspoon salt, or to taste
> Freshly ground black pepper to taste
> 2 teaspoons firmly packed dark brown sugar
> 1 batch Basic Bruschetta (recipe on page 48)

1. Heat oil in a large skillet over medium-high heat. Add onion, celery, green bell pepper, and garlic. Cook, stirring frequently, for 3 minutes, or until onion is translucent. Stir in curry powder, and cook for 1 minute, stirring constantly.
2. Add tomatoes, salt, pepper, and brown sugar. Reduce the heat to medium, and cook mixture, uncovered, for 15 minutes, or until tomatoes soften. Cool mixture to room temperature, or chill it.
3. To serve, mound the vegetable mixture onto toast slices, and serve immediately.

Note: The vegetable mixture can be prepared up to 1 day in advance and refrigerated, tightly covered.

Each serving contains:

297 calories | 95 calories from fat | 10.5 g fat | 1.5 g saturated fat | 0 mg cholesterol | 9 g protein | 44 g carbohydrates | 592 mg sodium

Variation:

- Substitute 2 teaspoons Italian seasoning or herbes de Provence for the curry powder.

Bean Bruschetta Provençale

Garbanzo beans are the nuttiest and meatiest of legumes, and they work so well when melded with tomatoes, olives, and herbs as a bruschetta topping. The mixture is thick because some of the beans are pureed while others are left whole.

Yield: 6 servings | **Active time:** 15 minutes | **Start to finish:** 15 minutes

> 2 (15-ounce) cans garbanzo beans, drained and rinsed, divided
> 1/3 cup olive oil
> 3 garlic cloves, peeled and minced
> 3 tablespoons chopped fresh parsley
> 1 teaspoon herbes de Provence
> 2 ripe plum tomatoes, rinsed, cored, seeded, and chopped
> 1/4 cup chopped pitted black olives, preferably oil-cured
> 1/2 teaspoon salt, or to taste
> Freshly ground black pepper to taste
> 1 batch Basic Bruschetta (recipe on page 48)

1. Combine 1/2 of the beans, oil, garlic, parsley, and herbes de Provence in a food processor fitted with the steel blade or in a blender. Puree until smooth, and scrape mixture into a mixing bowl.
2. Add remaining beans, tomatoes, olives, salt, and pepper to the mixing bowl, and stir well.
3. To serve, mound vegetable mixture onto toast slices, and serve immediately.

Note: The vegetable mixture can be prepared up to 1 day in advance and refrigerated, tightly covered.

Each serving contains:

493 calories | 177 calories from fat | 20 g fat | 3 g saturated fat | 0 mg cholesterol | 14 g protein | 67 g carbohydrates | 1,014 mg sodium

Variations:

- Substitute white beans for the garbanzo beans.
- Substitute green olives for the black olives and Italian seasoning for the herbes de Provence.

Southwestern Bruschetta

This bruschetta topping is similar to a salsa, but the vegetables other than the tomatoes are briefly cooked to mellow their flavor. You can alter the "heat" by adding additional chile or hot red pepper sauce.

Yield: 6 servings | **Active time:** 15 minutes | **Start to finish:** 30 minutes

> 3 tablespoons olive oil
> ¼ small red onion, peeled, halved lengthwise, and thinly sliced
> 2 garlic cloves, peeled and minced
> 1 small jalapeño or serrano chile, seeds and ribs removed, and finely chopped
> 6 ripe plum tomatoes, rinsed, cored, seeded, and diced
> 2 tablespoons chopped fresh cilantro
> ½ teaspoon salt, or to taste
> Freshly ground black pepper to taste
> 1 batch Basic Bruschetta (recipe on page 48)

1. Heat oil in a small skillet over medium-high heat. Add onion, garlic, and chile, and cook, stirring frequently, for 3 minutes, or until onion is translucent. Scrape mixture into a mixing bowl.
2. Add tomatoes, cilantro, salt, and pepper to the mixing bowl, and stir gently. Allow mixture to sit for 10 minutes before serving.
3. To serve, mound vegetable mixture onto toast slices, and serve immediately.

Note: The vegetable mixture can be prepared up to 1 day in advance and refrigerated, tightly covered.

Each serving contains:

292 calories | 104 calories from fat | 11.5 g fat | 2 g saturated fat | 0 mg cholesterol | 9 g protein | 41 g carbohydrates | 586 mg sodium

Variation:

- Substitute ½ cup finely chopped fresh pineapple or mango for 2 of the tomatoes.

Swiss Chard Bruschetta

Dried fruit is used extensively in Sicilian cooking, and the sweetness of the raisins balances the bitterness of the greens in this traditional bruschetta topping.

Yield: 6 servings | **Active time:** 20 minutes | **Start to finish:** 20 minutes

> ¼ cup chopped raisins
> ¼ cup dry white wine
> 3 tablespoons olive oil
> 3 garlic cloves, peeled and minced
> 1½ pounds Swiss chard, rinsed well, stemmed, and chopped
> ½ teaspoon salt, or to taste
> Freshly ground black pepper to taste
> ¼ cup freshly grated Parmesan cheese
> 1 batch Basic Bruschetta (recipe on page 48)

1. Combine raisins and wine in a small microwave-safe bowl, and microwave on High (100 percent power) for 30 seconds. Allow raisins to soak in hot wine.
2. Heat oil in a large skillet over medium-high heat. Add garlic, and cook for 1 minute, stirring constantly. Add Swiss chard, and cook for 3–5 minutes, or until chard is wilted and softens. Season with salt and pepper, and stir in raisins along with wine and Parmesan.
3. To serve, mound vegetable mixture onto toast slices, and serve immediately.

Note: The vegetable mixture can be prepared up to 1 day in advance and refrigerated, tightly covered. Serve it chilled, or reheat it over low heat, covered, until hot.

Each serving contains:

329 calories | 112 calories from fat | 12.5 g fat | 2 g saturated fat | 3 mg cholesterol | 11 g protein | 45 g carbohydrates | 873 mg sodium

Variations:
- Substitute escarole or kale for the Swiss chard.
- Substitute finely chopped dried apricots or dried currants for the raisins.

Tapenade

Shop at the olive bar of your supermarket to get just the amount of olives you'll need for this lusty dip from Provence flavored by garlic, herbs, and anchovy paste. Serve the tapenade on crackers, on toast slices, or as a dip for crudité.

Yield: 2 cups | **Active time:** 10 minutes | **Start to finish:** 10 minutes

> $1^3/_4$ cups pitted kalamata olives or other brine-cured black olives
> 2 garlic cloves, peeled and minced
> 2 tablespoons anchovy paste
> 1 tablespoon chopped parsley
> $^1/_2$ teaspoon dried thyme
> 3 tablespoons lemon juice
> $^1/_4$ cup olive oil
> Freshly ground black pepper to taste

1. Combine olives, garlic, anchovy paste, parsley, thyme, and lemon juice in a food processor fitted with the steel blade. Puree until smooth. Add olive oil through the feed tube, and mix well.
2. Scrape mixture into a mixing bowl, and season to taste with pepper. Serve immediately.

Note: The spread can be made up to 2 days in advance and refrigerated, tightly covered. Allow it to reach room temperature before serving.

Each $^1/_4$-cup serving contains:

96 calories | 89 calories from fat | 10 g fat | 1 g saturated fat | 0 mg cholesterol | 0 g protein | 3 g carbohydrates | 402 mg sodium

Variations:
- If you think anchovy paste will make the dish "too fishy," omit it and season the tapenade to taste with salt.
- If you can find good-quality brine-cured green olives at a lesser price, make the tapenade with them; both are authentic.

Spicy Chinese Eggplant Dip

This recipe is an adaptation of one I used to enjoy often when the late Barbara Tropp had her China Moon Café in San Francisco. There's a slightly sweet/sour/hot eating profile, and it's always a sensation with guests.

Yield: 2 cups | **Active time:** 15 minutes | **Start to finish:** 1½ hours, including 30 minutes for chilling

> 2 (1-pound) eggplants
> 6 garlic cloves, peeled and minced
> 2 tablespoons grated fresh ginger
> 6 scallions, white parts and 3 inches of green tops, rinsed, trimmed, and thinly sliced
> ½–1 teaspoon crushed red pepper flakes
> ⅓ cup reduced-sodium soy sauce
> ¼ cup firmly packed dark brown sugar
> 2 tablespoons rice wine vinegar
> 2 tablespoons hot water
> 2 tablespoons vegetable oil
> 2 tablespoons Asian sesame oil*

1. Preheat the oven to 450°F. Rinse eggplants under cold water, and prick them with a sharp meat fork or the tip of a paring knife. Bake 20 minutes, turn, and bake an additional 20 minutes, or until flesh is very soft when poked with a meat fork.
2. When eggplants are cool enough to handle, slice them in half and scrape out flesh. Add any juices from the baking pan. Puree in a food processor fitted with a steel blade or pass eggplant pulp through a food mill.
3. Combine garlic, ginger, scallions, and red pepper flakes in a small dish. Combine soy sauce, brown sugar, vinegar, and water in another small bowl, stirring to dissolve sugar.
4. Heat a wok or large, heavy skillet over high heat. Add vegetable oil and sesame oil, swirl to glaze the pan, and reduce heat to medium-high. Add scallion mixture, and stir-fry 15 seconds. Add liquid mixture, and stir until simmering. Add eggplant, and bring to a simmer. Simmer 2 minutes, stirring constantly.

*Available in the Asian aisle of most supermarkets and in specialty markets.

5. Allow dip to sit for 30 minutes to reach room temperature before serving.

Note: The dip can be made up to 2 days in advance and refrigerated, tightly covered. Allow it to reach room temperature before serving.

Each ¼-cup serving contains:

131 calories | 64 calories from fat | 7 g fat | 1 g saturated fat | 0 mg cholesterol | 3 g protein | 17 g carbohydrates | 263.5 mg sodium

Summer Tomato Salsa

You can make this salsa as mild or spicy as you want by cutting back or increasing the number of hot chiles. You can also vary it visually by using a combination of red and orange tomatoes.

Yield: 4 cups | **Active time:** 15 minutes | **Start to finish:** 1¼ hours, including 1 hour for chilling

> 5 large ripe tomatoes, rinsed, cored, seeded, and chopped
> ½ red onion, peeled and finely chopped
> ½ green bell pepper, seeds and ribs removed, and finely chopped
> 1–2 small jalapeño or serrano chiles, seeds and ribs removed, and finely chopped
> 4 garlic cloves, peeled and minced
> 3 tablespoons chopped fresh cilantro
> 1 teaspoon dried oregano
> ¼ cup red wine vinegar
> 2 tablespoons olive oil
> ½ teaspoon salt, or to taste
> Freshly ground black pepper to taste

1. Combine tomatoes, onion, green bell pepper, chiles, garlic, cilantro, oregano, vinegar, and olive oil in a glass or stainless steel bowl. Season with salt and pepper.
2. Stir gently, and refrigerate for at least 1 hour to blend the flavors. Serve chilled.

Note: The salsa can be prepared up to 1 day in advance and refrigerated, tightly covered.

Each ½-cup serving contains:

52 calories | 32 calories from fat | 4 g fat | 0.5 g saturated fat | 0 mg cholesterol | 1 g protein | 5 g carbohydrates | 151 mg sodium

Variations:
- Substitute chipotle chiles in adobo sauce, finely chopped, for the fresh chile peppers.
- Substitute 6 scallions, white parts and 3 inches of green tops, for the red onion.

Guacamole

Like purchased salsa, you are paying a premium for purchased guaca-mole, and it's usually loaded with preservatives, too. The cilantro adds a fresh aroma and finish to this creamy Mexican dip.

Yield: 2 cups | **Active time:** 10 minutes | **Start to finish:** 10 minutes

4 ripe avocados
1/2 small red onion, peeled and finely chopped
1–2 jalapeño or serrano chiles, seeds and ribs removed, and finely diced
1/2 cup chopped fresh cilantro
1 teaspoon ground cumin
3 tablespoons lime juice
1/2 teaspoon salt, or to taste
Freshly ground black pepper to taste

1. Place avocados, red onion, and chiles in a medium mixing bowl. Use a table fork to mash mixture together, leaving some avocado in chunks.
2. Add cilantro, cumin, and lime juice, season with salt and pepper, and mix well. Serve immediately.

Note: The dip can be prepared up to 8 hours in advance. Push a piece of plastic wrap directly into the surface to prevent discoloration, and then refrigerate.

Each 1/4-cup serving contains:

116 calories | 93 calories from fat | 10 g fat | 1 g saturated fat | 0 mg cholesterol | 1 g protein | 7 g carbohydrates | 151 mg sodium

---

An easy and efficient way to remove the flesh from avocados is to run a rubber spatula under the skin after the pit has been discarded. You can scrape out the flesh efficiently without the fear of tearing the skin, which would need to be picked out of the dip.

Salmon Cheese Balls

These tasty morsels made with canned salmon, cream cheese, and a variety of seasonings are a treat for any time of day. You can use the mixture as a spread for toasted bagels for brunch, too.

Yield: 10 servings | **Active time:** 15 minutes | **Start to finish:** 45 minutes, including 30 minutes for chilling

> 1 (15-ounce) can red salmon, drained, with skin and bones discarded
> 1 (8-ounce) package cream cheese, softened
> 2 tablespoons smoked Spanish paprika
> 2 tablespoons lemon juice
> 2 tablespoons grated onion
> 1 tablespoon prepared horseradish
> $\frac{1}{2}$ teaspoon salt, or to taste
> Freshly ground black pepper to taste
> $\frac{1}{2}$ cup chopped fresh parsley

1. Combine salmon, cream cheese, paprika, lemon juice, onion, horse-radish, salt, and pepper in a food processor fitted with the steel blade. Process until smooth. This can also be done by hand.
2. Form mixture into 1-tablespoon balls, and chill for at least 30 minutes, or until firm. Roll balls in parsley, and return to the refrigerator until ready to serve.

Note: The dish can be prepared up to 2 days in advance and refrigerated, tightly covered.

Each serving contains:

173 calories | 114 calories from fat | 13 g fat | 6 g saturated fat | 51 mg cholesterol | 11 g protein | 2 g carbohydrates | 233 mg sodium

Variation:
- Substitute 3 (5-ounce) cans light tuna, drained, for the salmon.

Tuna-Stuffed Deviled Eggs

These lunch or picnic treats are a cross between deviled eggs and tuna salad. The filling is punctuated with bits of colorful and flavorful olives, too.

Yield: 10 servings | **Active time:** 15 minutes | **Start to finish:** 1 hour

10 large eggs
⅓ cup mayonnaise
1 (5-ounce) can light tuna, drained and flaked
⅓ cup chopped pimiento-stuffed green olives, divided
2 teaspoons Worcestershire sauce
½ teaspoon salt, or to taste
Freshly ground black pepper to taste

1. Place eggs in a saucepan, and cover with cold water by 2 inches. Bring to a boil over high heat, uncovered. Boil for 1 minute, cover the pan, and remove the pan from the heat. Allow eggs to sit for 15 minutes, covered. Drain eggs, and fill pan with cold running water for 3 minutes to stop the cooking action. Allow eggs to sit in cold water for 10 minutes, then peel eggs and halve them lengthwise.
2. Carefully remove yolks from eggs, and place them in a food processor fitted with a steel blade. Add mayonnaise, and process until light and fluffy. This can also be done by hand using a fork to mash mixture. Stir in tuna, 2 tablespoons olives, Worcestershire sauce, salt, and pepper.
3. Pipe mixture into egg whites with a pastry bag fitted with a large fluted tip. Garnish eggs with remaining chopped olives.

Note: The deviled eggs can be assembled 3 hours in advance and refrigerated, tightly covered. Do not sprinkle them with olives until just before serving.

Each serving contains:

146 calories | 102 calories from fat | 11 g fat | 3 g saturated fat | 218 mg cholesterol | 10 g protein | 1 g carbohydrates | 336 mg sodium

Deviled Eggs

While the practice of mixing egg yolks with spices dates back to ancient Rome, we think of these treats as all-American. The best way to transport them is on a bed of shredded iceberg lettuce in a shallow covered container; the lettuce will keep them from rolling around.

Yield: 8 servings | **Active time:** 15 minutes | **Start to finish:** 1 hour

> 8 large eggs
> 1/4 cup mayonnaise
> 2 teaspoons Dijon mustard
> 1/4 cup finely chopped sweet pickles
> 1/4 cup finely chopped celery
> 1/2 teaspoon salt, or to taste
> Freshly ground black pepper to taste
> Paprika

1. Place eggs in a saucepan, and cover with cold water by 2 inches. Bring to a boil over high heat, uncovered. Boil for 1 minute, cover the pan, and remove the pan from the heat. Allow eggs to sit for 15 minutes, covered. Drain eggs, and fill pan with cold running water for 3 minutes to stop the cooking action. Allow eggs to sit in cold water for 10 minutes, then peel eggs and halve them lengthwise.

2. Carefully remove yolks from eggs, and place them in a food processor fitted with a steel blade. Add mayonnaise and mustard, and process until light and fluffy. This can also be done by hand using a fork to mash the mixture. Stir in pickles and celery, and season to taste with salt and pepper.

3. Pipe mixture into egg whites with a pastry bag fitted with a large fluted tip. Sprinkle with paprika, and serve immediately.

Note: The deviled eggs can be assembled 3 hours in advance and refrigerated, tightly covered. Do not sprinkle them with paprika until just before serving.

Each serving contains:

129 calories | 94 calories from fat | 10.5 g fat | 3 g saturated fat | 214 mg cholesterol | 6 g protein | 2 g carbohydrates | 315 mg sodium

Variations:

- Substitute 3 tablespoons chopped fresh dill for the pickles.
- Substitute 1 tablespoon dried tarragon and 1 finely chopped shallot for the celery and pickles.
- Omit the mustard and pickles, and add 2–3 finely chopped chipotle chiles in adobo sauce and 2 tablespoons chopped fresh cilantro.
- Substitute finely chopped sun-dried tomatoes for the pickles, and add 2 tablespoons chopped fresh chives.
- Substitute chopped green or black olives for the pickles, and omit the mustard.

The best place to store eggs is in their cardboard carton. The carton helps prevent moisture loss, and it shields the eggs from absorbing odors from other foods. If you're not sure if your eggs are fresh, submerge them in a bowl of cool water. If they stay on the bottom, they're fine. If they float to the top, it shows they're old, because eggs develop an air pocket at one end as they age.

Chapter 4:
The Lunch Bunch

Brown-bagging is a growing trend for American workers of all walks of life as an easy way to trim expenditures. While anticipating food for lunch might bump up the supermarket register tape a bit, you'll be saving money on your total food budget—which includes all food and not just what you cook. You'll also be saving money on gas if your office location means that you were always driving to forage for lunch food.

Nearly 15 percent of lunches were brought to work in 2008, and that was up from only 10 percent a year earlier. While food manufacturers are trying to lure you to the frozen-food shelves to take a lunch-size frozen entree to work, resist the temptation. While a serving might be less expensive than what you're now spending on lunch, you're still getting a lot of chemicals and preservatives.

Chances are a lot of the time you'll take leftovers from dinner the night before, and I encourage this as a way to ensure food isn't wasted. But there are other times when there aren't leftovers, and that's where the recipes in this chapter come into play.

In this chapter I've concentrated on three genres of dishes, all of which make great lunches. There are summer rolls made with rice paper pancakes, wrap sandwiches formed in tortillas, and soups. I agree with the old Spanish proverb, "Of soup and love, the first is best." The cold soups are light, and will keep you cool on even the most sultry summer day. And the hot soups are thick and hearty, so they are a meal in themselves.

Dishes that also make great lunches are the sushi rolls and bruschetta recipes in Chapter 3, and any cold entree salad recipe in Chapter 5.

LUNCH-POOLING

Do you have a group of coworkers with whom you have lunch a few times a week? If so, it only makes sense to start a lunch club for at least three days a week. That way you're enjoying both food and company, and providing the meal is someone else's responsibility most of the time. That's one of the reasons that the recipes in this chapter serve more than one person.

The times I've seen this be the most successful are when a group sets a budget and creates a theme around a different cuisine for each week. That makes lunch almost like going to an ethnic restaurant. What's important is that your group's members share the same taste in foods—whatever those tastes may be.

TOP LUNCH TIPS

Unlike taking food on a picnic, you've got all sorts of modern conveniences when taking lunch to the office. Even if there's no kitchen or refrigerator, there's certainly hot and cold running water! And there's your desk to use as a counter too. So there's no reason that food can't be presented at its optimal quality for your lunch; it's very different than packing the PB&J for your second grader. Here are some tips to help you enjoy gourmet-quality fare:

Keep real utensils and plates at the office. By bringing lunch from home you're already saving money, and this way you feel like an adult eating at your desk or in the lunch area. Remember that you have soap and water, and eating from a real plate with a metal fork elevates your lunch even further above fast food.

Buy a thermos. Preheat it by filling it with boiling water to heat it if bringing hot food to work, and chill it with ice water or keep it in the refrigerator overnight if bringing cold food.

Buy supplies at a restaurant supply store. Those tiny plastic cups for salad dressings and condiments cost merely pennies there, as do durable disposable plates and utensils if you don't want to keep a set of real ones at the office.

Buy reusable gel ice packs. As you learned in Chapter 2 in the section on food safety, cold food should never be out of refrigeration for more than two hours. If you have a long commute to work, or if there isn't a refrigerator, then these are the best way to keep food chilled.

Pack microwavable containers at home. While you want to reheat your food at the office, it only makes sense to bring it in a container that can go right into the microwave to get "nuked" at the right time.

Assemble your sandwiches and salads at the office. The wrap sandwich recipes in this chapter are sturdier than those made with slices of bread, and can be packed in the morning before you leave home. But if you're taking a traditional sandwich, pack the bread, filling, and condiments separately. For salads, segregate the hard, crisp ingredients from the softer foods, and of course keep the dressing separate.

Do your own single servings. You should realize from the proliferation of single-serving packages flooding the market in recent years that manufacturers are making more money on selling them rather than units with larger volume. Another advantage to packing your own single serving of snacks or sweets is that you can have variety, too. Throw in some bagel chips or pita crisps with those pretzels!

Chopped Tuna Salad on Croissant

One of the things that is so appealing about taking your lunch to work is that because you're saving so much money on the total cost, you can include a treat for the meal like a flaky croissant from a good bakery. It's on that French bun that this flavorful tuna salad is mounded.

Yield: 4 servings | **Active time:** 15 minutes | **Start to finish:** 15 minutes

> ½ cup chopped bread-and-butter pickles, or other sweet pickles
> ½ green bell pepper, seeds and ribs removed, and chopped
> 4 scallions, white parts and 3 inches of green tops, rinsed, trimmed, and sliced
> 1 small carrot, peeled and diced
> 1 celery rib, rinsed, trimmed, and chopped
> ⅓ cup mayonnaise
> 1 tablespoon cider vinegar
> 2 (5-ounce) cans light tuna, drained
> Freshly ground black pepper to taste
> 4 plain croissants, split
> 4 leaves romaine lettuce, rinsed and dried

1. Combine pickles, green bell pepper, scallions, carrot, celery, mayonnaise, and vinegar in a mixing bowl, and mix well. Gently fold in tuna, and season to taste with pepper.
2. To serve, divide lettuce onto the bottom of each croissant and top with a portion of salad. Replace croissant tops and serve immediately.

Note: The salad can be prepared up to 1 day in advance and refrigerated, tightly covered. Do not place it on the croissant until just prior to serving.

Each serving contains:

468 calories | 233 calories from fat | 26 g fat | 9 g saturated fat | 66 mg cholesterol | 24 g protein | 34 g carbohydrates | 948 mg sodium

Variation:
- Substitute 1¼ cups shredded cooked turkey or chicken for the tuna.

Tuna Niçoise Summer Rolls

This cross-cultural dish combines all the wonderful ingredients of a classic composed French tuna salad with the portability of an Asian summer roll. It contains eggs, tomatoes, and olives along with tuna.

Yield: 6 servings | **Active time:** 15 minutes | **Start to finish:** 30 minutes

1 ounce bean thread (sometimes called cellophane) noodles*
1/4 pound green beans, rinsed and stemmed
2 (5-ounce) cans light tuna, drained and flaked
1/4 cup balsamic vinegar
2 garlic cloves, peeled and minced
2 scallions, white parts and 3 inches of green tops, rinsed, trimmed, and chopped
1 tablespoon Dijon mustard
2 teaspoons anchovy paste (or 1/2 teaspoon salt)
Freshly ground black pepper to taste
1/3 cup olive oil
6 (8-inch) rice paper pancakes*
1 1/2 cups shredded iceberg lettuce
4 hard-cooked eggs, peeled and cut into 6 wedges each
2 ripe plum tomatoes, rinsed, cored, seeded, and thinly sliced
1/4 cup chopped pitted oil-cured black olives

1. Fill a 2-quart saucepan with water, and bring it to a boil over high heat. Have a bowl of ice water handy. Place noodles in a mixing bowl, cover them with 1/2 of the boiling water, and allow them to soak for 10 minutes. Drain well, and pat dry with paper towels. Transfer noodles to a mixing bowl.

2. Boil beans in remaining water for 3–5 minutes, or until crisp-tender. Drain beans, and plunge them into the bowl of ice water to stop the cooking action. Drain again, and set aside.

3. Add tuna to the mixing bowl with noodles. Combine vinegar, garlic, scallions, mustard, anchovy paste, and pepper in a jar with a tight-fitting lid, and shake well. Add olive oil, and shake well again. Pour 1/2 of the dressing into the bowl with noodles and tuna, and mix gently.

*Available in the Asian aisle of most supermarkets and in specialty markets.

4. Fill a wide mixing bowl with very hot tap water. Place a damp tea towel in front of you on the counter. Place rice paper pancakes on a plate, and cover with a barely damp towel.

5. Fill 1 rice paper pancake at a time, keeping remainder covered. Totally immerse pancake in the hot water for 2 seconds. Remove it and place it on the damp tea towel; it will become pliable within a few seconds. Sprinkle $\frac{1}{6}$ of the lettuce across bottom half of pancake, and then top with $\frac{1}{6}$ of the noodle and tuna mixture, 4 egg wedges, and $\frac{1}{6}$ of the tomatoes. Sprinkle $\frac{1}{6}$ of the olives over all.

6. Fold sides over filling, and roll tightly but gently, beginning with the filled side. Place roll on a plate, and cover with a damp paper towel. Continue until all rice paper pancakes are filled. To serve, cut each summer roll in half on the diagonal, and pass remaining dressing separately.

Note: Summer rolls can be prepared up to 6 hours prior to serving. Wrap each individually in a damp paper towel, and then refrigerate them in a heavy resealable plastic bag. Do not cut the rolls in half until ready to serve them.

Each serving contains:

295 calories | 149 calories from fat | 17 g fat | 3 g saturated fat | 166 mg cholesterol | 17 g protein | 20.5 g carbohydrates | 506 mg sodium

Variation:

- Substitute $1\frac{1}{2}$ cups chopped cooked chicken or turkey for the tuna.

Chicken and Vegetable Summer Rolls

Here's one of many ways you'll find in this book to use up leftover chicken in a delicious way. The chicken is combined with traditional silky Asian noodles and crunchy fresh vegetables, and it's then dipped into a flavorful sauce.

Yield: 6 servings | **Active time:** 25 minutes | **Start to finish:** 25 minutes

ROLLS

1 ounce bean thread (sometimes called cellophane) noodles*

3 tablespoons rice wine vinegar

2 teaspoons fish sauce (*nam pla*)*

2 teaspoons firmly packed light brown sugar

6 (8-inch) rice paper pancakes*

1/2 pound cooked chicken, cut into 1/2-inch strips

1/2 small cucumber, peeled, seeded, and thinly sliced lengthwise

12 scallions, green tops only

1 medium carrot, peeled and cut into 1/2-inch batons

DIPPING SAUCE

1/3 cup reduced-sodium soy sauce

2 tablespoons rice wine vinegar

2 teaspoons Asian sesame oil*

1. Place noodles in a mixing bowl, cover with boiling water, and allow them to soak for 10 minutes. Drain well, and pat dry with paper towels. Return noodles to the mixing bowl. While noodles soak, combine vinegar, fish sauce, and sugar in a small cup, and stir well to dissolve sugar. Toss liquid with noodles, and set aside.

2. Fill a wide mixing bowl with very hot tap water. Place a damp tea towel in front of you on the counter. Place rice paper pancakes on a plate, and cover with a barely damp towel.

3. Fill 1 rice paper pancake at a time, keeping remainder covered. Totally immerse pancake in the hot water for 2 seconds. Remove it and place it on the damp tea towel; it will become pliable within a few seconds. Arrange 1/6 of the flavored noodles, chicken, cucumber, scallions, and carrot across bottom third of pancake.

*Available in the Asian aisle of most supermarkets and in specialty markets.

4. Fold sides over filling, and roll tightly but gently, beginning with the filled side. Place roll on a plate, and cover with a damp paper towel. Continue until all rice paper pancakes are filled.
5. For sauce, combine soy sauce, vinegar, and sesame oil, and stir well. To serve, cut each summer roll in half on the diagonal, and pass sauce separately.

Note: Summer rolls can be prepared up to 6 hours prior to serving. Wrap each individually in a damp paper towel, and then refrigerate them in a heavy resealable plastic bag. Do not cut the rolls in half until ready to serve them.

Each serving contains:

168 calories | 27 calories from fat | 3 g fat | 1 g saturated fat | 32 mg cholesterol | 15 g protein | 21 g carbohydrates | 689 mg sodium

Variation:
- Substitute roast pork or turkey for the chicken.

Pork and Peanut Summer Rolls

Spicy peanut sauce plays a role in many Asian cuisines, and these slightly spicy rolls made with flavorful ground pork fit into that tradition. They appeal to children as well as adults.

Yield: 6 servings | **Active time:** 25 minutes | **Start to finish:** 25 minutes

SAUCE

¼ cup peanut butter

2 tablespoons very hot tap water

2 tablespoons reduced-sodium soy sauce

1 tablespoon hoisin sauce*

2 garlic cloves, peeled and minced

2 scallions, white parts and 4 inches of green tops, rinsed, trimmed, and chopped

1 teaspoon Chinese chile paste with garlic*

ROLLS

1 ounce bean thread (sometimes called cellophane) noodles*

¾ pound ground pork

2 large egg whites, lightly beaten

4 scallions, white parts and 4 inches of green tops, rinsed, trimmed, and chopped

2 garlic cloves, peeled and minced

3 tablespoons oyster sauce*

1–2 teaspoons Chinese chile paste with garlic*

2 tablespoons vegetable oil

6 (8-inch) rice paper pancakes*

1½ cups fresh bean sprouts, rinsed

½ green bell pepper, seeds and ribs removed, and cut into thin strips

6 sprigs fresh cilantro

1. For sauce, combine peanut butter, water, soy sauce, hoisin sauce, garlic, scallions, and chile paste in a small bowl. Whisk well, and set aside.

*Available in the Asian aisle of most supermarkets and in specialty markets.

2. Cover noodles with boiling water, and allow them to soak for 10 minutes. Drain well, and pat dry with paper towels. Set aside.

3. While noodles soak, combine pork, egg whites, scallions, garlic, oyster sauce, and chile paste in a mixing bowl, and mix well. Heat oil in a skillet over medium-high heat. Add pork mixture, breaking up lumps with a fork. Cook for 6–8 minutes, or until mixture is dry. Remove pork from the pan with a slotted spoon, and spread out onto a plate to cool.

4. Fill a wide mixing bowl with very hot tap water. Place a damp tea towel in front of you on the counter. Place rice paper pancakes on a plate, and cover with a barely damp towel.

5. Fill 1 rice paper pancake at a time, keeping remainder covered. Totally immerse pancake in the hot water for 2 seconds. Remove it and place it on the damp tea towel; it will become pliable within a few seconds. Spread $1/6$ of the peanut sauce across bottom half of pancake, and then top with $1/6$ of the noodles, pork, bean sprouts, pepper strips, and cilantro.

6. Fold sides over filling, and roll tightly but gently, beginning with the filled side. Place roll on a plate, and cover with a damp paper towel. Continue until all rice paper pancakes are filled. To serve, cut each summer roll in half on the diagonal, and pass sauce separately.

Note: Summer rolls can be prepared up to 6 hours prior to serving. Wrap each individually in a damp paper towel, and then refrigerate them in a heavy resealable plastic bag. Do not cut the rolls in half until ready to serve them.

Each serving contains:

318 calories | 174 calories from fat | 19 g fat | 5 g saturated fat | 33 mg cholesterol | 15 g protein | 22 g carbohydrates | 561 mg sodium

Variation:
- Substitute ground turkey for the ground pork.

Southwestern Chicken Wraps

The smoky flavor of chipotle chiles is matched by the fresh aroma of cilantro in the sauce that moistens this wrap sandwich filled with chicken as well as red onion.

Yield: 4 servings | **Active time:** 15 minutes | **Start to finish:** 15 minutes

> 1/2 cup mayonnaise
> 1/4 cup chopped fresh cilantro
> 1–2 chipotle chiles in adobo sauce, finely chopped
> 4 (10-inch) white or whole wheat flour tortillas
> 8 leaves romaine lettuce, rinsed and dried
> 1/2 small red onion, peeled and thinly sliced
> 3/4 pound thinly sliced cooked chicken

1. Combine mayonnaise, cilantro, and chiles in a small mixing bowl, and stir well. Set aside.
2. Soften tortillas, if necessary, by wrapping them in plastic wrap and heating them in a microwave oven on High (100 percent power) for 10–15 seconds, or until pliable. Place tortillas on a counter.
3. Arrange lettuce leaves on tortillas, and spread dressing on top of lettuce. Layer red onion and chicken on bottom half of each tortilla. Tuck sides of tortillas over filling, and roll gently but firmly beginning at the filled side. Cut in half on the diagonal prior to serving.

Note: The dressing can be made up to 1 day in advance and refrigerated, tightly covered.

Each serving contains:

528 calories | 266 calories from fat | 30 g fat | 5 g saturated fat | 75 mg cholesterol | 33 g protein | 31 g carbohydrates | 860 mg sodium

Variation:
- Substitute shredded red cabbage for the red onion.

Barbecued Turkey Salad Wraps

With hard-cooked eggs, corn, kidney beans, and Southwestern flavorings, this hearty wrap just zings with color and flavor. The combination of mayonnaise and barbecue sauce binds it together.

Yield: 4 servings | **Active time:** 15 minutes | **Start to finish:** 15 minutes

> 2 cups shredded roast turkey
> 3 hard-cooked eggs, peeled and diced
> 1 cup cooked corn kernels
> 1 (15-ounce) can red kidney beans, drained and rinsed
> 1/2 small red onion, peeled and chopped
> 3 ripe plum tomatoes, rinsed, cored, seeded, and diced
> 2 celery ribs, rinsed, trimmed, and thinly sliced
> 1/2 cup barbecue sauce
> 1/3 cup mayonnaise
> 2 garlic cloves, peeled and minced
> 2 tablespoons chopped fresh cilantro
> 4 (10-inch) white or whole wheat flour tortillas
> 8 leaves romaine lettuce, rinsed and dried

1. Combine turkey, eggs, corn, beans, onion, tomatoes, and celery in a mixing bowl.
2. Whisk together barbecue sauce, mayonnaise, garlic, and cilantro. Toss dressing with salad.
3. Soften tortillas, if necessary, by wrapping them in plastic wrap and heating them in a microwave oven on High (100 percent power) for 10–15 seconds, or until pliable. Place tortillas on a counter.
4. Arrange lettuce leaves on tortillas, and place 1/4 of the turkey salad on bottom half of tortillas. Tuck sides of tortillas over filling, and roll gently but firmly beginning at the filled side. Cut in half on the diagonal prior to serving.

Note: The salad can be prepared 1 day in advance and refrigerated, tightly covered.

Each serving contains:

617 calories | 200 calories from fat | 22 g fat | 5 g saturated fat | 219 mg cholesterol | 39 g protein | 77 g carbohydrates | 1,192 mg sodium

Buffalo Chicken Wraps

First there were wings to chew, and now the same hot and spicy chicken can be placed in a wrap sandwich with the traditional accompaniments of blue cheese dressing to cool it and celery sticks to give it crunch. There's enough lettuce inside the wrap, too, that your meal is really complete.

Yield: 4 servings | **Active time:** 15 minutes | **Start to finish:** 15 minutes

> ³/₄ pound boneless, skinless chicken breast halves
> ¹/₂ teaspoon salt, or to taste
> Freshly ground black pepper to taste
> 3 tablespoons unsalted butter
> 2–3 tablespoons hot red pepper sauce, or to taste
> ¹/₂ cup mayonnaise
> ¹/₂ cup sour cream
> ³/₄ cup crumbled blue cheese
> 1 tablespoon lemon juice
> 3 celery ribs, rinsed and trimmed
> 4 (10-inch) white or whole wheat flour tortillas
> 8 leaves romaine lettuce, rinsed and dried

1. Rinse chicken and pat dry with paper towels. Pound chicken to an even thickness of ¹/₂ inch between 2 sheets of plastic wrap. Cut chicken into 2-inch strips, and sprinkle with salt and pepper.
2. Melt butter in a large skillet over medium-high heat. Add chicken and cook for 2–3 minutes per side, turning strips with tongs. Chicken should be cooked through and no longer pink. Drizzle hot red pepper sauce over chicken, and shake the pan to distribute hot sauce.
3. While chicken cooks, combine mayonnaise, sour cream, blue cheese, and lemon juice in a mixing bowl. Whisk well. Cut each celery rib into 4 lengthwise strips, and cut pieces into 6-inch lengths. Set aside.
4. Soften tortillas, if necessary, by wrapping them in plastic wrap and heating them in a microwave oven on High (100 percent power) for 10–15 seconds, or until pliable. Place tortillas on a counter.
5. Arrange lettuce leaves on tortillas, and place celery sticks down the center of each tortilla. Place a portion of chicken on bottom half of tortillas, and top with dressing. Tuck sides of tortillas over filling, and roll gently but firmly beginning at the filled side. Cut in half on the diagonal prior to serving.

Note: The chicken can be cooked, and the dressing can be made, up to 1 day in advance and refrigerated, tightly covered.

Each serving contains:

598 calories | 370 calories from fat | 41 g fat | 15 g saturated fat | 116 mg cholesterol | 31 g protein | 37 g carbohydrates | 1,312 mg sodium

Variation:

- This dish can also be served as an entree salad by omitting the tortillas and doubling the amount of lettuce. Shred the lettuce, dice the celery, and mound the chicken and dressing on top.

Few dishes in American cuisine have an exact known parentage, but Buffalo chicken wings are one of them. They started at the Anchor Bar in Buffalo, New York, and were a totally serendipitous snack served one night by the owner to regular patrons.

Cobb Salad Wraps

Transforming salads from plate food to finger food is one of the trends of the late twentieth century that continues to grow in popularity. This wrap contains bacon, turkey, avocado, eggs, and tomatoes—all the components of a cobb salad—moistened with a blue cheese vinaigrette.

Yield: 4 servings | **Active time:** 20 minutes | **Start to finish:** 20 minutes

> 1/4 pound bacon
> 4 (10-inch) white or whole wheat flour tortillas
> 8 leaves romaine lettuce, rinsed and dried
> 1/2 pound thinly sliced turkey
> 4 hard-cooked eggs, shelled and sliced
> 3 ripe plum tomatoes, rinsed, cored, seeded, and sliced
> 1/2 ripe avocado, peeled and thinly sliced
> 3/4 cup crumbled blue cheese
> 3 tablespoons balsamic vinegar
> 1/2 teaspoon salt, or to taste
> Freshly ground black pepper to taste
> 3 tablespoons olive oil

1. Place bacon slices in a large skillet and cook over medium-high heat, turning slices with tongs, for 5–7 minutes, or until bacon is crisp. Drain bacon on paper towels, and set aside.

2. Soften tortillas, if necessary, by wrapping them in plastic wrap and heating them in a microwave oven on High (100 percent power) for 10–15 seconds, or until pliable. Place tortillas on a counter.

3. Arrange lettuce leaves on tortillas. Layer turkey, egg slices, tomato slices, and avocado slices on bottom half of each tortilla, and sprinkle with blue cheese. Combine vinegar, salt, and pepper in a small cup, and stir well. Add olive oil, and stir well again. Drizzle dressing over filling.

4. Tuck sides of tortillas over filling, and roll gently but firmly beginning at the filled side. Cut in half on the diagonal prior to serving.

Each serving contains:

665 calories | 375 calories from fat | 42 g fat | 13 g saturated fat | 293 mg cholesterol | 39 g protein | 44 g carbohydrates | 1,031 mg sodium

Variation:

- Substitute baked ham for the turkey.

BLT Blue Cheese Wraps

In late summer and fall, when tomatoes are ripe and local, my day isn't complete without a BLT sandwich. This wrap version is not only easier to transport and eat, it's also a variation on the theme because it includes sharp blue cheese.

Yield: 4 servings | **Active time:** 20 minutes | **Start to finish:** 20 minutes

> 1/3 pound bacon
> 4 ripe plum tomatoes, rinsed, cored, seeded, and thinly sliced
> 1/2 teaspoon salt, or to taste
> Freshly ground black pepper to taste
> 1/2 cup mayonnaise
> 1/2 cup crumbled blue cheese
> 4 (10-inch) white or whole wheat flour tortillas
> 8 large romaine leaves, rinsed and dried

1. Place bacon slices in a large skillet and cook over medium-high heat, turning slices with tongs, for 5–7 minutes, or until bacon is crisp. Drain bacon on paper towels, and set aside.
2. Toss tomatoes with salt and pepper, and allow to sit for 5 minutes. Combine mayonnaise and blue cheese, and set aside.
3. Soften tortillas, if necessary, by wrapping them in plastic wrap and heating them in a microwave oven on High (100 percent power) for 10–15 seconds, or until pliable. Place tortillas on a counter.
4. Arrange lettuce leaves on tortillas, and spread dressing on top of lettuce. Layer bacon slices and tomato slices on bottom half of each tortilla. Tuck sides of tortillas over filling, and roll gently but firmly beginning at the filled side. Cut in half on the diagonal prior to serving.

Note: The bacon can be cooked, and the dressing can be made, up to 1 day in advance and refrigerated, tightly covered. Reheat the bacon briefly in a microwave oven before assembling wraps.

Each serving contains:

611 calories | 417 calories from fat | 46 g fat | 13 g saturated fat | 48 mg cholesterol | 14 g protein | 35 g carbohydrates | 1,382 mg sodium

Chilled Garlicky Cream of Tomato Soup

This refreshing soup is like a cross between vichyssoise and cream of tomato; it contains potatoes that make it thick but also herbs, tomatoes, and garlic to enliven the flavor.

Yield: 6 servings | **Active time:** 15 minutes | **Start to finish:** 3½ hours, including 2½ hours for chilling

> 2 tablespoons olive oil
> 1 medium onion, peeled and diced
> 6 garlic cloves, peeled
> 4 cups Chicken Stock (recipe on page 22) or purchased stock
> 1½ pounds redskin potatoes, scrubbed and cut into ¾-inch cubes
> 1 (14.5-ounce) can diced tomatoes, undrained
> 1 tablespoon dried sage
> ½ teaspoon salt, or to taste
> ½ cup heavy cream
> Freshly ground black pepper to taste

1. Heat oil in a 4-quart saucepan over medium-high heat. Add onion and garlic, and cook, stirring frequently, for 3 minutes, or until onion is translucent. Add stock, potatoes, tomatoes, sage, and salt, and bring to a boil, stirring occasionally.
2. Reduce the heat to low, and simmer soup, partially covered, for 10–12 minutes, or until potatoes are tender.
3. Strain solids from soup, and puree in a food processor fitted with the steel blade or in a blender. Stir puree back into the pan, stir in cream, and season to taste with pepper. Chill until cold.

Note: The soup can be prepared up to 2 days in advance and refrigerated, tightly covered.

Each serving contains:

211 calories | 100 calories from fat | 11 g fat | 5 g saturated fat | 27 mg cholesterol | 4 g protein | 26 g carbohydrates | 446.5 mg sodium

When pureeing in a food processor or blender be careful to never fill the work bowl or beaker more than two-thirds full, and hold your hand on the cover to make sure it does not fly off.

Gazpacho

This traditional Spanish cold vegetable soup is emblematic of summer to me, and it's as welcome at a picnic as poured from your thermos for lunch. It's also incredibly low in calories, if dieting is part of your impetus to take lunch to the office.

Yield: 8 servings | **Active time:** 15 minutes | **Start to finish:** 1 hour, including 45 minutes for chilling

> 1 medium Bermuda or other sweet white onion, peeled and quartered
> 1 medium cucumber, peeled, seeded, and cut into 1-inch sections
> 1 green bell pepper, seeds and ribs removed, and diced
> 3 medium to large ripe tomatoes, seeded and diced, divided
> 3 large garlic cloves, peeled
> 1½ cups tomato juice
> ¼ cup olive oil
> 1 jalapeño or serrano chile, seeds and ribs removed, and sliced
> ¼ cup balsamic vinegar
> ¼ cup chopped fresh cilantro
> ½ teaspoon salt or to taste
> Freshly ground black pepper to taste

1. Finely chop onion, cucumber, green bell pepper, and 1 tomato in a food processor fitted with the steel blade using on-and-off pulsing. Scrape mixture into a large bowl.
2. Puree remaining tomatoes with garlic, tomato juice, olive oil, chile, and vinegar. Stir puree into vegetables, add cilantro, and season with salt and pepper. Chill well.

Each serving contains:

102 calories | 63 calories from fat | 7 g fat | 1 g saturated fat | 0 mg cholesterol | 1 g protein | 9 g carbohydrates | 292 mg sodium

---

Always available, green bell peppers are merely immature peppers picked before they turn color. They are less expensive than colored peppers because they are not as perishable in this young condition and are easier to transport. The flavor is not as sweet, however.

Minestrone

Every Italian soup filled with vegetables is called minestrone, and this hearty version includes some salami for flavor and a cornucopia of healthful vegetables and beans along with pasta. It will warm you on a chilly day.

Yield: 8 servings | **Active time:** 20 minutes | **Start to finish:** 1 hour

¼ cup olive oil
1 large onion, peeled and diced
1 large carrot, peeled and sliced
1 celery rib, rinsed, trimmed, and sliced
3 garlic cloves, peeled and minced
¼ pound Genoa salami, chopped
3 cups shredded green cabbage
4 cups Chicken Stock (recipe on page 22) or purchased stock
1 (14.5-ounce) can diced tomatoes, undrained
2 tablespoons tomato paste
¼ cup chopped fresh parsley
1 tablespoon Italian seasoning
1 (4-inch-square) piece Parmesan rind (optional)
2 zucchini, rinsed, trimmed, and diced
1 (15-ounce) can cannellini beans, drained and rinsed
¼ pound small shells or other small pasta
½ cup frozen peas, thawed
½ cup freshly grated Parmesan cheese
½ teaspoon salt, or to taste
Freshly ground black pepper to taste

1. Heat olive oil in a 4-quart saucepan over medium-high heat. Add onion, carrot, celery, garlic, and salami. Cook, stirring frequently, for 3 minutes, or until onion is translucent. Add cabbage, and cook for 1 minute.

2. Add stock, tomatoes, tomato paste, parsley, Italian seasoning, and Parmesan rind, if using. Stir well to dissolve tomato paste. Bring to a boil over medium-high heat, stirring occasionally. Reduce the heat to low, and simmer soup, partially covered, for 40 minutes. Add zucchini and beans, and simmer for an additional 15 minutes.

3. While soup simmers, bring a large pot of salted water to a boil over high heat. Cook pasta according to package directions until al dente. Drain, and set aside.

4. Remove and discard Parmesan rind, if using. Add pasta and peas to soup, stir in cheese, and season with salt and pepper. Serve hot.

Note: The soup can be prepared up to 2 days in advance and refrigerated, tightly covered. Reheat it, covered, over low heat, stirring frequently. Add the pasta just prior to serving.

Each serving contains:

276 calories | 120 calories from fat | 13 g fat | 4 g saturated fat | 19 mg cholesterol | 12 g protein | 29 g carbohydrates | 826 mg sodium

Variations:
- Substitute vegetable stock for the chicken stock, and omit the salami for a vegetarian soup.
- Substitute baked ham for the salami for milder flavor.
- Substitute ½ pound chopped kale for the cabbage.
- Use any beans you may have in the larder as a substitution for the cannellini beans.

When soups are made with pasta, the cooked pasta should be added just prior to serving. Otherwise it will absorb stock from the soup, and get mushy. You can cook the pasta at the same time you're cooking the soup, but refrigerate it separately.

Cabbage Soup with Italian Sausage and Potatoes

Cabbage is always in the bargain basement of the produce department, and it also has a very long life if refrigerated.

Yield: 6 servings | **Active time:** 20 minutes | **Start to finish:** 45 minutes

½ pound bulk sweet Italian sausage
1 medium onion, peeled and diced
2 garlic cloves, peeled and minced
2 carrots, peeled and diced
4 cups firmly packed shredded green cabbage
5 cups Chicken Stock (recipe on page 22) or purchased stock
1 (14.5-ounce) can diced tomatoes, undrained
1 pound redskin potatoes, scrubbed and cut into ¾-inch dice
2 tablespoons chopped fresh parsley
1 teaspoon Italian seasoning
½ teaspoon salt, or to taste
Freshly ground black pepper to taste

1. Heat a 4-quart saucepan over medium-high heat. Add sausage and cook, breaking up lumps with a fork, for 3–5 minutes, or until sausage is browned. Remove sausage from the pan with a slotted spoon, and set aside.
2. Add onion, garlic, and carrots to the pan, and cook, stirring frequently, for 3 minutes, or until onion is translucent. Add cabbage, and cook for an additional 2 minutes, or until cabbage begins to wilt.
3. Add stock, tomatoes, potatoes, parsley, and Italian seasoning. Bring to a boil over high heat, then reduce the heat to low and simmer soup, covered, for 20–25 minutes, or until vegetables are tender.
4. Season with salt and pepper, and serve hot.

Note: The soup can be prepared up to 2 days in advance and refrigerated, tightly covered. Reheat it over low heat, covered, until hot, stirring occasionally.

Each serving contains:

160 calories | 31 calories from fat | 3.5 g fat | 1 g saturated fat | 11 mg cholesterol | 9.5 g protein | 25 g carbohydrates | 674 mg sodium

Variation:
- Substitute ground pork or ground beef for the sausage.

Split Pea Soup with Ham

What could be a better lunch on a cold winter day? Thick, aromatic, and hearty with an undertone of smoky flavor, it's a meal in itself. If you're at the end of your ham, add the bone to the soup to achieve even more flavor.

Yield: 8 servings | **Active time:** 20 minutes | **Start to finish:** 1 hour

    1 pound dried green split peas
    2 tablespoons vegetable oil
    2 medium onions, peeled and chopped
    2 celery ribs, rinsed, trimmed, and chopped
    1 carrot, peeled and chopped
    2 garlic cloves, peeled and minced
    10 cups Chicken Stock (recipe on page 22) or purchased stock
    3 tablespoons chopped fresh parsley
    1 teaspoon dried thyme
    1 bay leaf
    ³/₄ pound baked ham, trimmed of fat and diced
    ½ teaspoon salt, or to taste
    Freshly ground black pepper to taste

1. Rinse peas under cold water and pick them over. Set aside.
2. Heat oil in a 3-quart saucepan over medium-high heat. Add onion, celery, carrot, and garlic, and cook, stirring frequently, for 3 minutes, or until onion is translucent. Add split peas to the pan, along with stock, parsley, thyme, and bay leaf. Bring to a boil over high heat, stirring occasionally.
3. Reduce the heat to low and simmer soup, partially covered, for 30 minutes. Add ham, and simmer for an additional 30–40 minutes, or until peas have disintegrated and soup is thick.
4. Discard bay leaf, season with salt and pepper, and serve hot.

Note: The soup can be prepared up to 3 days in advance and refrigerated, tightly covered. Reheat it, covered, over low heat, stirring frequently.

Each serving contains:

296 calories | 50 calories from fat | 6 g fat | 1 g saturated fat | 20 mg cholesterol | 22 g protein | 42 g carbohydrates | 713 mg sodium

Tuscan White Bean Soup with Sausage

This hearty soup is relatively fast to make because I developed the recipe using canned beans that require no soaking. The combination of the mild beans with the hearty sausage is delicious, and a tossed salad is all you need.

Yield: 8 servings | **Active time:** 20 minutes | **Start to finish:** 45 minutes

> 1 pound bulk Italian sausage (sweet or hot)
> 2 large onions, peeled and diced
> 4 garlic cloves, peeled and minced
> 4 celery ribs, rinsed, trimmed, and diced
> 2 carrots, peeled and diced
> 1 (6-inch) rind from Parmesan cheese, optional
> 4 cups Chicken Stock (recipe on page 22) or purchased stock
> 3 (15-ounce) cans white beans, drained and rinsed
> 1/4 cup chopped fresh parsley
> 1 1/2 teaspoons dried thyme
> 1 bay leaf
> 1 cup water
> 3/4 pound Swiss chard, rinsed, stemmed, and thinly sliced
> 1/2 cup freshly grated Parmesan cheese
> 1/2 teaspoon salt, or to taste
> Freshly ground black pepper to taste

1. Place a heavy 4-quart saucepan over medium-high heat. Add sausage, breaking up lumps with a fork. Cook, stirring frequently, for 3–5 minutes, or until sausage is browned and no longer pink. Remove sausage from the pan with a slotted spoon, and set aside. Discard all but 1 tablespoon sausage fat from the pan.

2. Add onions, garlic, celery, and carrots to the pan. Cook, stirring frequently, for 3 minutes, or until onion is translucent. Add sausage, Parmesan rind (if using), stock, 1/2 of the beans, parsley, thyme, and bay leaf to the pan. Bring to a boil over medium heat, and simmer, partially covered, for 20 minutes, or until carrots are soft.

3. While soup simmers, combine reserved beans and water in a blender or food processor fitted with a steel blade. Puree until smooth, and stir mixture into soup.

4. Add Swiss chard to soup, and simmer for 5 minutes. Remove and discard bay leaf and Parmesan rind (if using), and stir Parmesan cheese into soup. Season with salt and pepper, and serve hot.

Note: The soup can be made up to 3 days in advance and refrigerated, tightly covered. Reheat it, covered, over low heat, stirring frequently.

Each serving contains:

431 calories | 174 calories from fat | 19 g fat | 1 g saturated fat | 45 mg cholesterol | 21 g protein | 45 g carbohydrates | 767 mg sodium

Remember, in my kitchen nothing goes to waste! So I save the rinds from Parmesan cheese and use them for flavoring dishes such as soups and sauces. The rind will not melt into the dishes, but it will impart flavor. Remove and discard it before serving.

Chapter 5:
Picnic Panache

Summertime and the living is easy is not only a song from the Gershwins' immortal *Porgy and Bess*. It also describes Americans' casual lifestyle during warm weather. While those living in the South and parts of the West can appreciate the wonders of al fresco dining for a far longer time than those of us suffering through harsh winters, picnics in the summer—be they on a sandy beach at the shore or just on a grassy knoll in a local park—are treasured times for family and friends.

But food historians tell us that picnics weren't always casual fun. They evolved from the elaborate traditions of moveable outdoor feasts enjoyed by European aristocracy over the centuries. In the Middle Ages they were hunting feasts, and during the Renaissance the meals were outdoor country banquets.

In this chapter you'll find lots of wonderful dishes—American, European, and Asian—that are perfect picnic fare. But also look at the recipes for finger foods in Chapter 3 and the wraps and other hand-holdable creations in Chapter 4 for further inspiration.

Also consult the instructions in Chapter 2 on how to cut up chickens yourself to save money.

SAFE PICNICKING
Obviously all the rules for food safety and preventing food-borne illness detailed in Chapter 2 should be used for a picnic as well, but picnics—unless they're in your backyard—present other challenges to keep foods safe, because it's nary impossible to keep hot foods hot and cold foods cold without electricity. Here are some pointers:

- To keep your cold foods at 40°F, start by putting them in the freezer for 30–40 minutes before you leave the house. They won't freeze, but they will chill down to a lower temperature than can be provided by your refrigerator.

- Make your own freezer packs by freezing water in used milk containers or sturdy plastic containers. Use these ice packs between as well as around containers.

- Transport your cooler in the car and out of the sun rather than in the trunk of your car. The trunk of a car can reach 150°F or hotter on a summer day; your food needs air-conditioning even more than you do. When you arrive at the picnic site, place the cooler in the shade and put a blanket over it to insulate it against the heat.

- Pack raw food at the bottom of the cooler. If you're going to be grilling at your picnic, put that food at the bottom so raw meat or poultry juices can't drip on your cooked food. If possible, it's best to take raw food in a separate cooler.

- It's equally important to keep hot foods hot. Cook them just prior to leaving, and place those foods in the trunk. Hot foods—either homemade or purchased from a restaurant or store—should be eaten within two hours.

- Use chemicals before you unpack your food. If you have to spray for mosquitoes, do so before the picnic coolers are even removed from the car.

- Use small platters and refresh them frequently. Keep the majority of each dish in your cooler, and replenish small platters only as needed. Keep your utensils in the cooler too.

- Keep drinks in a separate cooler from the food. On a hot day, that will be the cooler that is opened frequently, so the food in the other cooler will be exposed to heat less often.

- Keep food covered with netting. Insects are not just annoying at a picnic, they can be dangerous; many insects carry harmful bacteria and viruses on their bodies.

- Keep your hands clean. Take a full bag of moist towelettes or a full jar of hand sanitizer and a lot of paper towels. And have everyone use them often.

- Ditch the leftovers. Many people don't get sick at the picnic, but they get sick the next day from eating leftovers that were left out of refrigeration for too long. As much as we don't like to see food wasted, it's even worse to see a trip to the emergency room. If there's still solid ice in the cooler when you get home, and a container of food never left the cooler, then transfer it immediately to the refrigerator. But when in doubt, throw it out.

Garlicky Tarragon Chicken

Tarragon is a refreshing herb with a slightly licorice flavor, and it blends very well with heady garlic. Especially if this chicken is served cold, it contains lots of flavor.

Yield: 6 servings | **Active time:** 15 minutes | **Start to finish:** 50 minutes

> 1 (3½–4-pound) frying chicken, cut into serving pieces, with each breast half cut in half crosswise
> ⅓ cup olive oil
> 6 garlic cloves, peeled and minced
> 3 tablespoons dried tarragon
> ½ teaspoon salt, or to taste
> Freshly ground black pepper to taste

1. Preheat the oven to 475°F, and line a 10 x 14-inch baking pan with heavy-duty aluminum foil.
2. Rinse chicken, and pat dry with paper towels. Combine olive oil, garlic, tarragon, salt, and pepper in a small bowl, and stir well. Rub oil mixture on all sides of chicken.
3. Bake chicken for 10 minutes, then reduce the oven temperature to 375°F. Bake for an additional 25–35 minutes, or until chicken registers 165°F on an instant-read thermometer and is cooked through and no longer pink. Serve hot, at room temperature, or chilled.

Note: The chicken can be prepared up to 2 days in advance and refrigerated, tightly covered.

Each serving contains:

455 calories | 217 calories from fat | 24 g fat | 6 g saturated fat | 231.5 mg cholesterol | 59 g protein | 0.5 g carbohydrates | 396 mg sodium

French Pressed Tuna Sandwich (Pan Bagnat)

The French name means "bathed bread," and this sandwich from the sun-drenched coast of Provence is basically a tuna salad pressed in a hollowed-out loaf of bread. Pan bagnat (pronounced *pahn bayn-yat*) is a wonderful dish to take on a picnic because it can be brought whole and carved into pieces just before you eat it.

Yield: 6 servings | **Active time:** 10 minutes | **Start to finish:** 20 minutes

1 (1-pound) loaf French bread, unsliced
2 tablespoons olive oil
1 cup firmly packed shredded iceberg lettuce
3 (5-ounce) cans light tuna packed in oil, undrained
3 ripe plum tomatoes, rinsed, cored, seeded, and diced
1/2 small red onion, peeled and chopped
1/2 cup chopped pitted kalamata olives
2 hard-cooked eggs, peeled and diced
3 tablespoons lemon juice
1/4 teaspoon salt, or to taste
Freshly ground black pepper to taste

1. Slice bread in half lengthwise. Using your hands, remove interior of loaf, leaving a 3/4-inch shell. Brush interior of both halves with olive oil and line both halves with lettuce.
2. Combine tuna, tomatoes, onion, olives, eggs, and lemon juice in a mixing bowl. Stir gently, and season with salt and pepper.
3. Spoon salad evenly into bottom bread shell. Cover with top bread shell, and wrap loaf tightly with plastic wrap. Place loaf in a shallow dish, top with a second dish, and weight top dish with cans. Allow loaf to sit for 10 minutes. To serve, cut into 2-inch slices.

Note: The loaf can be made up to 2 hours in advance and refrigerated.

Each serving contains:

403 calories | 115 calories from fat | 12.5 g fat | 2.5 g saturated fat | 102 mg cholesterol | 28 g protein | 48 g carbohydrates | 936 mg sodium

Thai Fish Salad

This salad is similar to one I recall eating in Thailand a few years ago. It's slightly spicy, but the chiles are balanced by the refreshing fresh basil. Since delicate cellophane noodles are part of the dish, they stretch the fish to feed a larger crowd.

Yield: 6 servings | **Active time:** 20 minutes | **Start to finish:** 1½ hours, including 1 hour to chill

SALAD

1¼ pounds cooked fish, broken into 1-inch pieces

8 ounces thin rice noodles, cooked according to package directions and chilled*

1 cucumber, peeled, halved lengthwise, seeded, and thinly sliced

½ small red onion, peeled and thinly sliced

4 cups shredded iceberg or romaine lettuce

DRESSING

⅓ cup lime juice

¼ cup fish sauce (*nam pla*)*

¼ cup vegetable oil

2 tablespoons granulated sugar

2 slices fresh ginger, about the size of a quarter, ¼ inch thick

2–3 jalapeño or serrano chiles, stemmed and seeded

3 garlic cloves, peeled

¾ cup firmly packed basil leaves

1. For salad, combine fish, cooked rice noodles, cucumber, red onion, and lettuce in a mixing bowl.
2. For dressing, combine lime juice, fish sauce, oil, sugar, ginger, chiles, garlic, and basil in a food processor fitted with the steel blade or in a blender. Puree until smooth. Refrigerate dressing until ready to use.
3. Add dressing to salad, and mix well. Serve chilled.

Note: The dressing can be prepared 1 day in advance and refrigerated, tightly covered. Do not dress the salad more than 2 hours before serving.

*Available in the Asian aisle of most supermarkets and in specialty markets.

Each serving contains:

387 calories | 128 calories from fat | 14 g fat | 2 g saturated fat | 52 mg cholesterol | 26 g protein | 39 g carbohydrates | 1,494 mg sodium

Variations:
- Substitute cooked chicken for the fish.
- Substitute fresh spinach for the lettuce.

Nam pla (pronounced *nam-PLA)*, a salty sauce with an extremely pungent odor, is made from fermented fish. It's used as a dipping sauce, condiment, and seasoning ingredient throughout Southeast Asia. *Nam pla* is the Thai term; it's known as *nuoc nam* in Vietnam and *shottsuru* in Japan.

Deviled Chicken

Back in the nineteenth century, something that was "deviled" meant it had an assertive flavor, usually mustard. That's why both this mustard-coated chicken and eggs flavored with mustard were called "deviled." This is a wonderful way to enjoy chicken, either hot or cold.

Yield: 6 servings | **Active time:** 20 minutes | **Start to finish:** 1¼ hours

> 1 (3 ½–4-pound) frying chicken, cut into serving pieces, with
>   each breast half cut in half crosswise
> ¼ pound (1 stick) unsalted butter, melted, divided
> ½ teaspoon salt, or to taste
> Freshly ground black pepper to taste
> ⅓ cup Dijon mustard
> 3 scallions, white parts and 3 inches of green tops, rinsed,
>   trimmed, and finely chopped
> ¾ teaspoon dried thyme
> 3 cups plain breadcrumbs

1. Preheat the oven to 400°F, and line a 10 x 14-inch baking pan with heavy-duty aluminum foil.
2. Rinse chicken and pat dry with paper towels. Brush chicken with 5 tablespoons butter, and sprinkle with salt and pepper. Bake chicken, skin side down, for 15 minutes.
3. While chicken bakes, combine mustard, scallions, thyme, and 3 tablespoons of remaining butter in a mixing bowl, and whisk well. Place breadcrumbs in a shallow bowl or on a sheet of plastic wrap or waxed paper.
4. Remove chicken pieces from the oven, and allow them to cool for 5 minutes. Using tongs, roll chicken in mustard mixture, and then place into crumbs, patting pieces so that crumbs adhere. Return chicken to the baking pan, skin side up.
5. Return chicken to the oven, and bake for 25–35 minutes, or until chicken registers 165°F on an instant-read thermometer and is cooked through and no longer pink. Serve hot, at room temperature, or chilled.

Note: The chicken can be prepared up to 2 days in advance and refrigerated, tightly covered.

Each serving contains:

556 calories | 187 calories from fat | 21 g fat | 7 g saturated fat | 237 mg cholesterol | 64 g protein | 26.5 g carbohydrates | 732 mg sodium

Variations:
- Substitute Italian bread crumbs for the plain bread crumbs.
- Substitute tarragon, basil, or oregano for the thyme.

While this chicken cooks partially before being coated, it is dangerous to start cooking poultry and then allow it to sit or to refrigerate it partially cooked. Salmonella bacteria, which is naturally occurring on chicken, must be cooked to 165°F to kill it.

Tortilla-Crusted Chicken

Here's a Southwestern variation on oven-baked chicken that uses crunchy tortilla chips as the breading. It's a great part of any picnic meal with other Hispanic flavors.

Yield: 6 servings | **Active time:** 15 minutes | **Start to finish:** 50 minutes

> 1 (3 $\frac{1}{2}$–4-pound) frying chicken, cut into serving pieces, with
>   each breast half cut in half crosswise
> $\frac{1}{2}$ teaspoon salt, or to taste
> $\frac{1}{2}$ teaspoon cayenne
> Freshly ground black pepper to taste
> 2 cups crushed corn tortilla chips
> 1 tablespoon chili powder
> 1 tablespoon smoked Spanish paprika
> 1 teaspoon ground cumin
> 2 large eggs, lightly beaten
> 1 cup vegetable oil, divided

1. Preheat the oven to 425°F, and place a 10 x 14-inch baking pan in the oven as it heats. Rinse chicken and pat dry with paper towels. Sprinkle chicken with salt, cayenne, and pepper.

2. Combine crushed tortilla chips, chili powder, paprika, and cumin in a shallow bowl, and mix well. Combine eggs and 2 tablespoons oil in another shallow bowl, and mix well.

3. Dip chicken pieces into egg mixture, letting any excess drip back into the bowl. Dip pieces into crumb mixture, coating all sides. Set aside.

4. Add remaining oil to the hot baking dish, and heat for 3 minutes. Add chicken pieces and turn gently with tongs to coat all sides with oil. Bake for a total of 25–35 minutes, turning pieces gently with tongs after 15 minutes, or until chicken registers 165°F on an instant-read thermometer and is cooked through and no longer pink. Remove chicken from the pan, and pat with paper towels. Serve hot, at room temperature, or chilled.

Note: The chicken can be prepared for baking up to 6 hours in advance and refrigerated, tightly covered.

Each serving contains:

602 calories | 328 calories from fat | 36 g fat | 8 g saturated fat | 267 mg cholesterol | 61 g protein | 9 g carbohydrates | 584 mg sodium

Variation:

- Substitute pork chops for the chicken, and reduce the baking time to a total of 20 minutes.

What creates a crispy coating on food is adding it to hot oil. When oven-frying, rather than deep-frying on top of the stove, it's crucial to heat the oil before adding the food or it will be greasy after baking.

Citrus Chicken

The marinade for these chickens contains three citrus juices as well as spices, and it produces a vibrantly flavored chicken that appeals to all generations. Serve it with any sort of cold vegetable salad.

Yield: 6 servings | **Active time:** 15 minutes | **Start to finish:** 4 hours, including 3 hours for marinating

> 1 (3 ½–4-pound) frying chicken, cut into serving pieces, with
>   each breast half cut in half crosswise
> 1 cup orange juice
> ¼ cup lemon juice
> ¼ cup lime juice
> ½ small onion, peeled and diced
> 3 garlic cloves, peeled
> 2 tablespoons smoked Spanish paprika
> 1 tablespoon dried oregano
> 2 teaspoons ground cumin
> ½ cup olive oil
> ½ teaspoon salt, or to taste
> Freshly ground black pepper to taste

1. Rinse chicken and pat dry with paper towels. Combine orange juice, lemon juice, lime juice, onion, garlic, paprika, oregano, cumin, and olive oil in a food processor fitted with the steel blade or in a blender. Puree until smooth. Season with salt and pepper.

2. Pour mixture into a heavy resealable plastic bag, and add chicken pieces. Marinate chicken, refrigerated, for a minimum of 3 hours or up to 6 hours, turning the bag occasionally.

3. Preheat the oven to 475°F, and line a 10 x 14-inch baking pan with heavy-duty aluminum foil.

4. Remove chicken from marinade and discard marinade. Bake chicken for 10 minutes, then reduce the oven temperature to 375°F. Bake for an additional 25–35 minutes, or until chicken registers 165°F on an instant-read thermometer and is cooked through and no longer pink. Serve hot, at room temperature, or chilled.

Note: The chicken can be prepared up to 2 days in advance and refrigerated, tightly covered.

Each serving contains:

538 calories | 226 calories from fat | 25 g fat | 7 g saturated fat | 298 mg cholesterol | 76 g protein | 2 g carbohydrates | 530 mg sodium

When using a marinade that's high in acid—like this one that uses both lemon juice and lime juice—it's important not to marinate it for more time than specified. The acid can alter the texture of the chicken and make it mushy after it's cooked.

Asian-Spiced Chicken Wings with Peanut Coconut Sauce

A creamy sauce mellows the spices of these chicken wings flavored with spices from both East and West. When serving chicken wings at a picnic, make sure you bring lots of hand wipes!

Yield: 6 servings | **Active time:** 15 minutes | **Start to finish:** 7 hours, including 6 hours for marinating

WINGS

18 chicken wings, separated into 2 pieces with wing tips reserved for stock

½ cup dry sherry

4 garlic cloves, peeled and minced

3 tablespoons grated onion

1 tablespoon Chinese five-spice powder*

1 tablespoon chili powder

½ teaspoon salt or to taste

Freshly ground black pepper to taste

⅓ cup vegetable oil

SAUCE

½ cup chunky peanut butter

⅓ cup well-stirred light coconut milk

¼ cup very hot tap water

2 tablespoons granulated sugar

1 tablespoon soy sauce

3 tablespoons chopped fresh cilantro

2 garlic cloves, peeled and minced

1. Rinse wings and pat dry with paper towels. Combine sherry, garlic, onion, five-spice powder, chili powder, salt, pepper, and vegetable oil in a small bowl, and stir well. Place wings in a heavy resealable plastic bag, and add marinade.
2. Marinate chicken wings, refrigerated, for at least 6 hours, preferably overnight, turning the bag occasionally.

*Available in the Asian aisle of most supermarkets and in specialty markets.

3. Preheat the oven to 425°F, and line 2 baking sheets with heavy-duty aluminum foil.
4. Remove wings from marinade and discard marinade. Arrange wings in a single layer on the baking sheet. Bake wings for 35–40 minutes, turning them with tongs after 20 minutes, or until wings are cooked through and no longer pink.
5. While wings bake, make sauce. Combine peanut butter, coconut milk, water, sugar, soy sauce, cilantro, and garlic in a mixing bowl, and whisk well. Set aside. Serve wings hot, at room temperature, or chilled.

Note: The wings can be cooked up to 2 days in advance and refrigerated, tightly covered. Serve them cold, or reheat them, uncovered, in a 350°F oven for 12–15 minutes, or until hot. The sauce can also be made up to 2 days in advance and refrigerated, tightly covered. Allow it to sit at room temperature for 30 minutes before serving.

Each serving contains:

539 calories | 358 calories from fat | 40 g fat | 9 g saturated fat | 113 mg cholesterol | 33 g protein | 11.5 g carbohydrates | 486 mg sodium

Variation:
- Substitute 1 pound boneless, skinless chicken breast, cut into 1-inch cubes, for the wings. Marinate cubes for 30 minutes, and then broil or grill for 3–4 minutes, or until cooked through and no longer pink.

There's a huge difference between the calories in light coconut milk and its fattier version, just labeled "coconut milk." Unless otherwise specified, I always use light coconut milk.

Thai Chicken Salad

This somewhat spicy salad contains blanched vegetables, and it's dressed with a mixture of ingredients characteristic of Thai cuisine, including fish sauce.

Yield: 6 servings | **Active time:** 20 minutes | **Start to finish:** 20 minutes

> 3 cups shredded green cabbage
> 2 carrots, peeled and thinly sliced
> 1/4 pound green beans, trimmed and cut into 1-inch lengths
> 1/4 cup lime juice
> 1/4 cup firmly packed light brown sugar
> 1/3 cup fish sauce (*nam pla*)*
> 2 tablespoons grated fresh ginger
> 2 garlic cloves, peeled and minced
> 1 jalapeño or serrano chile, seeds and ribs removed, and finely chopped
> 1/4 cup vegetable oil
> 2 tablespoons Asian sesame oil*
> 3 cups shredded cooked chicken
> Freshly ground black pepper to taste
> 1/2 cup chopped salted peanuts
> 1/4 cup chopped fresh cilantro

1. Bring a large pot of salted water to a boil over high heat, and have a bowl of ice water handy. Add cabbage and carrots, and cook for 3 minutes. Add green beans, and cook for 2 minutes more, or until vegetables are crisp-tender. Drain vegetables, and plunge into ice water to stop the cooking action. Drain well, and set aside.
2. While vegetables cook, make dressing. Combine lime juice and brown sugar in a small saucepan, and cook over medium-high heat until sugar dissolves. Pour mixture into a jar with a tight-fitting lid, and add fish sauce, ginger, garlic, and chile, and mix well. Add vegetable oil and sesame oil, and mix well again. Set aside.
3. Combine vegetables and chicken in a mixing bowl, and toss with dressing. Season to taste with pepper. Serve immediately, sprinkling each serving with chopped peanuts and cilantro.

*Available in the Asian aisle of most supermarkets and in specialty markets.

Note: The salad and dressing can both be made up to 1 day in advance and refrigerated, tightly covered. Do not dress the salad until just prior to serving.

Each serving contains:

284 calories | 149 calories from fat | 17 g fat | 2 g saturated fat
40 mg cholesterol | 17 g protein | 18 g carbohydrates | 1,322 mg sodium

While small packages of peanuts are more expensive per ounce than larger sizes, if you're not going to finish a large package, go for the smaller one. In this case, every convenience store has small snack packages of peanuts that are the perfect size for this recipe.

Peanut Chicken and Pasta Salad

If you want a one-dish picnic meal, here is one of your options. There are many fresh crisp vegetables as well as chicken and pasta in this salad flavored with a spicy peanut sauce.

Yield: 6 servings | **Active time:** 15 minutes | **Start to finish:** 30 minutes

> ³/₄ pound linguine, broken into 2-inch lengths
> ¹/₄ cup peanut butter
> ¹/₄ cup very hot tap water
> 4 tablespoons Asian sesame oil*
> 2 tablespoons soy sauce
> 2 tablespoons rice wine vinegar*
> 2 tablespoons firmly packed dark brown sugar
> 3 garlic cloves, peeled and minced
> 2 tablespoons grated fresh ginger
> 2 tablespoons chopped fresh cilantro
> 1–2 tablespoons Chinese chile paste with garlic*
> 2 cups shredded cooked chicken
> 6 scallions, white parts and 4 inches of green tops, rinsed, trimmed, and thinly sliced
> 1 cucumber, peeled, halved lengthwise, seeded, and thinly sliced
> 1 carrot, peeled and grated
> 1 cup bean sprouts, rinsed
> ¹/₂ cup finely chopped roasted peanuts

1. Bring a large pot of salted water to a boil. Add pasta, and cook according to package directions until al dente. Drain pasta, and rinse under cold running water until pasta is cool. Drain, and refrigerate.
2. While water heats, combine peanut butter and water in a mixing bowl, and whisk until smooth. Add sesame oil, soy sauce, vinegar, brown sugar, garlic, ginger, cilantro, and chile paste. Whisk well again.
3. Add sauce, chicken, scallions, cucumber, carrot, and bean sprouts to pasta. Mix well, and serve immediately sprinkled with peanuts.

Note: The salad can be prepared up to 1 day in advance and refrigerated, tightly covered.

*Available in the Asian aisle of most supermarkets and in specialty markets.

Each serving contains:

540 calories | 197 calories from fat | 22 g fat | 4 g saturated fat | 40 mg cholesterol | 28 g protein | 57 g carbohydrates | 578 mg sodium

Variations:
- Substitute shredded pork or beef for the chicken.
- Omit the chicken, and add 2 cups shredded Napa cabbage.

> While it may seem like a waste of water to chill cooked pasta under running water rather than soaking it in a mixing bowl, soaking it can cause the pasta to become mushy.

Jambalaya Salad

Cooking the rice in tomato juice is an easy way to achieve vivid flavor as well as color, making this a hearty one-dish picnic meal. Jambalaya is native to the Louisiana bayous, and many experts believe that the name comes from the Spanish word for ham, *jamón.*

Yield: 6 servings | **Active time:** 20 minutes | **Start to finish:** 1 hour, including 30 minutes to chill

SALAD

2 cups tomato juice

2 tablespoons chopped fresh parsley

$\frac{1}{2}$ teaspoon dried thyme

$\frac{1}{2}$ teaspoon hot red pepper sauce

1 bay leaf

$\frac{1}{2}$ teaspoon salt, or to taste

Freshly ground black pepper to taste

$1\frac{1}{4}$ cups long-grain rice

1 (10-ounce) package frozen peas, thawed

2 cups diced cooked chicken

$\frac{1}{4}$ pound baked ham, cut into $\frac{1}{2}$-inch dice

4 scallions, white parts and 3 inches of green tops, rinsed, trimmed, and thinly sliced

2 celery ribs, rinsed, trimmed, and thinly sliced

$\frac{1}{2}$ green bell pepper, seeds and ribs removed, and chopped

DRESSING

$\frac{1}{4}$ cup lemon juice

3 garlic cloves, peeled and minced

$\frac{1}{2}$ teaspoon salt, or to taste

Cayenne to taste

$\frac{1}{3}$ cup olive oil

1. Combine tomato juice, parsley, thyme, red pepper sauce, bay leaf, salt, and pepper in a saucepan, and bring to a boil over medium-high heat, stirring occasionally. Reduce the heat to low, and simmer mixture, uncovered, for 5 minutes. Add rice, and bring to a boil over medium-high heat. Cover the pan, reduce the heat to low, and cook

rice for 15 minutes. Add peas, and cook for an additional 5–7 minutes, or until rice is soft and liquid is absorbed. Spread rice onto a baking sheet, remove and discard bay leaf, and chill for at least 30 minutes.

2. Place chilled rice in a mixing bowl, and add chicken, ham, scallions, celery, and green pepper.

3. To prepare dressing, combine lemon juice, garlic, salt, and cayenne in a jar with a tight-fitting lid and shake well. Add olive oil and shake well again. Toss dressing with salad, and serve chilled.

Note: The salad and dressing can be prepared 1 day in advance and refrigerated, tightly covered. Do not toss the salad with the dressing until ready to serve.

Each serving contains:

404 calories | 132 calories from fat | 15 g fat | 2.5 g saturated fat | 44 mg cholesterol | 24 g protein | 44 g carbohydrates | 928 mg sodium

There's a reason why bay leaves should always be discarded. Although they add a pungent and woodsy flavor and aroma to dishes, they can be quite a bitter mouthful if you accidentally eat one. That's also why bay leaves are always added whole. If they were broken into pieces, it would be a real scavenger hunt to retrieve them.

Italian Chicken and Bread Salad

This salad is based on panzanella, a hearty Tuscan tomato and bread salad. The bread becomes soft, and the addition of lots of ripe tomatoes makes this a special meal.

Yield: 4 servings | **Active time:** 20 minutes | **Start to finish:** 2½ hours, including 2 hours for bread to soak

> 1 (½-pound) loaf Italian or French bread
> 2 cups very hot tap water
> ½ cup red wine vinegar, divided
> ½ teaspoon salt, or to taste
> Freshly ground black pepper to taste
> 3 large ripe tomatoes, rinsed, cored, seeded, and diced, divided
> 3 garlic cloves, peeled and minced
> ½ cup olive oil
> 2 cups diced cooked chicken
> ½ small red onion, peeled and diced
> 1 cucumber, peeled, halved lengthwise, seeded, and diced
> ½ cup firmly packed shredded fresh basil
> 2 tablespoons chopped fresh parsley

1. Cut bread into 1½-inch cubes, and place in a mixing bowl. Stir water and ¼ cup vinegar together, and pour over bread cubes. Stir cubes to moisten evenly, and sprinkle with salt and pepper. Set aside for 2 hours at room temperature. Drain bread, if necessary, and return it to the mixing bowl.

2. While bread soaks, combine remaining vinegar, ⅓ of the tomato, garlic, salt, and pepper in a food processor fitted with the steel blade or in a blender. Puree until smooth. Add olive oil, and mix well. Set aside.

3. Add remaining tomatoes, chicken, onion, cucumber, basil, and parsley to the mixing bowl with bread, and toss with dressing.

Note: The salad can be prepared up to 1 day in advance and refrigerated, tightly covered.

Each serving contains:

533 calories | 254 calories from fat | 28 g fat | 4 g saturated fat | 59.5 mg cholesterol | 30 g protein | 40 g carbohydrates | 724 mg sodium

Pollo Tonnato

Cold veal topped with a lemony tuna sauce is a classic in Italian cooking, and the sauce works equally well with far less expensive chicken. If you roast a chicken in advance, this recipe is ready in merely minutes.

Yield: 6 servings | **Active time:** 10 minutes | **Start to finish:** 10 minutes

1 (5-ounce) can light tuna packed in oil
¼ cup olive oil
¼ cup lemon juice
2 teaspoons anchovy paste (or ½ teaspoon salt)
Freshly ground black pepper to taste
1½ pounds chilled cooked chicken
Lemon slices (optional)

1. Combine tuna, oil, lemon juice, anchovy paste, and pepper in a food processor fitted with the steel blade or in a blender. Puree until smooth.
2. To serve, thinly slice chicken against the grain, and top each slice with a dollop of sauce. Garnish plates with lemon slices, if using.

Note: The sauce can be prepared up to 2 days in advance and refrigerated, tightly covered.

Each serving contains:

307 calories | 132 calories from fat | 15 g fat | 3 g saturated fat | 110 mg cholesterol | 42 g protein | 1 g carbohydrates | 375.5 mg sodium

Variation:
- Substitute cooked pork loin for the chicken.

Moroccan Chicken Salad

Tangy dried currants and succulent dried apricots meld with traditional Moroccan spices and add textural interest to the light couscous base of this toothsome chicken salad. It's refreshing on a summer day.

Yield: 6 servings | **Active time:** 20 minutes | **Start to finish:** 2$\frac{1}{2}$ hours, including 2 hours to chill

SALAD

3 cups water
$\frac{1}{2}$ teaspoon salt, or to taste
Freshly ground black pepper to taste
2 cups (12 ounces) plain couscous
$\frac{1}{2}$ cup dried currants
$\frac{1}{2}$ cup chopped dried apricots
2 cups shredded cooked chicken
1 (15-ounce) can garbanzo beans, drained and rinsed
$\frac{1}{2}$ cup chopped pitted kalamata olives
$\frac{1}{2}$ small red onion, peeled and diced
$\frac{1}{2}$ small fennel bulb, trimmed and diced

DRESSING

$\frac{1}{2}$ cup orange juice
2 tablespoons balsamic vinegar
$\frac{1}{4}$ cup chopped fresh cilantro
4 garlic cloves, peeled and minced
1 tablespoon ground cumin
$\frac{1}{2}$ teaspoon salt, or to taste
Freshly ground black pepper to taste
$\frac{1}{4}$ cup olive oil

1. For salad, bring water, salt, and pepper to a boil in a saucepan over high heat. Add couscous, currants, and apricots. Cover the pan, turn off the heat, and let couscous stand for 10 minutes. Fluff mixture with a fork and transfer it to a mixing bowl. Chill for at least 2 hours.
2. Add chicken, beans, olives, onion, and fennel to the couscous.

3. For dressing, combine orange juice, vinegar, cilantro, garlic, cumin, salt, and pepper in a jar with a tight-fitting lid, and shake well. Add olive oil and shake well again. Pour the dressing over the salad, and toss well. Serve chilled.

Note: The salad can be prepared 1 day in advance and kept refrigerated, tightly covered.

Each serving contains:

515 calories | 117 calories from fat | 13 g fat | 2 g saturated fat | 40 mg cholesterol | 27 g protein | 77 g carbohydrates | 794 mg sodium

---

Many people erroneously think that couscous is a grain, but it's really a very finely milled pasta. It's so fine that just stirring it into boiling water is enough to cook it. Or you can cook it in stock if you're going to serve it as a side dish.

Picnic Brisket with Herbed Mustard Sauce

You won't find many beef recipes in this chapter because the cuts of beef traditionally served cold, like tenderloin or rib eye roast, are too expensive to be included in this book. But I do adore this brisket, and cooking it in advance means that the fat can be easily discarded.

Yield: 8 servings | **Active time:** 20 minutes | **Start to finish:** 6 hours, including 3 hours to chill

BEEF

3 tablespoons olive oil

1 (2½–3-pound) beef brisket

1 small onion, peeled and diced

2 garlic cloves, peeled and minced

3 cups Beef Stock (recipe on page 24) or purchased stock

2 tablespoons chopped fresh parsley

½ teaspoon salt (omit if using purchased stock)

½ teaspoon thyme

1 bay leaf

Freshly ground black pepper to taste

SAUCE

¾ cup mayonnaise

¼ cup Dijon mustard

3 tablespoons chopped fresh parsley

1 tablespoon herbes de Provence

Freshly ground black pepper to taste

1. Preheat the oven to 350°F, and line a roasting pan with a large sheet of heavy-duty aluminum foil.

2. Heat oil in a large skillet over medium high heat. Sear beef on both sides, until very brown. Transfer beef to the roasting pan.

3. Add onion and garlic to the skillet, and cook, stirring frequently, for 3 minutes, or until onion is translucent. Add stock, parsley, salt (if using), thyme, bay leaf, and pepper to the skillet and bring to a boil over high heat. Pour mixture over beef, and seal foil around beef.

4. Bake beef for 2½–3 hours, or until beef is very tender. Remove beef from braising liquid, and save liquid for a future use. Chill beef well, cut off any layer of fat from the top, and then cut brisket into thin slices against the grain.

5. For sauce, combine mayonnaise, mustard, parsley, herbes de Provence, and pepper in a small mixing bowl, and stir well. Refrigerate until ready to serve. Serve beef chilled, passing sauce separately.

Note: The beef and sauce can be prepared up to 2 days in advance and refrigerated, tightly covered.

Each serving contains:

477 calories | 363 calories from fat | 40 g fat | 10 g saturated fat | 85 mg cholesterol | 22 g protein | 3 g carbohydrates | 2,176 mg sodium

Variations:
- Substitute tomato sauce for the mustard sauce.
- Substitute red wine for the beef stock.

The stock in which the beef is braised is a richly flavored treasure. Reduce it further to use it as a gravy, or save it to make a beef-based onion soup.

Asian Beef Salad

While I rarely send you to the line at the deli department, this salad is an exception. It makes far more sense to buy the roast beef than to make this small a quantity. The salad is full of crunchy vegetables, and the dressing is spicy and refreshing.

Yield: 6 servings | **Active time:** 20 minutes | **Start to finish:** 30 minutes

SALAD

> 1/4 pound fresh green beans, rinsed, trimmed, and cut into 1-inch lengths
> 1 pound rare roast beef, thinly sliced, trimmed of fat, and cut into thin strips
> 2 cups bean sprouts, rinsed
> 1 cucumber, peeled, halved lengthwise, seeded, and thinly sliced
> 1 green bell pepper, seeds and ribs removed, and thinly sliced
> 4 cups shredded Napa cabbage

DRESSING

> 1/3 cup rice wine vinegar
> 3 tablespoons reduced-sodium soy sauce
> 3 tablespoons Dijon mustard
> 3 tablespoons grated fresh ginger
> 2 tablespoons hoisin sauce*
> 1 tablespoon fermented black beans, finely chopped*
> 4 garlic cloves, peeled and minced
> 2 scallions, white parts and 4 inches of green tops, rinsed, trimmed, and chopped
> Freshly ground black pepper to taste
> 1/4 cup vegetable oil
> 1/4 cup Asian sesame oil*

1. Bring a pot of water to a boil over high heat, and have a bowl of ice water handy. Boil beans for 2–3 minutes, or until crisp-tender. Drain beans, and plunge them into ice water to stop the cooking action. Drain when cold, and set aside.

*Available in the Asian aisle of most supermarkets and in specialty markets.

2. Combine beans, beef, bean sprouts, cucumber, and green bell pepper in a mixing bowl.

3. To make the dressing, combine vinegar, soy sauce, mustard, ginger, hoisin sauce, fermented black beans, garlic, scallions, and pepper in a jar with a tight-fitting lid, and shake well. Add vegetable and sesame oils, and shake well again.

4. Toss beef mixture with $\frac{1}{2}$ of the dressing, and allow to sit for 5 minutes. Add cabbage, and toss well. Serve immediately, passing extra dressing separately.

Note: The salad and dressing can be prepared 1 day in advance and refrigerated, tightly covered. Do not toss the salad with the dressing until ready to serve.

Each serving contains:

348 calories | 219 calories from fat | 24 g fat | 5 g saturated fat | 39 mg cholesterol | 20 g protein | 13 g carbohydrates | 617 mg sodium

Fermented black beans are small black soybeans with a pungent flavor that have been preserved in salt before being packed. They should be chopped and soaked in some sort of liquid to soften them and release their flavor prior to cooking. Because they are salted as a preservative, they last for up to 2 years if refrigerated once opened.

Italian Meatloaf

Cold meatloaf is a wonderful cold dish to take on a picnic. While I'm sure you have a family favorite, I wanted to expand your repertoire with this dish. Tasty kalamata olives, creamy cheese, and Italian seasoning flavor this delicious meatloaf.

Yield: 6 servings | **Active time:** 20 minutes | **Start to finish:** 1½ hours

> 3 tablespoons olive oil
> 1 medium onion, peeled and chopped
> ½ green bell pepper, seeds and ribs removed, and chopped
> 3 garlic cloves, peeled and minced
> 1 large egg, lightly beaten
> ½ cup grated mozzarella cheese
> ½ cup Italian breadcrumbs
> ¾ cup marinara sauce, divided
> ¼ cup whole milk
> 2 tablespoons chopped fresh parsley
> 2 teaspoons Italian seasoning
> 1¼ pounds ground chuck
> ½ cup chopped kalamata olives
> ½ teaspoon salt, or to taste
> Freshly ground black pepper to taste

1. Preheat the oven to 350°F, and line a 9 x 13-inch baking pan with heavy-duty aluminum foil.
2. Heat oil in a medium skillet over medium-high heat. Add onion, green bell pepper, and garlic, and cook, stirring frequently, for 5–7 minutes, or until vegetables soften.
3. Combine egg, cheese, breadcrumbs, ¼ cup marinara sauce, milk, parsley, and Italian seasoning in a mixing bowl, and mix well. Add vegetable mixture, ground chuck, and olives to the mixing bowl, and mix well again. Season with salt and pepper. Form mixture into a loaf 9 inches long and 5 inches wide in the prepared pan. Spread top of meatloaf with remaining marinara sauce.
4. Bake meatloaf for 1–1¼ hours, or until an instant-read thermometer inserted into the center registers 165°F. Allow meatloaf to rest for 5 minutes, then serve hot, at room temperature, or chilled.

Note: The meatloaf mixture can be prepared up to 1 day in advance and refrigerated, tightly covered. Also, the meatloaf can be baked up to 2 days in advance and refrigerated, tightly covered.

Each serving contains:

323 calories | 177 calories from fat | 20 g fat | 5 g saturated fat | 117 mg cholesterol | 23 g protein | 14 g carbohydrates | 800 mg sodium

Variations:

- Cook 1 (10-ounce) package frozen chopped spinach according to package directions. Place spinach in a colander, and press with the back of a spoon to extract as much liquid as possible. Combine spinach with an additional ½ cup grated mozzarella cheese, and season to taste with salt and pepper. Form ½ of the meatloaf mixture into a loaf, and then create a line of spinach in the center of the loaf. Enclose spinach with remaining meatloaf mixture.
- Bake meatloaf with 4–6 hard-cooked eggs hidden in the middle of the loaf.

Scotch Eggs

Scotch eggs are a great gift from the British Isles to picnic food. The hard-cooked eggs are coated with flavorful sausage and then fried to cook the meat. The eggs then become a crispy treat.

Yield: 6 servings | **Active time:** 25 minutes | **Start to finish:** 1 hour

8 large eggs, divided
1 pound bulk American breakfast pork sausage
2 tablespoons chopped fresh parsley
2 tablespoons chopped fresh chives
2 teaspoons dried sage
$\frac{1}{2}$ teaspoon dried thyme
Cayenne to taste
2 tablespoons Dijon mustard
$\frac{1}{2}$ cup all-purpose flour
1 cup plain bread crumbs
Vegetable oil for frying

1. Place 6 eggs in a saucepan, and cover with cold water by 2 inches. Bring to a boil over high heat, uncovered. Boil for 1 minute, cover the pan, and remove the pan from the heat. Allow eggs to sit for 15 minutes, covered. Drain eggs, and fill pan with cold running water for 3 minutes to stop the cooking action. Allow eggs to sit in cold water for 10 minutes, then peel them.

2. Combine sausage, parsley, chives, sage, thyme, and cayenne in a mixing bowl. Beat 2 remaining eggs with mustard in a shallow bowl. Place flour on a sheet of plastic wrap or waxed paper, and place bread crumbs on another sheet of plastic wrap or waxed paper.

3. Dust peeled eggs with flour, then using wet hands, pat $\frac{1}{6}$ of the sausage mixture around each egg. Dip coated eggs into egg mixture, and then roll in bread crumbs, pressing gently to get crumbs to adhere. Refrigerate eggs for 30 minutes.

4. Heat 2 inches of oil in a deep-sided saucepan to a temperature of 350°F. Add 3 eggs to hot oil, and fry for 6–8 minutes, turning them gently with a slotted spoon occasionally, or until eggs are dark brown and sausage is cooked through. Remove eggs from the pan with a slotted spoon, and drain well on paper towels. Repeat with remaining 3 eggs. When cool enough to handle, cut eggs in half lengthwise. Serve at room temperature or chilled.

Note: The eggs can be prepared for frying up to 1 day in advance and refrigerated, tightly covered. They can be fully cooked up to 2 days in advance, and refrigerated, tightly covered.

Each serving contains:

341 calories | 204 calories from fat | 23 g fat | 6 g saturated fat | 302 mg cholesterol | 21 g protein | 11.5 g carbohydrates | 302 mg sodium

Variation:
- Substitute sweet or hot bulk Italian sausage for the American sausage, and substitute 2 teaspoons Italian seasoning for the sage and thyme.

> If you don't have access to fresh chives, you can substitute finely chopped scallion greens in any recipe.

Grilled Corn and Sausage Salad

It is not August at my table if fresh corn in some form is not part of the meal, and this salad is an especially appetizing way to prepare it. The sausage and simple dressing enhance the flavor of grilled corn. You can also serve this as a side dish with grilled meats or poultry.

Yield: 4 servings | **Active time:** 15 minutes | **Start to finish:** 1 hour

1 cup mesquite chips
4 ears fresh corn, unshucked
$^3/_4$ pound bulk pork sausage
1 small green bell pepper, seeds and ribs removed, and finely chopped
3 scallions, white parts and 3 inches of the green tops, rinsed, trimmed, and finely chopped
3 tablespoons olive oil
2 tablespoons lime juice
2 tablespoons pure maple syrup
$^1/_2$ teaspoon salt, or to taste
Freshly ground black pepper to taste
3 tablespoons chopped fresh cilantro

1. Light a gas or charcoal grill. If using a charcoal grill, soak mesquite chips in water for 30 minutes. If using a gas grill, create a packet for wood chips from heavy-duty aluminum foil, and poke holes in the foil.
2. Remove all but 1 layer of husks from corn and pull out the corn silks. Soak corn in cold water to cover for 10 minutes. Place wood chips on the grill. Grill corn, covered, for 10–15 minutes, turning with tongs occasionally. When cool enough to handle, discard husks, and cut kernels off cobs using a sharp serrated knife.
3. Cook sausage in a frying pan over medium heat, breaking up lumps with a fork. Cook until brown. Combine sausage and its fat with corn, green bell pepper, and scallions in a mixing bowl.
4. Combine olive oil, lime juice, maple syrup, salt, and pepper in a jar with a tight-fitting lid. Shake well, and toss with the corn mixture. Toss with cilantro, and serve at room temperature.

Note: The salad can be made up to 2 days in advance and refrigerated, tightly covered with plastic wrap. Allow it to sit at room temperature for a few hours to take the chill off. Do not add the cilantro until just before serving.

Each serving contains:

485 calories | 326 calories from fat | 36 g fat | 10.5 g saturated fat | 58 mg cholesterol | 13 g protein | 30 g carbohydrates | 902 mg sodium

Spanish Potato and Sausage Tortilla

A tortilla in Spain is really a baked omelet, similar to an Italian frittata; it has nothing to do with the thin breads of Mexico. Flavorful chorizo sausage and potatoes make this tortilla a robust picnic food.

Yield: 6 servings | **Active time:** 20 minutes | **Start to finish:** 40 minutes

½ pound Spanish chorizo sausage, thinly sliced
2 tablespoons olive oil
1 large onion, peeled and diced
2 garlic cloves, peeled and minced
1 pound redskin potatoes, scrubbed and thinly sliced
8 large eggs
½ cup sour cream
1½ cups grated cheddar cheese
½ teaspoon salt, or to taste
Freshly ground black pepper to taste

1. Preheat the oven to 400°F, and grease a 9 x 13-inch baking pan.
2. Heat a large skillet over medium-high heat. Add sausage, and cook, stirring frequently, for 3–5 minutes, or until sausage browns. Remove sausage from the skillet with a slotted spoon, and place it in the prepared pan.
3. Discard fat from the skillet, and heat oil over medium-high heat. Add onion and garlic, and cook, stirring frequently, for 3 minutes, or until onion is translucent. Add potatoes, cover the pan, and cook, stirring occasionally, for 10–12 minutes, or until potatoes are tender. Add potato mixture to the sausage, and stir to combine.
4. While potatoes cook, combine eggs, sour cream, and cheese in a mixing bowl. Season with salt and pepper, and whisk well.
5. Pour egg mixture on top of other ingredients in the pan. Bake for 20–25 minutes, or until eggs are set. Serve at room temperature or chilled.

Note: The dish can be cooked up to 2 days in advance and refrigerated, tightly covered.

Each serving contains:

514 calories | 344 calories from fat | 38 g fat | 16 g saturated fat | 353 mg cholesterol | 27 g protein | 16 g carbohydrates | 948 mg sodium

Ham and Egg Salad Bread Roll

Ham and eggs are as good a combo in a salad as they are on a plate at breakfast. You can use this technique of filling a hollowed out loaf of bread for any finely chopped salad.

Yield: 6 servings | **Active time:** 20 minutes | **Start to finish:** 2⅓ hours, including 2 hours for chilling

> 1 loaf French or Italian bread
> ½ cup mayonnaise, or more as needed
> 2 tablespoons Dijon mustard
> 2 cups finely chopped baked ham
> 4 hard-cooked eggs, peeled and finely chopped
> 2 celery ribs, rinsed, trimmed, and finely chopped
> 3 scallions, white parts and 3 inches of green tops, rinsed, trimmed, and finely chopped
> ½ cup chopped bread-and-butter pickles
> Freshly ground black pepper to taste

1. Cut both ends off of bread, and pull out inside, leaving a ¾-inch shell. Set aside. Mix mayonnaise and mustard, and stir well.
2. Combine ham, eggs, celery, scallions, and pickles in a mixing bowl, and add dressing. Stir well, and add additional mayonnaise if mixture seems dry. Season to taste with pepper.
3. Stuff salad mixture into bread shell. Wrap bread in foil and refrigerate for at least 2 hours, or up to 6 hours. Cut into slices.

Note: The salad can be made up to 2 days in advance and refrigerated, tightly covered. Do not stuff the bread more than 6 hours prior to serving.

Each serving contains:

444 calories | 188 calories from fat | 21 g fat | 5 g saturated fat | 174 mg cholesterol | 22 g protein | 38.5 g carbohydrates | 1,363 mg sodium

Variations:
- Substitute finely chopped cooked chicken or turkey for the ham, and season mixture to taste with salt.
- Substitute chopped pimiento-stuffed green olives for the pickles.

Chapter 6:
Supporting Players

Stellar side dishes can make a meal sparkle, and those are the recipes you'll find in this chapter. Just as every play has a lead actor and people playing smaller roles, so a meal should have exciting bit players too. I intentionally placed this chapter in between those dedicated to picnic foods and hot casseroles for potluck meals; they work for both eating occasions.

When starting to formulate a menu plan for any meal, first determine the entree. All other selections are made around that one dish, regardless of whether it is a picnic, a potluck dinner, or a party. As a general rule, you serve fancy side dishes with a simple entree and vice versa. If your main dish has a number of ingredients and a sauce, then the other portions of the meal should be created with restraint.

Think about the cuisine from which the main dish is drawn, and also how it is to be cooked. If you need the oven at one temperature to cook a casserole or bake some chicken, then you may choose to make side dishes that can be created on top of the stove, or need no cooking at all.

Some of these recipes are definitely side dishes, but some of the bean salads could easily be transformed into a vegetarian picnic entree or a first course for a dinner. For advice on some menus that I think work well together, turn to Chapter 10.

Fennel Salad

Fresh fennel is just beginning to enjoy the popularity in this country that it has held in Europe for centuries; its crisp texture and slightly licorice flavor make it a cooling delight as a summer salad.

Yield: 6 servings | **Active time:** 15 minutes | **Start to finish:** 15 minutes

> 2 medium fennel bulbs, well chilled
> ½ cup chopped fresh parsley
> ⅓ cup olive oil
> ¼ cup lemon juice
> 2 teaspoons anchovy paste or ½ teaspoon salt
> 2 garlic cloves, peeled and minced
> Freshly ground black pepper to taste

1. Trim ribs and root ends from fennel bulbs. Using the thin slicing disk of a food processor, slice the fennel. This can also be done on a mandoline or with a very sharp knife. Place fennel in a salad bowl and toss with parsley.
2. Place olive oil, lemon juice, anchovy paste or salt, garlic, and pepper in a jar with a tight-fitting lid, and shake well. Toss dressing with fennel, and serve immediately.

Note: The fennel can be sliced up to 6 hours in advance and refrigerated, tightly covered with plastic wrap.

Each serving contains:

135 calories | 109 calories from fat | 12 g fat | 2 g saturated fat | 0 mg cholesterol | 1 g protein | 7 g carbohydrates | 238 mg sodium

Variation:
- Substitute cilantro for the parsley and substitute lime juice for the lemon juice.

While the ribs attached to fennel bulbs are rarely used in cooking, they certainly have a role to play in salads. Use them in place of celery, and they'll give a slightly anise flavor but the same crisp texture.

Caponata

This classic Italian dish is extremely versatile. It can be served at any temperature and glamorizes any simple meal. It can also be served as an appetizer or as part of an antipasto buffet. The silky eggplant and crunchy celery are augmented with olives in a hearty tomato sauce.

Yield: 6 servings | **Active time:** 20 minutes | **Start to finish:** 1 hour

> 1 (1-pound) eggplant, peeled and cut into ¾-inch cubes
> Salt
> ⅓ cup olive oil, divided
> 2 celery ribs, rinsed, trimmed, and diced
> 1 medium onion, peeled and diced
> 4 garlic cloves, peeled and minced
> ¼ cup red wine vinegar
> 1 tablespoon granulated sugar
> 1 (14.5-ounce) can diced tomatoes, undrained
> 1 tablespoon tomato paste
> 2 tablespoons chopped fresh parsley
> ¼ cup chopped green olives
> 2 tablespoons anchovy paste (optional)
> Freshly ground black pepper to taste

1. Place eggplant in a colander and sprinkle liberally with salt. Place a plate on top of the eggplant cubes and weight the plate with cans. Place the colander in a sink or on a plate and allow eggplant to drain for 30 minutes. Rinse eggplant cubes and pat dry on paper towels.

2. Heat 2 tablespoons oil in a skillet over medium-high heat. Add celery, onion, and garlic, and cook, stirring frequently, for 3 minutes, or until onion is translucent. Remove vegetables from the pan with a slotted spoon, and set aside.

3. Pour remaining oil into the skillet and cook eggplant cubes over medium-high heat, stirring and turning them constantly, for 6 minutes, or until they are lightly browned.

4. Return celery mixture to the skillet, and add vinegar, sugar, tomatoes, tomato paste, parsley, olives, and anchovy paste, if using. Bring to a boil, reduce the heat to low, and simmer, uncovered, stirring frequently, for 15 minutes, or until vegetables are cooked but still retain texture. Season to taste with pepper, and add ½ teaspoon salt if not using anchovy paste. Serve at room temperature or chilled.

Note: The dish can be made 2 days in advance and refrigerated, tightly covered.

Each serving contains:

154 calories | 101 calories from fat | 11 g fat | 2 g saturated fat | 0 mg cholesterol | 2 g protein | 12 g carbohydrates | 352 mg sodium

Male eggplants are sweeter than female eggplants, since they have far fewer bitter seeds. To tell the difference, look at the base of the eggplant. The male has a rounded bottom with a smooth stem area, while the female eggplant is more elliptical, with a deeply indented stem area.

Gazpacho Salad

Garlicky gazpacho is a staple of summer soups, and this refreshing salad utilizes all the same ingredients and flavors. It works well with Mexican dishes, too.

Yield: 6 servings | **Active time:** 20 minutes | **Start to finish:** 2½ hours, including 2 hours for chilling

- 1 sweet onion, such as Vidalia or Bermuda, peeled and cut into ¼-inch dice
- 2 cucumbers, peeled, seeded, and cut into ½-inch dice
- 1 large green bell pepper, seeds and ribs removed, cut into ½-inch dice
- 4 medium tomatoes, cored, seeded, and cut into ½-inch dice
- 4 garlic cloves, peeled and minced
- 1 jalapeño or serrano chile, seeds and ribs removed, and finely chopped
- ¼ cup balsamic vinegar
- ½ teaspoon salt, or to taste
- Freshly ground black pepper to taste
- ⅓ cup olive oil
- ¼ cup chopped fresh cilantro

1. Place onion, cucumbers, green bell pepper, and tomatoes in a mixing bowl.
2. Combine garlic, chile, vinegar, salt, and pepper in a jar with a tight-fitting lid and shake well. Add olive oil and cilantro; shake well again.
3. Pour the dressing over the salad and refrigerate for 2–4 hours, tightly covered. Serve chilled.

Note: The salad should not be made more than 8 hours in advance.

Each serving contains:

169 calories | 111 calories from fat | 12 g fat | 2 g saturated fat | 0 mg cholesterol | 2 g protein | 13.5 g carbohydrates | 208 mg sodium

---

Here's an easy way to remove the seeds and ribs from bell peppers: Cut a slice off the bottom so the pepper stands up straight. You'll see that there are natural curves to the sections. Holding the pepper by its stem, cut down those curves.

Carrot Salad with Creamy Blue Cheese Dressing

Sweet and healthful carrots, dotted with bits of celery, are dressed with a light dressing flavored with sharp blue cheese.

Yield: 6 servings | **Active time:** 20 minutes | **Start to finish:** 20 minutes

> 1 pound carrots, peeled and grated
> 3 celery ribs, rinsed, trimmed, and chopped
> ¾ cup crumbled blue cheese, divided
> ⅓ cup mayonnaise
> ⅓ cup sour cream
> 2 tablespoons cider vinegar
> ½ teaspoon salt, or to taste
> Freshly ground black pepper to taste

1. Combine carrots and celery in a mixing bowl.

2. Combine ½ cup blue cheese, mayonnaise, sour cream, vinegar, salt, and pepper in a food processor fitted with the steel blade or in a blender. Puree until smooth.

3. Pour dressing over vegetables, and add remaining blue cheese. Toss to combine, and serve chilled.

Note: The salad and dressing can be prepared up to 1 day in advance and refrigerated, tightly covered. Do not dress the salad more than 2 hours prior to serving.

Each serving contains:

217 calories | 162 calories from fat | 18 g fat | 7 g saturated fat | 30 mg cholesterol | 6 g protein | 9.5 g carbohydrates | 623 mg sodium

Variation:

- Substitute plain yogurt for both the mayonnaise and sour cream to trim the calories from this recipe.

When you're peeling just 1 or 2 carrots, getting out the vegetable peeler makes sense. But for a whole pound, there's an easier way to do it. Pour boiling water over the carrots and allow them to sit for 3 minutes. Then drain them and run them under running water. The peels will slip right off.

Red Cabbage Slaw

This is an unusual slaw because it's made with vivid red cabbage, which is briefly steamed. The cabbage remains crunchy, but it won't provoke indigestion in people prone to that malady from eating raw cabbage.

Yield: 8 servings | **Active time:** 25 minutes | **Start to finish:** 3½ hours, including 2 hours to marinate and 1 hour to chill

> 1 (1½-pound) head red cabbage, cored and shredded
> 2 carrots, peeled and coarsely grated
> ½ red onion, peeled and thinly sliced
> 2 tablespoons grated fresh ginger
> ¾ cup cider vinegar
> 3 tablespoons honey
> 3 tablespoons vegetable oil
> ½ teaspoon salt, or to taste
> Freshly ground black pepper to taste
> ½ cup raisins, preferably golden raisins
> 3 scallions, rinsed, trimmed, and thinly sliced

1. Place cabbage, carrots, and red onion in a vegetable steamer set over boiling water. Steam for 5 minutes, drain, and place vegetables in a mixing bowl.

2. Combine ginger, vinegar, honey, oil, salt, and pepper in a jar with a tight-fitting lid. Shake well, and pour dressing over steamed vegetables. Marinate at room temperature for 2 hours, stirring occasionally.

3. Plump raisins in boiling water for 15 minutes. Drain and add to salad. Place salad in a colander set over another mixing bowl. Drain vegetables, pressing with the back of a spoon to extract as much juice as possible.

4. Place juice in a small saucepan and boil it over medium-high heat until only ½ cup remains. Stir reduced dressing back into the salad along with the scallions. Chill salad for at least 1 hour before serving.

Note: The salad can be made up to 1 day in advance and refrigerated, tightly covered.

Each serving contains:

106 calories | 17 calories from fat | 2 g fat | 0 g saturated fat | 0 mg cholesterol | 2 g protein | 23 g carbohydrates | 109 mg sodium

Variation:

- Substitute chopped dried apricots or dried cranberries for the raisins.

While dried fruit absorbs moisture when it is being cooked, I always recommend plumping it for uncooked recipes. You'll find there's a big difference in its softened texture that also brings out its natural sweetness.

Celery Seed Slaw

This is my signature coleslaw, and it's lower in calories than most because it doesn't contain mayonnaise. It's a crunchy sweet-and-sour slaw that is flavored with sharp mustard and tasty celery seed, and it goes with anything from simple burgers to fried chicken.

Yield: 8 servings | **Active time:** 20 minutes | **Start to finish:** 5⅓ hours, including 5 hours to marinate and chill

- ½ cup granulated sugar
- ½ cup cider vinegar
- ⅓ cup vegetable oil
- 1 tablespoon celery seeds
- 1 tablespoon mustard powder
- ½ teaspoon salt, or to taste
- Freshly ground black pepper to taste
- 1 (2-pound) head green cabbage, cored and shredded
- 1 small red onion, peeled and thinly sliced
- 1 large green bell pepper, seeds and ribs removed, and thinly sliced

1. Combine sugar, vinegar, and oil in a small saucepan, and bring to a boil over medium heat, stirring occasionally. Reduce the heat to low and stir in celery seeds, mustard, salt, and pepper. Simmer for 2 minutes, stirring occasionally.

2. Combine cabbage, onion, and green bell pepper in a large mixing bowl. Toss dressing with salad. Allow slaw to sit at room temperature for 2 hours, tossing it occasionally. Refrigerate slaw for 3–4 hours. Drain well before serving.

Note: The slaw can be made 1 day in advance and refrigerated, tightly covered with plastic wrap.

Each serving contains:

144 calories | 69 calories from fat | 8 g fat | 1 g saturated fat | 0 mg cholesterol | 2 g protein | 19 g carbohydrates | 168 mg sodium

Dilled Cucumbers

This is one of the most refreshing salads you could serve, and it is fat-free, which is always appreciated by diners.

Yield: 6 servings | **Active time:** 10 minutes | **Start to finish:** 2¼ hours, including 2 hours for marinating

> 3 cucumbers, peeled, halved, seeded, and thinly sliced
> ½ large sweet onion such as Vidalia or Bermuda, peeled and thinly sliced
> 1 cup rice wine vinegar
> 3 tablespoons chopped fresh dill
> 2 tablespoons granulated sugar
> ½ teaspoon salt, or to taste
> Freshly ground black pepper to taste

1. Combine cucumbers and onion in a heavy resealable plastic bag. Combine vinegar, dill, sugar, salt, and pepper in a jar with a tight-fitting lid. Shake well to dissolve sugar.
2. Add dressing to cucumbers and onion, and marinate for at least 2 hours, refrigerated, turning the bag occasionally. Drain salad from marinade, and serve chilled.

Note: The salad can be made up to 2 days in advance and refrigerated, tightly covered.

Each serving contains:

34 calories | 2 calories from fat | 0 g fat | 0 g saturated fat | 0 mg cholesterol | 1 g protein | 6.5 g carbohydrates | 199 mg sodium

Variation:

• Substitute thinly sliced zucchini for the cucumbers.

Thai Cucumber Salad

This spicy, crisp salad is a great accompaniment for any Asian meal, since it has so much flavor and virtually no calories. The amount of red pepper determines how spicy it becomes, so you can tone it down to suit your taste.

Yield: 6 servings | **Active time:** 10 minutes | **Start to finish:** 2³/₄ hours, including 2¹/₂ hours for marinating and chilling

> ³/₄ cup distilled white vinegar
> ¹/₄ cup firmly packed light brown sugar
> 1 tablespoon fish sauce (*nam pla*)*
> 1–2 teaspoons crushed red pepper flakes
> 3 cucumbers, peeled, halved, seeded, and thinly sliced
> 3 ripe plum tomatoes, cored, seeded, and diced

1. Combine vinegar, brown sugar, fish sauce, and red pepper flakes in a heavy resealable plastic bag. Mix well to dissolve sugar.
2. Add cucumbers and marinate for 2 hours, refrigerated, turning the bag occasionally. Add tomatoes, and marinate an additional 20 minutes. Drain salad from marinade, and serve chilled.

Note: The salad can be made up to 2 days in advance and refrigerated, tightly covered.

Each serving contains:

40 calories | 3 calories from fat | 0 g fat | 0 g saturated fat | 0 mg cholesterol | 1 g protein | 8 g carbohydrates | 65 mg sodium

*Available in the Asian aisle of most supermarkets and in specialty markets.

Red Onion Pickles

The red onions become a blushing shade of pink after they're poached in this mild Asian pickling liquid. I serve them along with a few other pickled dishes when the entree is simple.

Yield: 6 servings | **Active time:** 15 minutes | **Start to finish:** 30 minutes

> 1 pound small red onions
> 3 garlic cloves, peeled and halved
> ¾ cup rice wine vinegar
> ⅓ cup granulated sugar
> 1 tablespoon grated orange zest
> ½ teaspoon salt, or to taste
> ¼–½ teaspoon crushed red pepper flakes

1. Peel onions, cut them in half, and then slice each half into ¼-inch rings. Set aside.
2. Combine garlic, vinegar, sugar, orange zest, salt, and red pepper flakes in a 2-quart nonreactive saucepan. Bring to a boil over medium heat, stirring occasionally to dissolve sugar. Reduce heat to low and simmer for 3 minutes.
3. Add onions, and simmer for 4–5 minutes over medium heat, or until onions are soft. Remove and discard garlic cloves. Transfer onions and liquid to a storage container, and cool to room temperature. Refrigerate until cold, tightly covered.

Note: Refrigerate for up to 1 week, and serve onions chilled.

Each serving contains:

92 calories | 1 calorie from fat | 0 g fat | 0 g saturated fat | 0 mg cholesterol | 1 g protein | 20 g carbohydrates | 241 mg sodium

Variation:

• Substitute any sweet white onion, such as Bermuda or Vidalia, for the red onions.

Potato and Tomato Gratin

This is one of my favorite dishes, especially during the summer when tomatoes are ripe in my garden. The herbs and cheese enhance the flavor of both starring players.

Yield: 6 servings | **Active time:** 20 minutes | **Start to finish:** 1 hour

Vegetable oil spray

6 ripe plum tomatoes, rinsed, cored, halved lengthwise, and seeded

$\frac{1}{3}$ cup olive oil, divided

1 teaspoon granulated sugar

Freshly ground black pepper to taste

1$\frac{1}{2}$ pounds redskin potatoes, scrubbed and cut into $\frac{1}{4}$-inch slices

$\frac{1}{2}$ teaspoon salt, or to taste

$\frac{3}{4}$ cup Italian breadcrumbs

$\frac{1}{4}$ cup freshly grated Parmesan cheese

3 garlic cloves, peeled and minced

$\frac{1}{2}$ teaspoon dried basil

1. Preheat the oven to 275°F, line a baking sheet with heavy-duty aluminum foil, and grease the foil with vegetable oil spray.
2. Arrange tomato halves on the baking sheet, cut side up, and brush with 2 tablespoons olive oil. Sprinkle tomatoes with sugar and pepper. Bake tomatoes for 30 minutes, or until slightly softened. Remove tomatoes from the baking sheet, and reserve any juices that may have accumulated in the pan with the tomatoes.
3. Increase the oven temperature to 425°F, and line the baking sheet with another sheet of heavy-duty aluminum foil.
4. Toss potatoes with remaining olive oil, and arrange them on the baking sheet. Sprinkle potatoes with salt and pepper. Bake potato slices for 12–15 minutes, or until tender and lightly brown. Remove baking sheet from the oven, and reduce the oven temperature to 375°F.
5. While potato slices bake, combine breadcrumbs, Parmesan cheese, garlic, and basil in a mixing bowl.

6. Grease a 9 x 13-inch baking pan with vegetable oil spray. Arrange potato slices in the bottom of the pan, and then arrange tomato halves on top of potatoes; pour reserved tomato juices over tomatoes. Sprinkle breadcrumb mixture over all. Bake for 15–20 minutes, or until crumbs are lightly browned. Serve hot, at room temperature, or chilled.

Note: The dish can be prepared up to the final baking up to 1 day in advance and refrigerated, tightly covered. Bake it covered with foil for 10 minutes, then remove the foil and bake for 15–20 minutes.

Each serving contains:

269 calories | 116 calories from fat | 13 g fat | 2 g saturated fat | 3 mg cholesterol | 6 g protein | 34 g carbohydrates | 618 mg sodium

> Grating cheese is a snap in a food processor fitted with a steel blade. If you're doing it by hand with a box grater, spray the grater with vegetable oil spray, and the cheese will grate far more easily.

Gingered Carrot Pickles

Carrots add color to any table, and the combination of both ginger and chiles in the pickling liquid makes these zing in your mouth.

Yield: 6 servings | **Active time:** 15 minutes | **Start to finish:** 30 minutes

> 1 pound thick carrots, peeled
> 1/4 cup grated fresh ginger
> 2 small jalapeño or serrano chiles, seeds and ribs removed, and halved
> 1 1/2 cups rice wine vinegar
> 1/3 cup firmly packed light brown sugar
> 1/2 teaspoon salt, or to taste

1. Cut carrots on the diagonal into slices 1/16 inch thick. Set aside.
2. Combine ginger, chiles, vinegar, sugar, and salt in a 2-quart nonreactive saucepan. Bring to a boil over medium heat, stirring occasionally to dissolve sugar. Reduce heat to low, and simmer for 5 minutes.
3. Add carrots, and simmer for 3–4 minutes, or until carrots are crisp-tender. Remove and discard chiles. Transfer carrots and liquid to a storage container, and cool to room temperature.

Note: Refrigerate for up to 1 week, and serve carrots chilled.

Each serving contains:

110 calories | 2 calories from fat | 0 g fat | 0 g saturated fat | 0 mg cholesterol | 1 g protein | 22 g carbohydrates | 253 mg sodium

Variation:

- Substitute parsnips for the carrots.

Many a cook has suffered a scraped knuckle while grating fresh ginger. If the ginger knob is large, peel only the amount you think you'll need and hold onto the remainder. If you're down to a small part, impale it on a fork and use that as your grating handle.

Sweet Potato Salad with Mustard Dressing

Sweet potatoes make delicious cold salads, and their innate sweetness creates a complex flavor when dressed in a mustard vinaigrette.

Yield: 8 servings | **Active time:** 20 minutes | **Start to finish:** 1 hour

> 2 pounds sweet potatoes, peeled
> 1/4 cup finely chopped red onion
> 1/4 cup finely chopped green bell pepper
> 3 tablespoons white wine vinegar
> 2 tablespoons Dijon mustard
> 1 shallot, peeled and finely chopped
> 2 garlic cloves, peeled and minced
> 2 tablespoons sweet pickle relish
> 1/2 teaspoon salt, or to taste
> Freshly ground black pepper to taste
> 1/4 cup olive oil

1. Cut potatoes into quarters lengthwise, and then into 3/4-inch slices. Boil or steam potatoes for 10–15 minutes, or until tender. Transfer potatoes to a bowl and let them cool. Add onion and green bell pepper to the bowl.
2. Combine vinegar, mustard, shallot, garlic, pickle relish, salt, and pepper in a jar with a tight-fitting lid, and shake well. Add oil, and shake well again. Add dressing to the mixing bowl, and toss gently. Serve at room temperature or chilled.

Note: The salad can be made up to 1 day in advance and refrigerated, tightly covered with plastic wrap.

Each serving contains:

171 calories | 61 calories from fat | 7 g fat | 1 g saturated fat | 0 mg cholesterol | 2 g protein | 25 g carbohydrates | 321 mg sodium

> Dijon mustard is made from a combination of brown and black mustard seeds, and the essential ingredients are white wine and unfermented grape juice. Grey Poupon is a well-known American brand.

Janet's Potato Salad

This recipe comes from my dear friend, Janet Morell, who makes it every year to celebrate the Fourth of July; it always gets rave reviews. The refreshing cucumber added to the traditional vegetables makes it very special.

Yield: 8 servings | **Active time:** 20 minutes | **Start to finish:** 4 hours, including 3 hours to chill potatoes

> 2 pounds small redskin potatoes, scrubbed
> 1 cucumber, peeled
> 1 small green bell pepper, seeds and ribs removed
> 1 small red onion, peeled
> 3 celery ribs, rinsed and trimmed
> $\frac{1}{2}$ cup mayonnaise
> 3 tablespoons white wine vinegar
> $\frac{1}{2}$ teaspoon salt, or to taste
> Freshly ground black pepper to taste

1. Place potatoes in a large saucepan of cold salted water. Bring potatoes to a boil over high heat, reduce the heat to medium, and boil potatoes for 10–20 minutes, or until tender when pierced with the tip of a paring knife. Drain potatoes and chill well. Cut potatoes into $\frac{3}{4}$-inch cubes, and place them in a large mixing bowl.

2. Cut cucumber in half lengthwise and scrape out the seeds with a teaspoon. Slice cucumber into thin arcs, and add to potatoes. Cut green pepper into 1-inch sections and slice each section into thin strips. Add to the mixing bowl. Cut onion in half through the root end, and cut each half into thirds. Cut into thin slices and add to the mixing bowl. Cut each celery rib in half lengthwise and thinly slice the celery. Add to the mixing bowl.

3. Toss potato salad with mayonnaise and vinegar, and season with salt and pepper. Serve well chilled.

Note: The salad can be made 1 day in advance and refrigerated, tightly covered.

Each serving contains:

197 calories | 101 calories from fat | 11 g fat | 2 g saturated fat | 5 mg cholesterol | 3 g protein | 21 g carbohydrates | 241 mg sodium

White Bean Salad

While beans are a hearty accompaniment to meals, the bright flavors of parsley, scallions, and lemon juice make this a lighter bean salad than most. It pairs well with all Mediterranean dishes.

Yield: 8 servings | **Active time:** 10 minutes | **Start to finish:** 30 minutes, including 20 minutes for chilling

> 3 (15-ounce) cans white beans, drained and rinsed
> 1/3 cup finely chopped fresh parsley
> 4 scallions, white part and 3 inches of green tops, rinsed, trimmed, and chopped
> 1/3 cup lemon juice
> 2 garlic cloves, peeled and minced
> 1/2 teaspoon salt, or to taste
> Freshly ground black pepper
> 1/3 cup olive oil

1. Combine beans, parsley, and scallions in a mixing bowl.
2. Combine lemon juice, garlic, salt, and pepper in a jar with a tight-fitting lid, and shake well. Add olive oil, and shake well again.
3. Toss salad with dressing, and refrigerate salad for at least 20 minutes before serving.

Note: The salad can be made 1 day in advance and refrigerated, tightly covered.

Each serving contains:

267 calories | 85 calories from fat | 9 g fat | 1 g saturated fat | 0 mg cholesterol | 12 g protein | 36 g carbohydrates | 156 mg sodium

Variation:
- To make this salad into an entree, add 3 (5-ounce) cans light tuna packed in oil. Break the tuna into chunks, and use the oil from the cans as part of the oil in the dressing.

Hash-Brown Potato Salad

Crusty potatoes are not inconsistent with potato salad, as you'll find when making this easy recipe. The mustard and herbs in the dressing are wonderful too.

Yield: 6 servings | **Active time:** 20 minutes | **Start to finish:** 45 minutes

> 1 1/2 pounds boiling potatoes, peeled, quartered lengthwise, and
>   cut crosswise into 1-inch slices
> 1/4 pound bacon, cut into 1/2-inch slices
> 1 teaspoon dried rosemary, crumbled
> 3 tablespoons cider vinegar, divided
> 1/2 small red onion, peeled and finely chopped
> 1 celery rib, rinsed, trimmed, and thinly sliced
> 1/3 cup mayonnaise
> 2 teaspoons Dijon mustard
> 2 tablespoons chopped fresh parsley
> 1/2 teaspoon salt, or to taste
> Freshly ground black pepper to taste

1. Steam potatoes in a steamer set over boiling water, covered, for 6–8 minutes, or until barely tender. Remove potatoes from the steamer, and set aside.

2. While potatoes steam, cook bacon in a large skillet over medium-high heat for 5–7 minutes, or until crisp. Remove bacon from the pan with a slotted spoon, drain on paper towels, and discard all but 3 tablespoons bacon grease.

3. Add potatoes and rosemary to the skillet, and cook, turning potatoes carefully, for 10 minutes. Add 2 tablespoons vinegar and cook potatoes, turning carefully, for 5 minutes, or until crusty and golden.

4. Transfer potatoes to a large bowl, and cool. Add onion and celery to potatoes. Thin mayonnaise with remaining 1 tablespoon vinegar and mustard, add it to salad along with bacon, parsley, salt, and pepper. Toss salad gently, and serve salad at room temperature.

Note: The salad can be made 1 day in advance and refrigerated, tightly covered. Allow the salad to come back to room temperature before serving.

Each serving contains:

270 calories | 165 calories from fat | 18 g fat | 5 g saturated fat | 17 mg cholesterol | 5 g protein | 21 g carbohydrates | 471 mg sodium

Variation:

- Substitute sweet potatoes for the boiling potatoes.

While most dried herbs need no preparation prior to adding them to dishes, one of the exceptions is rosemary. The long hard needles should be crushed to release their flavor.

Garlicky Potato Salad

The best aioli sauce I've ever tasted was in Provence, where it was used as the dressing for a colorful potato salad. Every time I taste a garlicky bite of this dish, I see fields of sunflowers and hillsides of lavender.

Yield: 8 servings | **Active time:** 15 minutes | **Start to finish:** 4 hours, including 3 hours to chill potatoes

> 2 pounds small redskin potatoes, scrubbed
> 1 (10-ounce) package frozen peas and carrots
> 1 green bell pepper, seeds and ribs removed, and finely chopped
> 6 garlic cloves, peeled
> 2 large egg yolks, at room temperature
> $^3/_4$ cup olive oil
> 1 tablespoon lemon juice
> $^1/_2$ teaspoon salt, or to taste
> Freshly ground black pepper to taste

1. Place potatoes in a large saucepan of cold salted water. Bring potatoes to a boil over high heat, reduce the heat to medium, and boil potatoes for 10–20 minutes, or until they are tender when pierced with the tip of a paring knife. Drain potatoes, and chill well. Cut potatoes into $^3/_4$-inch cubes and place them in a large mixing bowl.

2. Cook peas and carrots according to package directions, and add them to the bowl with potatoes to chill. Add green bell pepper to the bowl.

3. To prepare aioli sauce, combine garlic cloves and egg yolks in a food processor fitted with the steel blade or in a blender. Puree, then very slowly add olive oil through the feed tube of the food processor or the top of the blender. When the sauce has emulsified and thickened, add lemon juice and season with salt and pepper.

4. Combine sauce with salad, and serve chilled.

Note: The salad can be made 1 day in advance and refrigerated, tightly covered.

Each serving contains:

306 calories | 196 calories from fat | 22 g fat | 3 g saturated fat | 52 mg cholesterol | 5 g protein | 25.5 g carbohydrates | 194 mg sodium

Black Bean and Orange Salad

This easy-to-make salad captures all the flavors of the tropics—with citrus juices and savory seasonings paired with luscious fruit.

Yield: 6 servings | **Active time:** 20 minutes | **Start to finish:** 35 minutes

2 (15-ounce) cans black beans, drained and rinsed

2 navel oranges, peeled and cut into $\frac{1}{2}$-inch dice

$\frac{1}{2}$ medium jicama, peeled and cut into $\frac{1}{2}$-inch dice

$\frac{1}{2}$ green bell pepper, seeds and ribs removed, cut into $\frac{1}{2}$-inch dice

$\frac{1}{4}$ cup chopped fresh cilantro

3 garlic cloves, peeled and minced

3 scallions, white part and 3 inches of green tops, rinsed, trimmed, and chopped

1 teaspoon ground cumin

$\frac{1}{4}$ teaspoon ground cinnamon

$\frac{1}{3}$ cup orange juice

3 tablespoons lime juice

3 tablespoons cider vinegar

$\frac{1}{2}$ teaspoon salt, or to taste

Cayenne to taste

$\frac{1}{3}$ cup olive oil

1. Combine beans, oranges, jicama, green bell pepper, and cilantro in a mixing bowl.
2. Combine garlic, scallions, cumin, cinnamon, orange juice, lime juice, vinegar, salt, and cayenne in a jar with a tight-fitting lid, and shake well. Add olive oil, and shake well again.
4. Toss salad with dressing, and refrigerate salad for at least 15 minutes before serving.

Note: The salad can be made 1 day in advance and refrigerated, tightly covered.

Each serving contains:

243 calories | 109 calories from fat | 12 g fat | 2 g saturated fat | 0 mg cholesterol | 7 g protein | 33 g carbohydrates | 735 mg sodium

Jasmine Rice Salad

This colorful salad is the perfect summer side dish if you are serving any entree with Asian flavors. You can also add some leftover chicken or fish to the rice and serve it as an appetizer or lunch dish.

Yield: 8 servings | **Active time:** 20 minutes | **Start to finish:** 3 hours, including 2 hours for chilling

1½ cups jasmine rice*
½ cup vegetable oil, divided
4 garlic cloves, peeled and minced
1 large shallot, peeled and minced
3 cups water
¾ teaspoon salt
½ cup rice wine vinegar
¼ cup firmly packed dark brown sugar
2 tablespoons fish sauce (*nam pla*)*
1–2 teaspoons Chinese chile paste with garlic*
1 large carrot, peeled and shredded
1 green bell pepper, seeds and ribs removed, and cut into a fine julienne
6 scallions, rinsed, trimmed, cut into 1-inch sections, and cut into a fine julienne

1. Rinse rice in a sieve under cold running water until water runs clear. Heat 2 tablespoons oil in a large saucepan over medium heat. Add garlic and shallot and cook, stirring constantly, for 3 minutes, or until shallot is translucent. Add rice, water, and salt, and cover the pan. Bring rice to a boil over high heat. Reduce the heat to low and simmer rice for 20 minutes, or until liquid is absorbed. Remove the pan from the heat. Allow rice to rest, covered, for 10 minutes, then fluff rice with a fork.

2. While rice cooks, prepare dressing. Combine vinegar, brown sugar, fish sauce, and chile paste in a jar with a tight-fitting lid, and shake well until sugar dissolves. Add remaining oil, and shake well again.

3. Place rice in a mixing bowl or serving dish, and pour dressing over hot rice. Add carrot, green bell pepper, and scallions. Mix well to combine. Refrigerate salad for 2 hours, or until chilled, tightly covered with plastic wrap.

*Available in the Asian aisle of most supermarkets and in specialty markets.

Note: The salad can be made up to 2 days in advance.

Each serving contains:

249 calories | 87 calories from fat | 10 g fat | 1 g saturated fat | 0 mg cholesterol | 3 g protein | 39 g carbohydrates | 698 mg sodium

Variation:
- Substitute green beans and celery or sliced cooked asparagus for the carrot and scallions.

Julienne and batonnet are long, rectangular cuts that are used for vegetables. For hard vegetables like carrots or potatoes, trim them so that the sides are straight, which will make it easier to make even cuts. Slice the vegetable lengthwise, using parallel cuts of the proper thickness. Stack the slices, aligning the edges, and make parallel cuts of the same thickness through the stack. To make batonnet, the cuts should be thick. To make a fine julienne, the cuts should be very thin.

Baked Beans

For picnics or potluck dinners, if you're only going to serve one hot side dish, make it baked beans. Everyone loves them, and they go with everything.

Yield: 8 servings | **Active time:** 15 minutes | **Start to finish:** 5½ hours

> 1 pound dried navy beans
> ¼ pound bacon, cut into ½-inch pieces
> 1 large onion, peeled and diced
> 2 garlic cloves, peeled and minced
> 6 cups water
> 1 cup ketchup
> ½ cup firmly packed dark brown sugar
> ¼ cup apple cider vinegar
> 2 tablespoons dry mustard
> Salt and freshly ground black pepper to taste

1. Rinse beans in a colander and place them in a mixing bowl covered with cold water. Allow beans to soak overnight. Or place beans into a saucepan and bring to a boil over high heat. Boil 1 minute. Turn off the heat, cover the pan, and soak beans for 1 hour. With either soaking method, drain beans, discard soaking water, and begin cooking as soon as possible.
2. Preheat the oven to 350°F.
3. Place bacon in a Dutch oven, and cook over medium-high heat until crisp. Remove bacon from the pan with a slotted spoon, and set aside. Discard all but 2 tablespoons of bacon grease from the pan. Add onion and garlic to the pan, and cook, stirring frequently, for 3 minutes, or until onion is translucent.
4. Return beans and bacon to the pan, and add water, ketchup, sugar, vinegar, mustard, salt, and pepper. Stir well, and bring to a boil over medium heat, stirring occasionally.
5. Transfer the pan to the oven, and bake for 3 ½–4 hours, stirring occasionally, or until beans soften and liquid thickens. Serve hot.

Note: The beans can be baked up to 3 days in advance and refrigerated, tightly covered. Reheat them in a 300°F oven for 40 minutes, covered, or until hot.

Each serving contains:

347 calories | 65 calories from fat | 7 g fat | 2 g saturated fat | 10 mg cholesterol | 22.5 g protein | 58 g carbohydrates | 511 mg sodium

The reason why these beans take so long to cook—even though they've been pre-soaked—is because food containing acid, like vinegar and the tomatoes in the ketchup, retard beans from softening.

Garbanzo Bean Salad Provençale

I frequently serve this salad as a vegetarian entree. It's colorful with flecks of dark olive and bright red cabbage, and the beans are nutty and meaty.

Yield: 6 servings | **Active time:** 15 minutes | **Start to finish:** 30 minutes

    2 (15-ounce) cans garbanzo beans, drained and rinsed
    3/4 cup chopped pitted Niçoise or other oil-cured black olives
    5 scallions, white part and 3 inches of green tops, rinsed,
        trimmed, and chopped
    1 1/2 cups chopped red cabbage
    1/4 cup red wine vinegar
    1/4 cup orange juice
    3 garlic cloves, peeled and minced
    3 tablespoons chopped fresh parsley
    1 tablespoon herbes de Provence
    1 teaspoon dried rosemary
    1/2 teaspoon dried thyme
    1/2 teaspoon dried oregano
    1/2 teaspoon salt, or to taste
    Freshly ground black pepper to taste
    1/3 cup olive oil

1. Combine beans, olives, scallions, and red cabbage in a mixing bowl.
2. Combine vinegar, orange juice, garlic, parsley, herbes de Provence, rosemary, thyme, oregano, salt, and pepper in a jar with a tight-fitting lid, and shake well. Add olive oil, and shake well again.
3. Toss dressing with salad, and chill for 15 minutes to blend flavors.

Note: The salad and dressing can be made 1 day in advance and refrigerated, tightly covered. Do not toss until just prior to serving.

Each serving contains:

312 calories | 138 calories from fat | 15 g fat | 2 g saturated fat | 0 mg cholesterol | 8 g protein | 37 g carbohydrates | 773 mg sodium

Variation:
- Substitute white beans for the garbanzo beans, and substitute pimiento-stuffed green olives for the black olives.

Gemelli with White Beans, Tomatoes, and Sage

This cold pasta salad is simultaneously hearty and refreshing. The garlic and sage add savory flavor to the pasta and beans. Serve it with any Mediterranean meal.

Yield: 8 servings | **Active time:** 15 minutes | **Start to finish:** 30 minutes

> 1 pound gemelli or penne pasta
> ⅓ cup olive oil
> 4 garlic cloves, peeled and minced
> 2 tablespoons dried sage
> 4 ripe plum tomatoes, rinsed, cored, seeded, and chopped
> 1 (15-ounce) can cannellini beans, drained and rinsed
> ½ teaspoon salt, or to taste
> Freshly ground black pepper to taste
> ½ cup freshly grated Parmesan cheese, optional

1. Bring a large pot of salted water to a boil. Add pasta, and cook according to package directions until al dente. Drain pasta, and rinse under cold running water until pasta is cool. Drain, and refrigerate.

2. While water is heating, heat olive oil in a large skillet over medium-high heat. Add garlic and sage, and cook, stirring constantly, for 1 minute. Scrape mixture into a large mixing bowl, and add tomatoes and beans.

3. Add pasta to mixing bowl, season with salt and pepper, and serve at room temperature or chilled. Toss with Parmesan cheese just prior to serving, if using.

Note: The salad can be prepared up to 1 day in advance and refrigerated, tightly covered.

Each serving contains:

386 calories | 104 calories from fat | 11.5 g fat | 2 g saturated fat | 4 mg cholesterol | 14 g protein | 57 g carbohydrates | 231 mg sodium

Canned beans should always be added close to the end of the cooking time. They are already fully cooked, and if they're simmered for more than 30 minutes they can become mushy.

Tabbouleh

Tabbouleh, pronounced *ta-BOOL-ah,* is the potato salad of the Middle East; it is served as an accompaniment to almost everything. The characteristic ingredients are bulgur, parsley, and lemon juice. From that base it is open to interpretation.

Yield: 8 servings | **Active time:** 20 minutes | **Start to finish:** 2 hours, including 1 hour for chilling

> 1 pound bulgur wheat
> 3/4 cup lemon juice
> 3 cups very hot water
> 1 cucumber, peeled, halved, seeded, and chopped
> 4 ripe plum tomatoes, rinsed, cored, seeded, and chopped
> 1 small red onion, peeled and chopped
> 2 garlic cloves, peeled and minced
> 1 cup chopped fresh parsley
> 3 tablespoons chopped fresh mint
> 1/2 cup olive oil
> 1 cup crumbled feta cheese (optional)
> 1/2 teaspoon salt, or to taste
> Freshly ground black pepper to taste

1. Place bulgur in a large mixing bowl and add lemon juice and hot water. Let stand for 30 minutes or until bulgur is tender. Drain off any excess liquid.
2. Add cucumber, tomatoes, onion, garlic, parsley, and mint to bulgur and toss to combine. Add olive oil a few tablespoons at a time to make salad moist but not runny. Stir in feta, if using, and season with salt and pepper.
3. Refrigerate tabbouleh for at least 1 hour. Serve cold or at room temperature.

Note: The salad can be prepared up to 1 day in advance and refrigerated, tightly covered.

Each serving contains:

345 calories | 131 calories from fat | 14.5 g fat | 2 g saturated fat | 0 mg cholesterol | 8 g protein | 50.5 g carbohydrates | 59 mg sodium

Chapter 7:
The Casserole Connection

Potluck suppers with a bountiful buffet table are part of American life, and the concept of everyone bringing a dish is now more entrenched than ever because time and money vie for importance in our lives. While many of the side dishes for a potluck or participatory dinner can be cold, traditionally the main dish is some sort of hot casserole. Those are the recipes you'll find in this chapter.

Potluck as a word and culinary tradition has two meanings. The earliest citation is from 16th-century England, and the intent was food given away to guests. In that regard it was a casual meal, or "come for supper and it's potluck—whatever we have in the pot you'll share."

The use of the term *potluck* to mean a participatory meal, also called a covered-dish dinner in some parts of the country, comes from the Native American custom of potlatch, which was a ceremonial feast.

In developing recipes for this chapter, I selected only those that can be at least doubled successfully, if not tripled; the term for this is *scaling-up* in the professional kitchen. If the original recipe calls for a 9 x 13-inch baking pan, the doubled recipe will fit into a 10 x 14-inch baking pan or a shallow roasting pan. If the dish initially calls for a 10 x 14-inch pan, you'll have to use a roasting pan.

REFINING THE CONCEPT

The most important part of the success of a potluck meal is coordination. One person should always serve as dinner coordinator and assign different categories of food.

As potlucks gain popularity, there have been subtle variations on the theme, and I've used many of them in my own life. Here are two ideas:

The progressive dinner. This is only feasible if everyone lives within a mile of each other. There's one course served at each of four or fives homes. As an added bonus, the group hires a single babysitter, who watches everyone's kids at the home that is serving dessert.

The themed dinner. This variation is a wonderful way to explore ethnic cuisines. The organizer picks a country or region, sets the menu, and then assigns specific recipes to the participants.

Tex-Mex Tuna Casserole

The custard makes this brunch or supper casserole almost like a cross between an enchilada and a quiche. It's mildly spiced, so it appeals to all generations, too.

Yield: 6 servings | **Active time:** 15 minutes | **Start to finish:** 45 minutes

2 tablespoons (1/4 stick) unsalted butter

1 medium onion, peeled and diced

2 garlic cloves, peeled and minced

1 1/2 teaspoons dried oregano

1 (4-ounce) can diced mild green chiles, drained

8 (6-inch) corn tortillas, cut into 1/2-inch strips

1 cup grated Monterey Jack cheese

3 (5-ounce) cans light tuna, drained

3 large eggs

1 1/2 cups whole milk

1/4 cup chopped fresh cilantro

1/2 teaspoon salt, or to taste

Freshly ground black pepper to taste

1. Preheat the oven to 350°F, and grease a 9 x 13-inch baking pan.
2. Melt butter in a small skillet over medium-high heat. Add onion, garlic, and oregano. Cook, stirring frequently, for 3 minutes or until onions are translucent. Stir green chiles into onion mixture, and set aside.
3. Place 1/2 of the tortilla strips in the prepared baking pan, and top with 1/2 of the Monterey Jack cheese, 1/2 of the tuna, and 1/2 of the onion mixture. Repeat with second layer. Whisk eggs with milk and cilantro, and season with salt and pepper. Pour egg mixture into the baking pan, and cover the pan with aluminum foil.
4. Bake for 15 minutes, remove the foil, and bake for an additional 15 minutes, or until top is browned and a toothpick inserted in the center comes out clean.

Note: The casserole can be prepared for baking up to 1 day in advance and refrigerated, tightly covered. Add 10 minutes to the covered baking time if chilled.

Each serving contains:

279 calories | 132 calories from fat | 15 g fat | 8 g saturated fat | 162.5 mg cholesterol | 22 g protein | 16 g carbohydrates | 592 mg sodium

Heat releases the flavor and aroma of dried herbs and spices. For blends such as curry powder or chili powder, it also removes any "raw" taste. Add these dried ingredients at the beginning of the cooking process. Add fresh herbs more toward the end.

Oven-Baked Chicken and Garden Pea Risotto

Risotto is a traditional Italian rice dish that dates back to the Renaissance. The key ingredient is Arborio rice, which is a short, fat-grained Italian rice with a high starch content. Traditional risotto recipes require countless minutes of laborious stirring, but this recipe achieves the same results with far less work.

Yield: 6 servings | **Active time:** 15 minutes | **Start to finish:** 50 minutes

> 4 cups Chicken Stock (recipe on page 22) or purchased stock, divided
> 1 (1-pound) package frozen peas, thawed and drained, divided
> 1 pound boneless, skinless chicken breast halves, cut into 1-inch cubes
> 1/2 teaspoon salt, or to taste
> Freshly ground black pepper to taste
> 3 tablespoons unsalted butter
> 1 large onion, peeled and chopped
> 1 garlic clove, peeled and chopped
> 2 cups Arborio rice
> 1/2 cup dry white wine
> 2 teaspoons dried tarragon
> 3/4 cup freshly grated Parmesan cheese

1. Preheat the oven to 400°F, and grease a 10 x 14-inch baking pan.
2. Combine 1 cup stock and 1/3 of the peas in a food processor fitted with the steel blade or in a blender. Puree until smooth, and set aside.
3. Rinse chicken, pat dry with paper towels, and sprinkle with salt and pepper. Heat butter in a large skillet over medium-high heat. Add chicken and cook, stirring frequently, for 2 minutes, or until chicken is opaque. Remove chicken from the pan with a slotted spoon, and set aside. Add onion and garlic to the pan, and cook for 3 minutes, stirring frequently, or until onion is translucent. Add rice to the pan, and cook for 2 minutes, stirring constantly.
4. Add wine to the pan, raise the heat to high, and cook for 3 minutes, stirring constantly, or until wine is almost evaporated. Add stock and pea puree, remaining stock, chicken, and tarragon to the pan, and bring to a boil. Scrape mixture into prepared pan, cover pan with aluminum foil, and bake for 15 minutes.

5. Remove foil, stir in remaining peas, and return the pan to oven for 10–15 minutes, or until rice is soft and has absorbed liquid. Stir in Parmesan cheese, and serve immediately.

Note: The dish can be cooked up to 2 days in advance and refrigerated, tightly covered. Reheat in a 350°F oven, covered, for 20–25 minutes, or until hot.

Each serving contains:

452 calories | 102 calories from fat | 11 g fat | 6 g saturated fat | 77 mg cholesterol | 27 g protein | 59 g carbohydrates | 475 mg sodium

Variation:
- Substitute frozen chopped broccoli for the peas.

> Bags of frozen vegetables are less expensive per ounce than cardboard boxes, so if you use a vegetable regularly, buy the plastic bags. Each individual vegetable is different, so measure the contents and take note of what portion of the bag equals the volume of a 10-ounce box.

Turkey Tetrazzini

This grandmother of all leftover poultry casseroles was named for Italian singer Luisa Tetrazzini, who was the toast of the American opera circuit in the early 1900s. Where the dish was created, and by whom, is not known.

Yield: 8 servings | **Active time:** 20 minutes | **Start to finish:** 50 minutes

1 pound thin spaghetti, broken into 2-inch lengths
4 tablespoons ($\frac{1}{2}$ stick) unsalted butter, divided
2 tablespoons olive oil
1 small onion, peeled and chopped
2 garlic cloves, peeled and minced
2 celery ribs, rinsed, trimmed, and thinly sliced
$\frac{1}{2}$ pound mushrooms, wiped with a damp paper towel, trimmed, and sliced
3 tablespoons all-purpose flour
$\frac{1}{2}$ cup dry sherry
1 cup Chicken Stock (recipe on page 22) or purchased stock
$1\frac{1}{2}$ cups half-and-half
3 cups shredded turkey
1 cup freshly grated Parmesan cheese, divided
$\frac{1}{2}$ teaspoon salt, or to taste
Freshly ground black pepper to taste
$\frac{1}{2}$ cup plain breadcrumbs

1. Preheat the oven to 350°F, and grease a 10 x 14-inch baking pan. Bring a large pot of salted water to a boil, and cook pasta according to package directions until al dente. Drain, and place pasta in the prepared pan.

2. Heat 2 tablespoons butter and olive oil in a large skillet over medium-high heat. Add onion, garlic, and celery, and cook, stirring frequently, for 3 minutes, or until onion is translucent. Add mushrooms, and cook for 3 minutes, or until mushrooms soften. Add vegetables to the pan with pasta.

3. Heat remaining butter in saucepan over low heat. Stir in flour and cook, stirring constantly, for 2 minutes. Whisk in sherry, and bring to a boil over medium-high heat, whisking constantly. Simmer 3 minutes, then add stock and half-and-half, and simmer 2 minutes.

4. Stir turkey and ³/₄ cup Parmesan cheese into sauce, and season with salt and pepper. Combine mixture with pasta and vegetables in the prepared pan. Cover pan with aluminum foil, and bake for 15 minutes. Combine remaining Parmesan cheese with breadcrumbs. Uncover the pan, sprinkle breadcrumb mixture on top, and bake an additional 15–20 minutes, or until bubbly and top is browned. Serve immediately.

Note: The dish can be prepared up to baking 1 day in advance and refrigerated, tightly covered. Add 10 minutes to covered bake time if filling is chilled.

Each serving contains:

549 calories | 183 calories from fat | 20 g fat | 10 g saturated fat | 81 mg cholesterol | 30.5 g protein | 56 g carbohydrates | 421 mg sodium

Variation:

- Reduce the mushrooms to ¼ pound, and add 1 (10-ounce) package frozen mixed vegetables, thawed.

Mushrooms are relatively expensive, so you don't want them to go to waste. Always store mushrooms in a paper bag rather than a plastic bag. Plastic causes mushrooms to become moist and soggy. An alternative method is to line a bowl with paper towels, add the mushrooms, then cover the bowl with more paper towels.

Chicken and Jalapeño Jack Strata

Jalapeño Jack, which is a Monterey Jack cheese that comes already imbedded with flecks of fiery pepper, is not a convenience food; it's a real cheese, and it's the same price as its mild cousin. But it is a convenience to have the peppers included, and they really enliven this strata.

Yield: 6 servings | **Active time:** 15 minutes | **Start to finish:** 1¼ hours

6 large eggs
2½ cups whole milk
½ teaspoon salt, or to taste
Freshly ground black pepper to taste
1¼ cups grated jalapeño Jack cheese
½-pound loaf French or Italian bread, cut into ½-inch slices
2 tablespoons olive oil
1 medium onion, peeled and diced
2 garlic cloves, peeled and minced
½ green bell pepper, seeds and ribs removed, and chopped
2 teaspoons ground cumin
1 teaspoon dried oregano
3 cups diced cooked chicken
1 (10-ounce) package frozen corn, thawed and drained
Vegetable oil spray

1. Preheat the oven to 350°F, and grease a 9 x 13-inch baking pan with vegetable oil spray.
2. Combine eggs, milk, salt, and pepper in mixing bowl, and whisk well. Stir in cheese. Arrange bread slices in the prepared pan, and pour egg mixture over them, pressing down so that bread will absorb liquid.
3. Heat oil in a medium skillet over medium-high heat. Add onion, garlic, and green bell pepper, and cook, stirring frequently, for 5–7 minutes, or until vegetables are soft. Add cumin and oregano, and cook for 1 minute, stirring constantly. Stir vegetables, chicken, and corn into bread mixture.
4. Cover the baking pan with aluminum foil, and bake in the center of the oven for 30 minutes. Remove the foil, and bake for an additional 15–20 minutes, or until a toothpick inserted in the center comes out clean and the top is lightly browned. Allow to rest for 5 minutes, and then serve.

Note: The strata can be prepared for baking up to 1 day in advance and refrigerated, tightly covered. Add 10 minutes to the covered baking time if the strata is cold. Also, the strata can be baked up to 3 days in advance; reheat it in a 325°F oven, covered, for 20–25 minutes, or until hot.

Each serving contains:

562 calories | 216 calories from fat | 24 g fat | 10 g saturated fat | 302 mg cholesterol | 43 g protein | 43 g carbohydrates | 636 mg sodium

Variations:

- Substitute Monterey Jack cheese for all or some of the jalapeño Jack for a milder dish.
- Substitute 1 (15-ounce) can kidney beans, drained and rinsed, for the corn.
- Substitute a savory cornbread for the white bread.

While you have to make sure that raw chicken never touches other foods, the same is not true for eggs. Any egg dish, such as this strata, can be prepared in advance.

Chicken and Cheese Enchiladas

These rolls of chicken bound with seasoned cream cheese in a creamy sauce are a real crowd pleaser. And they are excellent for a buffet meal because they can be cut with a fork.

Yield: 6 servings | **Active time:** 20 minutes | **Start to finish:** 50 minutes

2 tablespoons olive oil
1 medium onion, peeled and chopped
2 garlic cloves, peeled and minced
1 jalapeño or serrano chile, seeds and ribs removed, and finely chopped
2 tablespoons chili powder
1 teaspoon ground cumin
1 teaspoon dried oregano
2 tablespoons canned diced mild green chiles, drained
3 cups shredded cooked chicken
1 (3-ounce) package cream cheese, softened
1 1/2 cups grated Monterey Jack cheese, divided
1/2 teaspoon salt, or to taste
Freshly ground black pepper to taste
3 tablespoons unsalted butter
3 tablespoons all-purpose flour
3/4 cup Chicken Stock (recipe on page 22) or purchased stock
3/4 cup half-and-half
12 (6-inch) corn tortillas
Vegetable oil spray

1. Preheat the oven to 400°F, and grease a 9 x 13-inch baking pan.
2. Heat oil in a small skillet over medium-high heat. Add onion, garlic, and chile, and cook, stirring frequently, for 3 minutes, or until onion is translucent. Add chili powder, cumin, and oregano. Cook for 1 minute, stirring constantly. Add canned chiles, and set aside.
3. Combine chicken, cream cheese, and 3/4 cup Monterey Jack cheese in a mixing bowl. Season with salt and pepper, and set aside.
4. Heat butter in a saucepan over low heat. Stir in flour, and cook, stirring constantly, for 2 minutes. Whisk in stock, and bring to a boil over medium-high heat, whisking constantly. Add half-and-half, and simmer 2 minutes. Stir in cooked vegetables, and season to taste with salt and pepper.

5. Heat a large nonstick skillet over medium heat. Spray tortillas lightly with vegetable oil spray, and cook for 10 seconds per side, turning gently with tongs. Tortillas should be pliable, but not crisp.

6. Place ⅓ of the sauce in the bottom of the prepared pan. Divide chicken mixture among tortillas, and roll each gently. Arrange enchiladas seam side down in the pan. Pour remaining sauce over top, and cover pan with aluminum foil. Bake for 10 minutes, uncover pan, sprinkle with remaining cheese, and bake for 15–20 minutes, or until bubbly and browned. Allow to sit for 5 minutes before serving.

Note: The dish can be prepared up to baking 1 day in advance and refrigerated, tightly covered. Add 10 minutes to covered bake time if filling is chilled.

Each serving contains:

534 calories | 268 calories from fat | 30 g fat | 15 g saturated fat | 127 mg cholesterol | 34.5 g protein | 32 g carbohydrates | 533 mg sodium

Variations:

- Substitute 2–3 (5-ounce) cans tuna, drained and flaked, for the chicken.
- Substitute 2–3 cups canned kidney beans, drained and rinsed, for the chicken, and substitute Vegetable Stock (recipe on page 23) for Chicken Stock.

Be careful when cooking hot chiles that the steam from the pan doesn't get in your eyes. The potent oils in the peppers can be transmitted in the vapor.

Chicken and Sausage Jambalaya

Jambalaya is a staple of cooking in Louisiana, where culinary traditions of France, Spain, Italy, and the New World, among others, blended. Jambalaya was a local adaptation of the Spanish rice dish paella, and became a favorite among the Cajuns, French transplants who settled in the Louisiana bayous.

Yield: 6 servings | **Active time:** 20 minutes | **Start to finish:** 55 minutes

1 (3½–4-pound) frying chicken, cut into serving pieces, with each breast half cut in half crosswise

½ teaspoon salt, or to taste

Freshly ground black pepper to taste

3 tablespoons olive oil

½ pound kielbasa or other smoked sausage, cut into ½-inch-thick slices

2 celery ribs, rinsed, trimmed, and chopped

1 large onion, peeled and diced

½ green bell pepper, seeds and ribs removed, and diced

4 garlic cloves, peeled and minced

2 (5-ounce) packages yellow rice

1½ cups Chicken Stock (recipe on page 22) or purchased stock

2 tablespoons chopped fresh parsley

1 teaspoon dried thyme

1 bay leaf

1 cup frozen green peas, thawed

1. Rinse chicken, pat dry with paper towels, and sprinkle chicken with salt and pepper. Heat oil in a large skillet over medium-high heat. Add chicken pieces to the skillet, and brown well on all sides, turning gently with tongs, and being careful not to crowd the pan. Remove chicken from the skillet, and set aside.

2. Add kielbasa, celery, onion, green pepper, and garlic to the skillet, and cook, stirring frequently, for 3 minutes, or until onion is translucent. Add rice to the skillet, and cook for 1 minute, stirring constantly. Add stock, parsley, thyme, and bay leaf to the skillet, and bring to a boil over high heat, stirring frequently.

3. Return chicken to the skillet, cover the skillet, reduce the heat to medium-low, and cook for 25–35 minutes, or until chicken is cooked through and no longer pink, and almost all liquid has been absorbed.

4. Stir peas into the skillet, recover the pan, and cook for 2–3 minutes, or until hot and remaining liquid is absorbed. Remove and discard bay leaf, and serve immediately.

Note: The dish can be cooked up to 2 days in advance and refrigerated, tightly covered. Reheat in a 350°F oven, covered, for 30–35 minutes, or until hot.

Each serving contains:

751 calories | 290 calories from fat | 32 g fat | 9.5 g saturated fat | 254.5 mg cholesterol | 69 g protein | 45 g carbohydrates | 1,588 mg sodium

Variation:

- Substitute baked ham, cut into ½-inch dice, for the sausage.

Chile Relleño Bake

Authentic chile rellenos are really time-consuming to make because each individual pepper is stuffed. This casserole contains all the same wonderful flavors, but it's ready to cook in minutes.

Yield: 6 servings | **Active time:** 20 minutes | **Start to finish:** 1¼ hours

BEANS

- 2 tablespoons olive oil
- 1 small onion, peeled and chopped
- 2 garlic cloves, peeled and minced
- 1 small jalapeño or serrano chile, seeds and ribs removed, and finely chopped
- 1 tablespoon ground cumin
- 1 (15-ounce) can kidney beans, drained with liquid reserved
- 2 tablespoons chopped fresh cilantro
- Freshly ground black pepper to taste

DISH

- 1¼ pounds lean ground beef
- 2 tablespoons olive oil
- 1 medium onion, peeled and diced
- 2 garlic cloves, peeled and minced
- 2 teaspoons ground cumin
- 1 teaspoon dried oregano
- 2 (4-ounce) cans diced mild green chiles, drained
- ½ teaspoon salt, or to taste
- Freshly ground black pepper to taste
- 2 cups shredded Monterey Jack cheese
- 1½ cups whole milk
- 3 large eggs
- ¼ cup yellow cornmeal
- Hot red pepper sauce to taste

1. Preheat the oven to 350°F, and grease a 9 x 13-inch baking pan.
2. For the beans, heat oil in a medium skillet over medium-high heat. Add onion, garlic, and chile, and cook, stirring frequently, for 3 minutes, or

until onion is translucent. Add cumin and cook for 1 minute, stirring constantly. Add beans, with 3 tablespoons of reserved liquid, and heat until beans begin to simmer. Turn off the heat, and mash the beans with a potato masher or the back of a heavy spoon. Stir in cilantro, and season to taste with pepper. Set aside.

3. For the dish, heat a large skillet over medium-high heat. Add beef, and cook until browned, breaking up lumps with a fork. Remove beef from the skillet with a slotted spoon, and set aside in a bowl. Discard fat from the skillet.

4. Heat oil in the skillet, and add onion and garlic. Cook, stirring frequently, for 3 minutes, or until onion is translucent. Add cumin and oregano, and cook for 1 minute, stirring constantly. Remove the pan from the heat; add beef, beans, and green chiles. Season with salt and pepper, stir, and set aside.

5. Spread $\frac{1}{2}$ of the beef mixture into the bottom of the prepared baking pan, and sprinkle $\frac{1}{2}$ of the Monterey Jack cheese over top. Repeat with remaining beef mixture and Monterey Jack cheese.

6. In a medium-size mixing bowl, whisk together milk, eggs, cornmeal, and hot red pepper sauce. Pour mixture over casserole.

7. Cover the pan with aluminum foil, and bake for 15 minutes. Remove the foil and bake for an additional 30 minutes. Allow to sit for 5 minutes; then serve immediately.

Note: The dish can be baked up to 1 day in advance and refrigerated, tightly covered. Reheat it, covered with foil, in a 350°F oven for 20–25 minutes, or until hot.

Each serving contains:

567 calories | 303 calories from fat | 34 g fat | 14 g saturated fat | 207 mg cholesterol | 38 g protein | 28 g carbohydrates | 856 mg sodium

Variations:
- Substitute 1 (15-ounce) can kidney beans, drained and rinsed, and 2 small zucchini for the ground beef.
- Substitute ground turkey or ground pork for the ground beef.
- Substitute jalapeño Jack cheese for some or all of the Monterey Jack cheese for a spicier dish.

Greek Macaroni and Beef (Pastitsio)

The use of a touch of cinnamon is characteristic of traditional Greek cooking, and this classic dish is a one-pot meal. Half of the pasta is coated with a rich, cinnamon-scented tomato sauce, and the other half is mixed into cheese sauce.

Yield: 6 servings | **Active time:** 20 minutes | **Start to finish:** 50 minutes

PASTA

$^{2}/_{3}$ pound macaroni

BEEF

3 tablespoons olive oil, divided
1 pound lean ground beef
1 medium onion, peeled and diced
1 garlic clove, peeled and minced
1 (28-ounce) can crushed tomatoes, undrained
2 tablespoons chopped fresh parsley
1 teaspoon dried oregano
$^{1}/_{2}$ teaspoon ground cinnamon
$^{1}/_{2}$ teaspoon salt, or to taste
Freshly ground black pepper to taste

CHEESE SAUCE

3 tablespoons unsalted butter
3 tablespoons all-purpose flour
2 cups whole milk
$^{3}/_{4}$ cup crumbled feta cheese
$^{1}/_{4}$ teaspoon salt, or to taste
Freshly ground black pepper to taste
2 large eggs

1. Bring a large pot of salted water to a boil over high heat. Cook pasta according to package directions until al dente. Drain, and set aside.
2. While pasta cooks, heat 1 tablespoon oil in a large skillet over medium-high heat. Add beef, breaking up lumps with a fork, and brown well. Remove meat from the skillet with a slotted spoon, discard grease, and set aside.

3. Heat remaining oil in the skillet, and add onion and garlic. Cook, stirring frequently, for 3 minutes, or until onion is translucent. Return beef to the skillet, and add tomatoes, parsley, oregano, and cinnamon. Bring to a boil, then reduce the heat to low, and simmer mixture, partially covered, for 20 minutes. Season with salt and pepper.
4. Preheat the oven to 400°F, and grease a 9 x 13-inch baking pan.
5. While beef simmers, make cheese sauce. Melt butter in a saucepan over low heat. Add flour, and cook for 2 minutes, stirring constantly. Stir in milk, and bring to a boil over medium heat, whisking constantly. Reduce the heat to low, and simmer sauce, stirring frequently, for 3 minutes. Add feta, salt, and pepper, and stir until cheese melts.
6. Whisk eggs well in a large mixing bowl, and then slowly whisk hot sauce into eggs. Add 1/2 of the pasta to the mixing bowl with cheese sauce.
7. Place remaining pasta in the prepared pan, and add beef sauce. Stir well, and spread into an even layer. Spoon pasta in cheese sauce over pasta in beef sauce.
8. Bake dish for 25–30 minutes, or until bubbling and top is browned. Allow to sit for 5 minutes, then serve immediately.

Note: The dish can be cooked up to 2 days in advance and refrigerated, tightly covered. Reheat, covered with foil, in a 350°F oven for 35–40 minutes, or until hot.

Each serving contains:

603 calories | 261 calories from fat | 29 g fat | 12 g saturated fat | 155.5 mg cholesterol | 33 g protein | 55 g carbohydrates | 980 mg sodium

Variations:
- Substitute ground lamb for the ground beef.
- Add 1 small eggplant, rinsed and cut into 3/4-inch dice, to the meat sauce along with the tomatoes.
- Substitute freshly grated Parmesan cheese for the feta cheese.
- Add 1/4 cup chopped fresh dill to the cheese sauce.

Baked Pasta with Beef and Beans (Pasta e Fagioli)

This homey Italian casserole is a great way to "sneak" some vegetables into kids because the beans are part of the dish. This is a great candidate for a potluck because it can be multiplied many times.

Yield: 6 servings | **Active time:** 15 minutes | **Start to finish:** 45 minutes

⅔ pound mostaccioli or penne pasta

½ pound bulk hot or sweet Italian sausage, or link sausage with casings discarded

½ pound ground chuck

2 tablespoons olive oil

1 large onion, peeled and chopped

2 garlic cloves, peeled and minced

1 (28-ounce) can diced tomatoes, drained

2 tablespoons tomato paste

1 (15-ounce) can kidney beans, drained and rinsed

1 teaspoon dried oregano

½ teaspoon dried thyme

½ teaspoon salt, or to taste

Freshly ground black pepper to taste

½ cup freshly grated Parmesan cheese

¼ cup chopped fresh parsley

1 cup grated whole-milk mozzarella cheese

1. Preheat the oven to 400°F, and grease a 9 x 13-inch baking pan. Bring a large pot of salted water to a boil. Boil pasta according to package directions until al dente. Drain, and place pasta in the prepared pan.

2. While pasta cooks, heat a large skillet over medium-high heat. Add sausage and beef, breaking up lumps with a fork, and brown well. Remove meats from the skillet with a slotted spoon, discard grease, and set aside.

3. Heat oil in the skillet, and add onion and garlic. Cook, stirring frequently, for 3 minutes, or until onion is translucent. Add tomatoes, tomato paste, kidney beans, oregano, and thyme, and simmer 5 minutes. Season with salt and pepper. Stir in Parmesan and parsley, and stir mixture into pasta.

4. Cover the pan with aluminum foil, and bake for 15 minutes. Uncover the pan, sprinkle with mozzarella cheese, and bake for an additional 15 minutes, or until bubbly and cheese is melted. Serve immediately.

Note: The dish can be cooked up to 2 days in advance and refrigerated, tightly covered. Reheat, covered with foil, in a 350°F oven for 30–35 minutes, or until hot.

Each serving contains:

507 calories | 151 calories from fat | 17 g fat | 8 g saturated fat | 58 mg cholesterol | 32 g protein | 57.5 g carbohydrates | 1,179 mg sodium

Variation:
- Substitute ground turkey for the ground beef.

The main difference between sweet and hot Italian sausage is red pepper flakes. You can't remove them if you want a milder flavor, but you can certainly add them to make a dish hotter.

Tex-Mex Tamale Pie

This is one of my favorite dishes to bring to a potluck dinner with a Hispanic theme because the cornbread topping is stunning when the casserole is put on the table, and all generations love it.

Yield: 6 servings | **Active time:** 15 minutes | **Start to finish:** 1 hour

FILLING

1 1/4 pounds ground chuck

2 tablespoons olive oil

1 large onion, peeled and chopped

2 celery ribs, rinsed, trimmed, and sliced

1/2 green bell pepper, seeds and ribs removed, and chopped

1 jalapeño or serrano chile, seeds and ribs removed, and finely chopped

2 garlic cloves, peeled and minced

2 tablespoons chili powder

1 tablespoon smoked Spanish paprika

1 (14.5-ounce) can diced tomatoes, undrained

1 (8-ounce) can tomato sauce

1/2 teaspoon salt, or to taste

Freshly ground black pepper to taste

1 cup fresh corn kernels or frozen corn kernels, thawed

TOPPING

2 large eggs, lightly beaten

1 cup buttermilk

1/4 cup vegetable oil, bacon grease, or melted butter

1 1/2 cups yellow cornmeal

1/2 cup all-purpose flour

2 1/2 teaspoons baking powder

1/2 teaspoon salt

1. Preheat the oven to 400°F, and grease a 9 x 13-inch baking pan.
2. For filling, heat a large skillet over medium-high heat. Add beef, breaking up lumps with a fork, and brown well. Remove beef from the skillet with a slotted spoon, discard grease, and set aside.

3. Heat oil in the skillet, and add onion, celery, bell pepper, chile, and garlic. Cook, stirring frequently, for 3 minutes, or until onion is translucent. Stir in chili powder and paprika, and cook for 1 minute, stirring constantly.

4. Return beef to the skillet, add tomatoes and tomato sauce, and season with salt and pepper. Bring to a boil, and simmer, uncovered, for 10 minutes. Add corn, and simmer 5 minutes. Spread mixture into the prepared pan.

5. While filling simmers, prepare topping. Combine eggs, buttermilk, oil, cornmeal, flour, baking powder, and salt in a mixing bowl, and whisk well. Spoon batter over filling, leaving a ½-inch margin around the edges.

6. Bake for 15 minutes, or until golden and a toothpick inserted into the topping comes out clean. Serve immediately.

Note: The filling can be prepared up to 2 days in advance and refrigerated, tightly covered. Reheat it over low heat until hot before baking.

Each serving contains:

504 calories | 204 calories from fat | 23 g fat | 4 g saturated fat | 128 mg cholesterol | 27 g protein | 49 g carbohydrates | 978.5 mg sodium

Variations:
- Substitute 1 (15-ounce) can kidney beans, drained and rinsed, for the corn.
- Substitute ground turkey for the ground beef.
- Sprinkle ½ cup grated cheddar or Monterey Jack cheese on top of the cornbread for the last 3 minutes of baking.

Chili powder is actually a spice blend, and can be made as follows: Combine 2 tablespoons ground red chile, 2 tablespoons paprika, 1 tablespoon ground coriander, 1 tablespoon garlic powder, 1 tablespoon onion powder, 2 teaspoons ground cumin, 2 teaspoons ground red pepper or cayenne, 1 teaspoon ground black pepper, and 1 teaspoon dried oregano.

Johnny Marzetti

If you grew up in the Midwest, or lived there like I did, you certainly encountered this casserole. Named for Marzetti's Restaurant in Columbus, Ohio, it always contains some sort of pasta or noodles and a tomato sauce. This version is made with a combination of ground beef and Italian sausage, and all you need to complete the meal is a tossed salad.

Yield: 6 servings | **Active time:** 20 minutes | **Start to finish:** 1¼ hours

> ½ pound macaroni
> 3 tablespoons olive oil, divided
> ½ pound ground beef
> ½ pound mild or spicy bulk Italian sausage
> 1 large onion, peeled and diced
> 2 garlic cloves, peeled and minced
> ½ small green bell pepper, seeds and ribs removed, and diced
> 1 celery rib, rinsed, trimmed, and diced
> ½ pound fresh mushrooms, wiped with a damp paper towel, trimmed, and sliced
> 1 (28-ounce) can crushed tomatoes in tomato puree
> 2 tablespoons chopped fresh parsley
> 2 teaspoons Italian seasoning
> ½ teaspoon salt, or to taste
> Freshly ground black pepper to taste
> 1½ cups grated sharp cheddar cheese, divided
> ½ cup Italian breadcrumbs
> ¼ cup freshly grated Parmesan cheese
> 2 tablespoons unsalted butter, melted

1. Preheat the oven to 350°F, and grease a 9 x 13-inch baking pan. Bring a large pot of salted water to a boil over high heat. Cook macaroni according to package directions until al dente. Drain, and set aside.

2. Heat 1 tablespoon oil in a deep skillet over medium-high heat. Add beef and sausage, breaking up lumps with a fork. Cook meats for 3–5 minutes, or until browned. Remove meat from the skillet with a slotted spoon, and set aside. Discard grease from the pan.

3. Heat remaining oil in the skillet over medium-high heat. Add onion, garlic, green bell pepper, celery, and mushrooms. Cook, stirring frequently, for 3 minutes, or until onion is translucent. Add meats to the skillet, along with tomatoes, parsley, and Italian seasoning.

4. Bring to a boil over medium-high heat, then reduce the heat to medium, and simmer mixture, uncovered, for 12–15 minutes, or until slightly thickened. Season with salt and pepper.

5. Spread 1/2 of the meat mixture on the bottom of the prepared pan, and top with 1/2 of the macaroni and 3/4 cup of the cheddar cheese. Repeat layering. Combine breadcrumbs, Parmesan cheese, and butter in a small bowl. Sprinkle crumbs on top of pan.

6. Bake for 30–40 minutes, or until bubbly. Serve immediately.

Note: The dish can be prepared for baking up to 1 day in advance and refrigerated, tightly covered. Add 10 minutes to the baking time if chilled. It can also be baked up to 2 days in advance and refrigerated, tightly covered. Reheat it in a 350°F oven, covered, for 30–35 minutes, or until hot.

Each serving contains:

657 calories | 337 calories from fat | 37.5 g fat | 16 g saturated fat | 97 mg cholesterol | 30 g protein | 46 g carbohydrates | 1,115 mg sodium

Variation:

- Substitute mozzarella or Monterey Jack for the cheddar cheese.

Reuben Sandwich Bake

Although now defunct, Reuben's Delicatessen was a New York institution that opened in the late 1890s. Legend has it that owner Arthur Reuben invented the Reuben sandwich there in 1914 for the cast of a Charlie Chaplin film. This casserole contains all the elements of the iconic sandwich, but it can be done ahead, and it's great to feed a crowd.

Yield: 6 servings | **Active time:** 10 minutes | **Start to finish:** 45 minutes

1 cup mayonnaise

⅓ cup bottled chili sauce

2 tablespoons lemon juice

2 scallions, white parts and 3 inches of green tops, rinsed, trimmed, and chopped

2 tablespoons sweet pickle relish

2 tablespoons Dijon mustard

Freshly ground black pepper to taste

1 (2-pound) package sauerkraut

5 tablespoons unsalted butter

1 small onion, peeled and diced

2 teaspoons caraway seeds (optional)

3 cups shredded Swiss cheese

1⅓ cups bottled Thousand Island salad dressing

1 pound thinly sliced cooked corned beef, coarsely chopped

6 slices rye bread, cut into 1-inch strips

1. Preheat the oven to 375°F, and grease a 9 x 13-inch baking pan. Combine mayonnaise, chili sauce, lemon juice, scallions, pickle relish, mustard, and pepper in a mixing bowl. Whisk well, and set aside.

2. Place sauerkraut in a colander, and press with the back of a spoon to extract as much liquid as possible. Rinse sauerkraut under cold running water for 2 minutes. Then place sauerkraut in a large mixing bowl and fill bowl with cold water. Soak sauerkraut for 5 minutes.

3. While sauerkraut soaks, heat butter in a small skillet over medium heat until melted. Pour off and reserve 3 tablespoons butter. Add onion to remaining butter and cook, stirring frequently, over medium-high heat for 3 minutes, or until onion is translucent.

4. Drain sauerkraut in a colander again, pressing with the back of a spoon to extract as much liquid as possible. Place sauerkraut in the prepared baking pan and top with onions and caraway seeds, if using.

5. Layer with ½ of the Swiss cheese, ½ of the dressing, and corned beef. Then layer with remaining dressing and Swiss cheese. Brush bread strips with reserved melted butter. Place bread strips on top of Swiss cheese.

6. Cover the pan with aluminum foil and bake for 10 minutes. Remove the foil, and bake for an additional 25 minutes, or until bread is browned and cheese is melted. Serve immediately.

Note: The casserole can be prepared for baking up to 1 day in advance and refrigerated, tightly covered. Add 10 minutes to the covered baking time if chilled.

Each serving contains:

1,028 calories | 710 calories from fat | 79 g fat | 24 g saturated fat | 161 mg cholesterol | 40 g protein | 38 g carbohydrates | 3,406 mg sodium

Contrary to its name, chili sauce is closer to a chunky ketchup than a fiery sauce. It's a tomato-based condiment that contains onions, green peppers, vinegar, sugar, and spices. It serves as the basis for traditional cocktail sauce, too, so it's worth it to keep a bottle in the house.

Mac' and Cheese with Ham

While Italians have all sorts of pasta dishes made with cheeses, mac' and cheese is our home-grown American favorite. Delicious in and of itself, it is also a great way to use up leftover ham.

Yield: 8 servings | **Active time:** 15 minutes | **Start to finish:** 50 minutes

1 pound elbow macaroni
4 tablespoons ($\frac{1}{2}$ stick) unsalted butter
$\frac{1}{4}$ cup all-purpose flour
1 tablespoon paprika
1 teaspoon dry mustard
$\frac{1}{2}$ cup Chicken Stock (recipe on page 22) or purchased stock
$2\frac{1}{2}$ cups whole milk
1 pound grated sharp cheddar cheese, divided
$\frac{1}{2}$ teaspoon salt, or to taste
Freshly ground black pepper to taste
1 pound cooked ham, trimmed of fat and cut into $\frac{1}{2}$-inch cubes

1. Preheat the oven to 375°F, and grease a 9 x 13-inch baking pan. Bring a large pot of salted water to a boil. Add macaroni, and cook for 2 minutes less than package directions. Drain, and place macaroni in the prepared pan.

2. Melt butter in a saucepan over low heat. Stir in flour, paprika, and mustard, and stir constantly for 2 minutes. Whisk in chicken stock, and bring to a boil over medium-high heat, whisking constantly. Whisk in milk, and bring to a boil again, stirring frequently. Reduce the heat to low and simmer for 2 minutes. Stir in all but $\frac{1}{2}$ cup grated cheese, stirring until cheese melts, and season with salt and pepper.

3. Stir ham and sauce into macaroni, and sprinkle with remaining $\frac{1}{2}$ cup cheese. Bake for 25–30 minutes, or until bubbly. Allow to sit for 5 minutes, then serve immediately.

Note: The dish can be prepared up to baking 2 days in advance and refrigerated, tightly covered. Reheat it, covered with foil, for 15 minutes before removing foil and baking for 25 minutes.

Each serving contains:

609 calories | 269 calories from fat | 30 g fat | 18 g saturated fat | 108 mg cholesterol | 36 g protein | 50 g carbohydrates | 1,466 mg sodium

Variations:
- Substitute cooked chicken or turkey for the ham.
- Substitute 2 cups sautéed mushrooms for the ham, and substitute Vegetable Stock (recipe on page 23) for Chicken Stock.

When a dish containing pasta is baked for more than 20 minutes, and the dish contains a lot of liquid, it's better to slightly undercook the pasta. That way it won't be mushy after baking.

Italian Pork

Pork loin is a great inexpensive stand-in for veal; it has the same delicate flavor and texture. In this dish it's layered with cheese, salami, and sage for a version of vitello saltimbocca.

Yield: 6 servings | **Active time:** 15 minutes | **Start to finish:** 30 minutes

> 1¼ pounds boneless pork loin
> ½ teaspoon salt, or to taste
> Freshly ground black pepper to taste
> 2 garlic cloves, peeled and minced
> 1 teaspoon Italian seasoning
> 1 teaspoon dried sage
> ¼ pound thinly sliced Genoa salami
> ½ cup Chicken Stock (recipe on page 22) or purchased stock
> ½ pound whole-milk mozzarella cheese, thinly sliced

1. Preheat the oven to 425°F, and line a 9 x 13-inch baking pan with aluminum foil. Rinse pork and pat dry with paper towels. Slice pork into ⅓-inch slices against the grain, and arrange slices in the pan, overlapping them slightly. Sprinkle pork with salt and pepper.

2. Combine garlic, Italian seasoning, and sage in a small cup. Sprinkle mixture on top of pork. Layer salami on top of seasonings, and drizzle stock over all. Top with cheese.

3. Bake for 15–20 minutes, or until pork is cooked through and cheese is bubbly. Serve immediately.

Note: The dish can be prepared for baking up to 1 day in advance and refrigerated, tightly covered. Add 10 minutes to baking time if chilled.

Each serving contains:

342 calories | 194 calories from fat | 22 g fat | 10 g saturated fat | 97.5 mg cholesterol | 33 g protein | 2 g carbohydrates | 786 mg sodium

Variation:
- Substitute boneless, skinless chicken breast halves, cut into ½-inch slices, for the pork.

Chapter 8:
Exciting Hot Hors d'Oeuvres

An array of tantalizing nibbles and noshes is usually the first part of a potluck meal. The dishes in this chapter will all serve the purpose of whetting the appetite without filling the guests for the meal to come.

These recipes are drawn from many cuisines—from subtly seasoned classic French to lusty Latin and a veritable pu-pu platter of Asian options. While I do believe that a dinner menu should not mix parts of the world, I think that the sky is the limit when it comes to hors d'oeuvres.

PARTY PLANNING POINTERS

How much food to make for a cocktail party, and what those dishes should be, can be perplexing. While there is not a mathematic formula, there are some general guidelines that will help you plan so that no one leaves hungry and you're not deluged with leftovers:

- If the hors d'oeuvres are a prelude to dinner, make two or three varieties and plan on one hour. During that time your guests will probably eat two of each hors d'oeuvre. These can be passed hors d'oeuvres for a large group or a platter that's put on the coffee table if you're sitting around the living room. Keep the hors d'oeuvres light so no one will fill up before being called to the table.

- For a cocktail party at which no dinner will be served, you should consider that most guests view your offerings as dinner, and plan accordingly. Assuming that a party has a duration of two to three hours, you should make about six different hors d'oeuvres and count on two or three of each per person. Choose some vegetable items for the increasing number of vegetarians, and then weight the menu more toward fish than meats; fish gives the illusion of being extravagant, and you use very little of it.

- Vary the fare between passed dishes and those that sit on tables, and hot and cold dishes. All of the hot recipes in this chapter can be prepared in advance and then briefly reheated.

Miniature Cheese Puffs

Gougères are a classic French hors d'oeuvre hailing from Burgundy; they are cheese puffs flavored with expensive, imported Gruyère cheese. I've discovered that they are equally delicious made with less expensive, domestic Swiss cheese, and they keep well in the freezer so you can have a supply on hand.

Yield: 3 dozen puffs | **Active time:** 15 minutes | **Start to finish:** 40 minutes

> 1 cup water
> 6 tablespoons (³/₄ stick) unsalted butter, cut into thin slices
> ½ teaspoon salt
> ¼ teaspoon dry mustard
> Pinch of cayenne
> 1 cup all-purpose flour
> 4 large eggs
> ³/₄ cup grated Swiss cheese

1. Preheat the oven to 400° F, and grease 2 cookie sheets.
2. Combine water, butter, salt, mustard, and cayenne in a saucepan, and bring to a boil over medium-high heat, stirring occasionally. Remove the pan from the heat, and add flour all at once. Using a wooden paddle or wide wooden spoon, beat flour into liquid until it is smooth. Then place the saucepan over high heat and beat mixture constantly for 1–2 minutes, until it forms a mass that leaves the sides of the pan and begins to film the bottom of the pot.
3. Transfer mixture to a food processor fitted with the steel blade. Add eggs, 1 at a time, beating well between each addition and scraping the sides of the work bowl between each addition. This can also be done by hand. Then add cheese, and mix well again.
4. Scrape dough into a pastry bag, and pipe mounds 1 inch in diameter and ½ inch high onto the baking sheets, allowing 2 inches between puffs. Bake puffs for 20–25 minutes, or until puffs are golden brown and crusty to the touch.
5. Remove the pans from the oven, and using the tip of a paring knife, cut a slit in the side of each puff to allow the steam to escape. Turn off the oven, and place baked puffs back into the oven with the oven door ajar for 10 minutes to finish crisping. Remove puffs from the oven and serve immediately.

Note: The puffs can be made up to 2 days in advance and refrigerated, tightly covered; they can also be frozen for up to 2 weeks. Reheat chilled puffs in a 350°F oven for 10 minutes and frozen puffs for 15 minutes.

Each 3-puff serving contains:

141 calories | 89 calories from fat | 10 g fat | 6 g saturated fat | 93 mg cholesterol | 5 g protein | 8 g carbohydrates | 166 mg sodium

Variations:

- Substitute cheddar, jalapeño Jack, or blue cheese for the Swiss cheese.
- Add 2 teaspoons herbes de Provence or Italian seasoning to the dough.
- Add 1–3 tablespoons Dijon mustard for a very spicy puff.
- Add ½ cup crumbled cooked bacon or finely chopped ham to the dough.
- Add ½ cup finely chopped sun-dried tomatoes to the dough.

Cheddar Crackers

Admittedly, reading crushed potato chips in the ingredient list is unusual, but they make these the crunchiest as well as most flavorful cheese crackers you'll ever taste. I serve them before a hearty meal because they're tasty but light.

Yield: 2 dozen crackers | **Active time:** 10 minutes | **Start to finish:** 30 minutes

> 1 (5.5-ounce) bag potato chips
> 1½ cups grated sharp cheddar cheese
> 5 tablespoons unsalted butter, melted
> ⅓ cup all-purpose flour
> ½ teaspoon cayenne, or to taste

1. Preheat the oven to 350°F. Place potato chips in a food processor fitted with the steel blade. Coarsely chop chips, using on-and-off pulsing. This can also be done by placing chips in a heavy resealable plastic bag and hitting chips with the bottom of a heavy skillet.

2. Scrape potato chip crumbs into a mixing bowl, and add cheese, butter, flour, and cayenne. Stir until mixture is combined and holds together when pressed in the palm of your hand.

3. Form 1 tablespoon of mixture into a ball. Place it on an ungreased baking sheet and flatten it into a circle with the bottom of a floured glass or with your fingers. Repeat with remaining dough, leaving 1 inch between circles.

4. Bake for 15–18 minutes, or until browned. Cool crackers on the baking sheet for 2 minutes, then transfer to a cooling rack with a spatula to cool completely. Serve at room temperature.

Note: The crackers can be made 2 days in advance and kept at room temperature in an airtight container.

Each 2-cracker serving contains:

181 calories | 127 calories from fat | 14 g fat | 6.5 g saturated fat | 28 mg cholesterol | 5 g protein | 10 g carbohydrates | 171 mg sodium

Variations:

- Substitute Gruyère or Swiss cheese for the cheddar.
- Substitute crushed corn tortilla chips for the potato chips, and jalapeño Jack cheese for the cheddar.
- For additional flavor, substitute a flavored potato chip such as barbecue or sour cream and onion for the plain chips.

When a recipe calls for grated cheese, don't use processed cheese like Velveeta. Processed cheese will not melt correctly and form crisp crackers.

Potato and Cheese Sticks

These tasty and crunchy morsels are much easier and less expensive to make than traditional cheese sticks.

Yield: 30 sticks | **Active time:** 15 minutes | **Start to finish:** 40 minutes

> ½ pound russet potatoes, peeled and cut into 1-inch dice
> ⅔ cup all-purpose flour
> ¼ pound (1 stick) unsalted butter, softened and cut into small pieces
> 1 large egg, lightly beaten
> 1 cup grated sharp cheddar cheese
> ½ teaspoon salt, or to taste
> Cayenne to taste

1. Preheat the oven to 425°F, and grease 2 baking sheets.
2. Boil potatoes in salted water for 10–12 minutes, or until very tender when pierced with a knife. Drain potatoes, shaking the colander vigorously to extract as much liquid as possible. Return potatoes to the pan, and mash well or put potatoes through a ricer.
3. Cook mashed potatoes over low heat for 1–2 minutes, or until they begin to form a film on the bottom of the pan. Beat in flour, then butter, bit by bit, beating well to ensure that butter melts; place the pan over low heat if butter is not melting. Beat in egg, cheese, and salt, and season to taste with cayenne.
4. Transfer potato mixture to a pastry bag fitted with a ½-inch fluted tip, and pipe out dough into 2-inch lengths. Bake sticks for 12–15 minutes, or until browned. Serve hot.

Note: The sticks can be prepared up to 2 days in advance and refrigerated, tightly covered. Reheat them in a 375°F oven for 3–5 minutes, or until hot. Undercook sticks slightly if you're planning on reheating them.

Each 3-stick serving contains:

61 calories | 41 calories from fat | 4.5 g fat | 3 g saturated fat | 19 mg cholesterol | 2 g protein | 4 g carbohydrates | 65 mg sodium

Variations:
- Substitute Swiss cheese for the cheddar cheese.
- Add 1 teaspoon Italian seasoning or herbes de Provence to the potato mixture.

Basic Pizza Dough

Here's your basic pizza crust, with some ways to personalize it at the end. It's a foolproof recipe I've used for years.

Yield: 1¼ pounds (enough for one 12-inch pizza or 10 servings) | **Active time:** 10 minutes | **Start to finish:** 1½ hours

> 1 tablespoon active dry yeast
> ¾ cup plus 2 tablespoons warm water, 100–110°F
> 1 teaspoon granulated sugar
> 2¾ cups all-purpose flour, plus additional for working dough
> 1 teaspoon salt
> 1 tablespoon olive oil

1. Combine yeast, water, and sugar in a small cup; stir well to dissolve yeast. Let stand 10 minutes, or until foamy.
2. Combine flour and salt in a mixing bowl or in a food processor fitted with the steel blade. Add in yeast mixture and then knead dough until elastic. Place dough in a mixing bowl coated with oil, cover tightly wth plastic wrap, and then allow dough to rise until doubled.
3. Shape dough as specified in the recipe, and allow it to rise for an additional 20 minutes, covered with a damp towel. Top and bake dough according to individual recipes.

Note: The dough can be made up to deflating it after rising 1 day in advance. Wrap the ball loosely in plastic wrap, and refrigerate. Allow dough to reach room temperature before rolling and topping.

Each serving contains:

142 calories | 16 calories from fat | 2 g fat | 0 g saturated fat | 0 mg cholesterol | 4 g protein | 27 g carbohydrates | 234.5 mg sodium

Variations:

- Add 2 tablespoons chopped fresh herbs (such as basil or oregano) or 1 tablespoon dried herbs to the flour and salt mixture before adding the yeast.
- Substitute whole wheat flour for the all-purpose flour.
- Use 2½ cups all-purpose flour and ⅓ cup finely ground yellow cornmeal in place of the 2¾ cups flour.

Onion Pizza Niçoise (Pissaladière)

Caramelized onions are an inexpensive treat that everyone loves, and they form the crowning glory for this Provençal pizza dotted with succulent olives.

Yield: 20 pieces | **Active time:** 25 minutes | **Start to finish:** 1 hour

> 1 recipe Basic Pizza Dough (recipe on page 185) or 1¼ pounds purchased pizza dough
> 3 tablespoons unsalted butter
> ½ cup olive oil, divided
> 4 large sweet onions such as Bermuda or Vidalia, peeled and thinly sliced
> 2 teaspoons granulated sugar
> ½ teaspoon salt, or to taste
> Freshly ground black pepper to taste
> ½ cup chopped fresh parsley
> ½ cup Italian bread crumbs
> 4 tablespoons anchovy paste
> 3 garlic cloves, peeled and minced
> 1 large egg yolk
> 1 tablespoon cider vinegar
> 1 tablespoon lemon juice
> ½ cup chopped oil-cured black olives

1. Preheat the oven to 425°F, and place a baking stone or baking sheet on the bottom of the oven. Form pizza dough into 1 large pizza. Allow crust to rise for 20 minutes, lightly covered with a damp towel.

2. Melt butter and 2 tablespoons oil in a large skillet over medium heat. Add onions, sugar, salt, and pepper, and toss to coat onions. Cover the skillet, and cook for 10 minutes, stirring occasionally. Uncover the skillet, and cook over medium-high heat for 20–30 minutes, or until onions are browned.

3. While onions cook, combine parsley, bread crumbs, anchovy paste, garlic, egg yolk, and vinegar in a food processor fitted with the steel blade or in a blender. Puree until smooth. Slowly add remaining olive oil, and continue to process until smooth and thick.

4. Spread crust with bread crumb mixture, stopping 1 inch from the edge. Arrange onions on top.

5. Bake pizza on pizza stone or baking sheet for 10 minutes. Reduce the oven temperature to 400°F, and sprinkle pizza with olives. Bake for an additional 10–15 minutes, or until crust is golden. Cut pizza into small squares, and serve hot.

Note: The pizza can be baked up to 1 day in advance and refrigerated, tightly covered. Reheat it in a 375°F oven for 6–8 minutes, or until hot. Do not cut it into pieces until ready to serve.

Each 2-piece serving contains:

163 calories | 67 calories from fat | 7 g fat | 2 g saturated fat | 14 mg cholesterol | 3 g protein | 21 g carbohydrates | 342 mg sodium

The most time-consuming part of this dish is caramelizing the onions, and there's no reason you couldn't do a double or triple batch and freeze what's not needed for this recipe. With the leftovers, future onion soup or any number of dishes are just moments away from completion.

Corn Fritters

These crispy treats have an interesting flavor even without a dipping sauce of any kind because there are spices and aromatic cilantro right in the batter.

Yield: 12 servings | **Active time:** 25 minutes | **Start to finish:** 25 minutes

> 2 pounds whole corn kernels (either cut fresh from the cob or frozen and thawed; do not use canned corn)
> 3 large eggs
> 2 medium onions, peeled and chopped
> 2 scallions, white parts only, rinsed, trimmed, and chopped
> 1 garlic clove, peeled and minced
> 3 tablespoons chopped fresh cilantro
> 1¼ cups all-purpose flour
> ½ cup yellow cornmeal
> 1 tablespoon granulated sugar
> 1½ tablespoons baking powder
> 1½ tablespoons ground coriander
> ¾ teaspoon salt
> Freshly ground black pepper to taste
> 3–4 cups vegetable oil for frying

1. Place corn in a saucepan, and cover with salted water. Bring to a boil over high heat, and cook for 2 minutes. Drain, and place corn in a blender or in a food processor fitted with the steel blade. Add eggs, and puree until smooth. Scrape mixture into a mixing bowl.
2. Stir onions, scallions, garlic, and cilantro into corn. Combine flour, cornmeal, sugar, baking powder, coriander, salt, and pepper in another mixing bowl, and whisk well. Stir dry ingredients into corn mixture, stirring until just combined.
3. Heat oil in a deep-sided saucepan or deep-fryer to a temperature of 350°F. Preheat the oven to 150°F, and line a baking sheet with paper towels.
4. Using a rubber spatula, push batter off carefully into hot fat, about 1 tablespoonful at a time. Fry fritters until they are a deep golden brown, turning them in the hot fat to brown both sides. Remove fritters from the pan with a slotted spoon, and drain on paper towels. Keep fritters warm in the oven on a prepared baking sheet while frying remaining batter. Serve hot.

Note: The fritters can be prepared up to 2 days in advance and refrigerated, tightly covered. Reheat in a 375°F oven for 5–7 minutes, or until hot and crispy.

Each serving contains:

202 calories | 58 calories from fat | 6 g fat | 1 g saturated fat | 53 mg cholesterol | 6 g protein | 34 g carbohydrates | 198 mg sodium

Baking powder doesn't last forever, and how long it's effective depends on many factors. If you can't remember when you bought your can, stir a few teaspoons into a cup of cold water. If it doesn't bubble furiously, toss it.

Sauerkraut Balls with Mustard Sauce

While sauerkraut itself is German, these balls are a treasured treat of Midwestern cooking due to the large number of German settlers in the region. The sauerkraut is mixed with potato, and the dipping sauce has lots of mustard.

Yield: 4 dozen balls | **Active time:** 30 minutes | **Start to finish:** 30 minutes

> 1 pound potatoes, peeled
> 1 pound sauerkraut, drained well
> 2 large eggs
> ³/₄ cup whole grain Dijon mustard, divided
> 3 scallions, white parts and 2 inches of green tops, rinsed, trimmed, and chopped
> 2 tablespoons chopped fresh parsley
> ½ teaspoon salt
> Freshly ground black pepper to taste
> 1 cup plain breadcrumbs
> 3 cups vegetable oil for frying
> ½ cup mayonnaise
> ½ cup sour cream

1. Dice potatoes into 1-inch cubes, and boil in salted water for 10–15 minutes, or until very tender. Drain potatoes, shaking in a colander to get out as much water as possible. Mash potatoes until smooth, and set aside.

2. While potatoes boil, soak sauerkraut in cold water, changing the water every 3 minutes for a total of 3 times. Drain sauerkraut, pressing with the back of a spoon to extract as much liquid as possible, and coarsely chop sauerkraut.

3. Whisk eggs and ¼ cup mustard in a mixing bowl, and add potatoes, sauerkraut, scallions, and parsley. Mix well, and season with salt and pepper.

4. Place breadcrumbs in a shallow bowl. Form mixture into 1-inch balls, roll balls in breadcrumbs, and repeat until all of sauerkraut mixture is used.

5. Heat oil in a deep-sided saucepan to a temperature of 375°F. Preheat the oven to 150°F, and line a baking sheet with paper towels.

6. While oil heats, mix remaining ½ cup mustard with mayonnaise and sour cream, and whisk well. Set aside.

7. Add sauerkraut balls to saucepan, being careful not to crowd the pan. Cook sauerkraut balls for 3–4 minutes, or until browned. Remove balls from the pan with a slotted spoon, and drain well on paper towels. Keep fried sauerkraut balls warm on prepared baking sheet in the oven while frying remaining balls. Serve immediately with sauce.

Note: The sauerkraut balls can be prepared for frying up to 1 day in advance and refrigerated, tightly covered. They can also be fried in advance; reheat them in a 400°F oven for 5–7 minutes, or until hot and crusty again.

Each 4-ball serving contains:

204 calories | 131 calories from fat | 15 g fat | 3 g saturated fat | 43 mg cholesterol | 3 g protein | 12 g carbohydrates | 838 mg sodium

Variations:
- Add 1 cup chopped ham or cooked, crumbled sausage, such as smoked kielbasa.
- Add ½ cup grated cheese, such as cheddar or smoked cheddar.

Fish Satay with Thai Peanut Sauce

Satay is part of many Asian cultures, and these morsels of tender fish are inspired by Thai cooking. Because the food is woven onto bamboo skewers, many kids will eat this fish even if they wouldn't eat a whole fillet, and the peanut butter in the sauce makes it seem familiar.

Yield: 6 servings | **Active time:** 15 minutes | **Start to finish:** 1½ hours, including 1 hour for marinating

SATAY

6 (8-inch) bamboo skewers

1½ pounds thick firm-fleshed white fish fillets

½ cup soy sauce

½ cup firmly packed dark brown sugar

¼ cup freshly squeezed lime juice

2 teaspoons Chinese chile paste with garlic*

2 garlic cloves, peeled and minced

1 tablespoon Asian sesame oil*

SAUCE

1 cup chunky peanut butter

½ cup very hot tap water

½ cup firmly packed dark brown sugar

⅓ cup freshly squeezed lime juice

¼ cup soy sauce

2 tablespoons Asian sesame oil*

2 tablespoons Chinese chile paste with garlic*

2 garlic cloves, peeled and minced

3 scallions, white parts and 4 inches of green tops, rinsed, trimmed, and chopped

¼ cup chopped fresh cilantro

1. Soak bamboo skewers in cold water. Rinse fish and pat dry with paper towels. Cut fish into 1-inch cubes.
2. Combine soy sauce, brown sugar, lime juice, chile paste, garlic, and sesame oil in a heavy resealable plastic bag, and blend well. Add

*Available in the Asian aisle of most supermarkets and in specialty markets.

fish cubes and marinate, refrigerated, for 1 hour, turning the bag occasionally.

3. While fish marinates, make sauce. Combine peanut butter, water, brown sugar, lime juice, soy sauce, sesame oil, and chile paste in a mixing bowl. Whisk until well combined. Stir in garlic, scallions, and cilantro, and chill well before serving.

4. Light a charcoal or gas grill, or preheat the oven broiler. Remove fish from marinade, and discard marinade. Thread fish onto skewers. Grill or broil fish for a total of 3–5 minutes, turning skewers with tongs, or until fish is cooked through and flakes easily. Serve at room temperature or chilled, passing sauce separately.

Note: The sauce can be made up to 3 days in advance and refrigerated, tightly covered. Bring it back to room temperature before serving.

Each serving contains:

429 calories | 203 calories from fat | 22.5 g fat | 4 g saturated fat | 49 mg cholesterol | 30 g protein | 30 g carbohydrates | 1,535 mg sodium

Variation:

- Substitute boneless, skinless chicken thighs or chicken breast, or cubes of boneless pork loin, for the fish. Marinate chicken or pork for 2–4 hours, and cook chicken until it is cooked through and no longer pink.

Baked Fish Toast Rolls

When I wrote a book titled *All Wrapped Up* in 1998, I was experimenting with various wrappers, and discovered that rolled-out slices of basic white bread worked wonderfully! These flavorful Asian morsels are crunchy from water chestnuts as well as from the toast covering.

Yield: 36 pieces | **Active time:** 20 minutes | **Start to finish:** 30 minutes

Vegetable oil spray
12 slices white sandwich bread
¾ pound thin white-fleshed fish fillets
2 tablespoons grated fresh ginger
1 tablespoon Asian sesame oil*
1 large egg white
1 tablespoon dry sherry
2 tablespoons cornstarch
2 tablespoons reduced-sodium soy sauce
2 scallions, white parts and 4 inches of green tops, rinsed, trimmed, and sliced
⅓ cup finely chopped canned water chestnuts
Freshly ground black pepper to taste

1. Preheat the oven to 425°F, cover a baking sheet with heavy-duty aluminum foil, and spray the foil with vegetable oil spray.
2. Remove crusts from bread slices using a serrated bread knife. Roll each slice with a rolling pin until bread slice is thin, but still pliable. Set aside.
3. Combine fish, ginger, sesame oil, egg white, sherry, cornstarch, and soy sauce in a food processor fitted with the steel blade or in a blender. Puree until smooth, stopping a few times to scrape the sides of the work bowl. Scrape mixture into a mixing bowl, and stir in scallions and water chestnuts. Season to taste with pepper.
4. Spread bread slices out on a counter and place 1 heaping tablespoon filling in a line across the long side of each slice. Roll bread around filling so that edges meet, and place rolls, seam side down, on the prepared baking sheet. Spray tops with vegetable oil spray.

*Available in the Asian aisle of most supermarkets and in specialty markets.

5. Bake rolls for 5 minutes, turn over gently with tongs, and bake for 4 minutes, or until browned. Cut each into 3 sections with a serrated knife, and serve immediately.

Note: The fish mixture can be prepared 1 day in advance and refrigerated, tightly covered. Fill bread and bake the rolls just prior to serving.

Each 3-piece serving contains:

115 calories | 20 calories from fat | 2 g fat | 0 g saturated fat | 12 mg cholesterol | 8 g protein | 15 g carbohydrates | 276 mg sodium

> If you don't have a rolling pin, or you're using it to prop open a window, you can use any glass bottle—like wine or vinegar—to roll out the bread slices.

Curried Caribbean Meatballs

While we think of curry powder in relation to Indian food, it's also at home in the West Indies. These meatballs have a hot and sweet flavor profile from the fresh fruit as well as chutney in the sauce.

Yield: 36 meatballs | **Active time:** 25 minutes | **Start to finish:** 1 hour

Vegetable oil spray
3 tablespoons vegetable oil
1 medium onion, peeled and chopped
3 garlic cloves, peeled and minced
1 egg
2 tablespoons whole milk
3 slices white bread
$1/2$ teaspoon ground ginger
$1/4$ teaspoon ground nutmeg
$1 1/4$ pounds ground turkey
$1/2$ teaspoon salt, or to taste
Freshly ground black pepper to taste
1 tablespoon curry powder
1 (8-ounce) can crushed pineapple packed in juice, undrained
1 cup pineapple juice
$1/2$ cup Chicken Stock (recipe on page 22) or purchased stock
$1/3$ cup mango chutney, chopped
1 tablespoon cornstarch
1 tablespoon cold water

1. Preheat the oven broiler, line a rimmed baking sheet with heavy-duty aluminum foil, and grease the foil with vegetable oil spray.

2. Heat oil in a large skillet over medium-high heat. Add onion and garlic and cook, stirring frequently, for 3 minutes, or until onion is translucent. While onion mixture cooks, combine egg and milk in a mixing bowl, and whisk until smooth. Break bread into tiny pieces and add to mixing bowl along with ginger and nutmeg, and mix well.

3. Add $1/2$ of the onion mixture and turkey, season with salt and pepper, and mix well again. Make mixture into $1 1/4$-inch meatballs, and arrange meatballs on the prepared pan. Spray tops of meatballs with vegetable oil spray.

4. Broil meatballs 6 inches from the broiler element, turning them with tongs to brown all sides. While meatballs brown, add curry powder to onion mixture remaining in the skillet, and cook over low heat for 1 minute, stirring constantly. Add pineapple with juice, pineapple juice, stock, and chutney to the skillet. Bring to a boil over medium-high heat, stirring occasionally. Simmer sauce over medium heat, uncovered, for 10 minutes.

5. Remove meatballs from the baking pan with a slotted spoon, and add meatballs to sauce. Bring to a boil, and simmer meatballs over low heat, covered, turning occasionally with a slotted spoon, for 15 minutes. Mix cornstarch with water in a small cup, and add to sauce. Simmer for 1–2 minutes, or until slightly thickened. Serve hot.

Note: The meatball mixture can be prepared up to 1 day in advance and refrigerated, tightly covered. Also, the dish can be cooked up to 2 days in advance and refrigerated, tightly covered. Reheat it in a 350°F oven, covered, for 15–20 minutes, or until hot.

Each 3-meatball serving contains:

168 calories | 63 calories from fat | 7 g fat | 2 g saturated fat | 55 mg cholesterol | 10 g protein | 16 g carbohydrates | 145.5 mg sodium

Variation:

- Substitute fresh diced mango for the pineapple; add it along with the meatballs, and add an additional ½ cup pineapple juice to the sauce.

The English word *pineapple* evolved because of the fruit's resemblance to a pinecone rather than anything to do with its flavor or color. The Tupi word for the fruit was *anana*, which means "excellent fruit." Hummingbirds, which are native to the tropics, are the natural pollinators for pineapple.

Vietnamese Spring Rolls

Cha gio, crispy Vietnamese spring rolls wrapped in rice paper, are one of my favorite dishes, and baking instead of frying them makes them much quicker to prepare and lighter.

Yield: 36 pieces | **Active time:** 25 minutes | **Start to finish:** 1 hour

> 5 large dried shiitake mushrooms
> 1 ounce bean thread (sometimes called cellophane) noodles*
> Vegetable oil spray
> 1/2 pound ground pork
> 1 cup fresh bean sprouts, rinsed and cut into 1-inch lengths
> 1 small carrot, peeled and grated
> 5 scallions, white parts and 4 inches of green tops, rinsed, trimmed, and chopped
> 6 garlic cloves, peeled and minced
> 3 tablespoons fish sauce (*nam pla*)*
> 2 large eggs, lightly beaten
> 1 teaspoon granulated sugar
> Freshly ground black pepper to taste
> 18 (8-inch) rice paper pancakes*

1. Soak dried mushrooms and bean thread noodles in separate bowls of very hot tap water for 30 minutes. Drain mushrooms, and squeeze well to extract as much water as possible. Discard stems, and finely chop mushrooms. Drain bean thread noodles. Place them on a cutting board in a long log shape, and cut into 1-inch pieces. Measure out 1/2 cup, and discard any additional.

2. Preheat the oven to 400°F, cover a baking sheet with heavy-duty aluminum foil, and grease the foil with vegetable oil spray.

3. Place mushrooms and noodles in a mixing bowl, and add pork, bean sprouts, carrot, scallions, garlic, fish sauce, eggs, and sugar. Season to taste with pepper, and mix well.

4. Fill a wide mixing bowl with very hot tap water. Place a damp tea towel in front of you on the counter. Place rice paper pancakes on a plate, and cover with a barely damp towel.

*Available in the Asian aisle of most supermarkets and in specialty markets.

5. Fill 1 rice paper pancake at a time, keeping remainder covered. Totally immerse pancake in the hot water for 2 seconds. Remove it and place it on the damp tea towel; it will become pliable within a few seconds. Gently fold the front edge of the pancake $1/3$ of the way to the top. Place about 2 tablespoons filling on the folded-up portion, and shape it into a log, leaving a 2-inch margin on each side. Lightly spray the unfilled part of the pancake with vegetable oil spray. Fold the sides over the filling, and roll tightly but gently, beginning with the filled side. Place roll on the prepared baking sheet, and continue until all rice paper pancakes are filled. Spray tops and sides of rolls with vegetable oil spray.

6. Bake for 12 minutes, then turn rolls gently with tongs, and bake an additional 10–12 minutes, or until rolls are browned. Remove the pan from the oven, and blot rolls with paper towels. Slice each in half on the diagonal, and serve immediately.

Note: The rolls can be baked up to 2 days and refrigerated, tightly covered. Reheat them, uncovered, in a 375°F oven for 5–7 minutes, or until hot. Do not slice them prior to reheating.

Each 2-piece serving contains:

97 calories | 30 calories from fat | 3 g fat | 1 g saturated fat | 32 mg cholesterol | 4 g protein | 13 g carbohydrates | 256 mg sodium

Variations:
- Add 1–2 tablespoons Chinese chile paste with garlic to the filling for a spicy dish.
- Substitute ground chicken for the pork.

I serve these, as well as other Asian finger food dishes, in a bamboo steamer. I line the steamer with plastic wrap and then with leaves of green or red head lettuce.

Dilled Swedish Meatballs

Allspice and nutmeg, in addition to a combination of meats and a creamed sauce, define the quintessential Swedish meatball, called *köttbullar* in Sweden. Variations on this recipe have been served at American cocktail parties for generations, and they're still delicious.

Yield: 36 meatballs | **Active time:** 20 minutes | **Start to finish:** 45 minutes

Vegetable oil spray
4 tablespoons unsalted butter, divided
1 small onion, peeled and chopped
1/4 cup whole milk
1 large egg
1 large egg yolk
3 slices white bread
1/4 teaspoon ground allspice
1/4 teaspoon freshly grated nutmeg
1 1/4 pounds ground pork
1/2 teaspoon salt
Freshly ground black pepper to taste
1/4 cup all-purpose flour
2 1/2 cups Chicken Stock (recipe on page 22) or purchased stock
1/2 cup heavy cream
1/4 cup chopped fresh dill

1. Preheat the oven broiler, line a rimmed baking sheet with heavy-duty aluminum foil, and grease the foil with vegetable oil spray.
2. Heat 2 tablespoons butter in a large skillet over medium-high heat. Add onion, and cook, stirring frequently, for 3 minutes, or until onion is translucent. Combine milk, egg, and egg yolk in a mixing bowl, and whisk until smooth. Break bread into tiny pieces and add to mixing bowl along with allspice and nutmeg, and mix well.
3. Add onion and pork, season with salt and pepper, and mix well again. Make mixture into 1-inch meatballs, and arrange meatballs on the prepared pan. Spray tops of meatballs with vegetable oil spray.

4. Broil meatballs 6 inches from the broiler element, turning them with tongs to brown all sides. While meatballs brown, add remaining butter to the skillet and heat over low heat. Stir flour into the skillet, and cook over low heat for 2 minutes, stirring constantly. Raise the heat to medium-high, whisk in stock and cream, and bring to a boil over medium-high heat, whisking constantly.

5. Remove meatballs from the baking pan with a slotted spoon, and add meatballs and dill to sauce. Bring to a boil, and simmer meatballs, covered, over low heat, turning occasionally with a slotted spoon, for 15 minutes. Serve immediately.

Note: The meatball mixture can be prepared up to 1 day in advance and refrigerated, tightly covered. Also, the dish can be cooked up to 2 days in advance and refrigerated, tightly covered. Reheat in a 350°F oven, covered, for 15–20 minutes, or until hot.

Each 3-meatball serving contains:

234 calories | 163 calories from fat | 18 g fat | 8 g saturated fat | 89 mg cholesterol | 10 g protein | 7 g carbohydrates | 187 mg sodium

Variations:
- Substitute ground turkey for the pork.
- Substitute 2 tablespoons chopped fresh parsley and ³/₄ teaspoon dried thyme for the dill.

Oven-browning meatballs is a great trick to use for all meatball recipes. One of the pitfalls of making meatballs is that they tend to fall apart when browned in a skillet, and using this method helps them retain their shape. Another bonus is that you don't have a messy skillet to wash.

Mexican Beef and Chile Dip (Chile con Queso)

Here's a hearty dip that kids as well as adults love, and celery ribs or cucumber slices make good dippers if you want a vegetable rather than chips.

Yield: 8 servings | **Active time:** 15 minutes | **Start to finish:** 25 minutes

1 tablespoon olive oil
1 small onion, peeled and diced
2 garlic cloves, peeled and minced
½ pound lean ground beef
2 ripe plum tomatoes, rinsed, cored, seeded, and chopped
2 chipotle chiles in adobo sauce, finely chopped
¼ cup heavy cream
1 cup grated Monterey Jack cheese
1 cup grated cheddar cheese
2 teaspoons cornstarch
1 tablespoon cold water
Freshly ground black pepper to taste

1. Heat oil in a large, heavy skillet over medium-high heat. Add onion, garlic, and ground beef. Cook, breaking up lumps with a fork, for 3–5 minutes, or until brown and no pink remains. Add tomatoes and chipotle chiles, and cook for an additional 3 minutes. Remove the contents of the skillet with a slotted spoon, and discard grease from the skillet.

2. Return mixture to the skillet, and add cream, Monterey Jack cheese, and cheddar cheese. Cook the mixture over low heat, stirring frequently, for 3 minutes, or until cheeses melt and are bubbly.

3. Combine cornstarch and water in a small bowl, and stir to dissolve cornstarch. Add mixture to dip and bring to a simmer, stirring constantly. Cook over low heat for 1–2 minutes, or until dip thickens. Season to taste with pepper.

Note: The dip can be prepared up to 2 days in advance and refrigerated, tightly covered. Reheat it over low heat, covered, until hot, stirring occasionally.

Each serving contains:

220 calories | 146 calories from fat | 16 g fat | 9 g saturated fat | 56 mg cholesterol | 13 g protein | 5 g carbohydrates | 205 mg sodium

Variation:
- Substitute 1 (8-ounce) package seasoned taco cheese for the Monterey Jack and cheddar cheeses to add additional seasoning to the dip.

A can of chipotle chiles in adobo sauce goes a long way. Chances are you use less than a half-dozen chiles in a given recipe. To save the remainder of the can, place a few chiles with a teaspoon of sauce in ice-cube trays. When they're frozen, transfer them to a heavy resealable plastic bag. Be sure to wash the ice-cube tray well.

Chapter 9:
Desserts for Delivery

Luscious homemade baked goods make every meal special, and having to pack and trek with a sweet is not an impediment to enjoying a wonderful dessert—as long as the recipe is carefully selected. As I've said in other chapters of this book, the operative word is *sturdy.* But that doesn't mean that only rock-hard biscotti will do!

Certainly such foods as soufflés are out. As are multi-level cakes or any dessert requiring careful refrigeration or freezing. But that eliminates just a tiny number of treats, as you'll see when cooking the recipes in this chapter.

Certain desserts are also more appropriate for potluck dinners than picnics. For example, I find that pies are wonderful at a potluck dinner, but a real pain to both serve and eat at a picnic. Dense bundt cakes, cookies, and variations on cobblers are the best choices for treats that travel for all occasions. They are also very easy to make, although especially the cakes take time to bake.

TRICKS FOR TRAVEL

Even though these desserts are not fragile, caution always needs to be taken when transporting baked goods to any location away from your house. Here are some tips to help you avoid arriving with a box full of crumbs:

- Plain popped corn is a great insulating material. Use it like Styrofoam peanuts to hold cakes and cookies in place.

- Bundt cakes are best transported in the pans in which they were baked. Remove cake from the pan and allow it to cool, and then glaze it if that's part of the recipe. Wash out the bundt pan, grease it lightly with vegetable oil spray, and place it upside down over the cake.

- If a cake is to be frosted, transport it in components and assemble it on the spot. Pack your cake layers and frosting, along with a platter and icing spatula, and put it together when you arrive.

- Create a cage with bamboo skewers for cakes. If you want to frost a cake in advance of carrying it, poke bamboo skewers into the sides and top, and then create a tent with plastic wrap.

- Shallow containers for cookies are better than deeper ones. What crushes cookies is the weight of the cookies themselves. So if you have a shallow container, there's less chance they'll break.

COOKIE DOUGH CACHE

Here's another trick from my catering kitchen—you can successfully freeze cookie dough and bake individual cookies or a whole batch at a moment's notice. Your friends and family will be thrilled to walk into your kitchen to the aroma of cinnamon from an oatmeal cookie or the chocolaty richness of a chocolate chip cookie.

If you want to freeze a whole batch of dough, do so in a heavy resealable plastic bag. Allow it to thaw overnight in the refrigerator. But I find it's much easier to freeze individual dough balls.

Cover a baking sheet with plastic wrap, and form the proper size balls of dough on the cookie sheet. You can place them very close together because they're not going to spread. Once they are frozen solid, transfer them to a heavy resealable plastic bag. It's not necessary to allow time for frozen dough balls to thaw. Just add two to three minutes to the baking time of the cookie.

FRESH FROM THE FREEZER

There's nothing like the flavor and aroma of fresh fruit, but if your favorite fruit is out of season, it's better to use dry-packed frozen fruit rather than canned fruit or unripe fruit. Frozen fruits are picked and frozen at the peak of ripeness, and for any dessert that will be baked, it doesn't really matter that the fruits were frozen.

Stock up on fruits when they are either in season locally or attractively priced, and freeze them yourself.

The best way to freeze fruit is to first prepare the fruit by cleaning, slicing, peeling, or sectioning, as appropriate. Then simply arrange $\frac{1}{2}$- to 1-inch pieces on a baking sheet covered with plastic wrap, and put them into the freezer until they're frozen. After the fruit is frozen, transfer it to a heavy, resealable plastic bag. Mark the date on the bag, and use the fruit within two months.

Picnic Apple Cake

This moist cake is my answer to taking an apple pie on a picnic. It has the same intense apple flavor, enhanced by aromatic Chinese five-spice powder, but it's also hand-holdable.

Yield: 8 servings | **Active time:** 20 minutes | **Start to finish:** 2 hours, including time for cooling

CAKE

  ³/₄ cup raisins
  ¼ cup rum
  ¼ pound (1 stick) unsalted butter, melted and cooled
  2 large eggs, at room temperature
  1 cup granulated sugar
  2 teaspoons Chinese five-spice powder*
  1½ teaspoons baking powder
  ½ teaspoon salt
  1½ cups all-purpose flour
  3 Granny Smith apples

GLAZE

  1 cup confectioners' sugar
  3 tablespoons dark rum

1. Preheat the oven to 350°F. Grease and flour a 10-inch ring pan or bundt pan. Combine raisins and rum in a small microwave-safe bowl, and heat on High (100 percent) power for 45 seconds. Stir, and allow raisins to plump.
2. Combine butter, eggs, sugar, five-spice powder, baking powder, and salt in a mixing bowl. Whisk by hand until smooth. Add flour, and stir well; the batter will be very thick.
3. Peel, core, and quarter apples. Cut each apple quarter in half lengthwise, and then thinly slice apples. Add apples to batter, and stir to coat apples evenly. Pack batter into the prepared pan.

*Available in the Asian aisle of most supermarkets and in specialty markets.

4. Bake cake in the center of the oven for 1 hour, or until a toothpick inserted in the center comes out clean. Cool cake in the pan set on a rack for 20 minutes, or until cool. Invert cake onto a serving platter.
5. Combine confectioners' sugar and rum in a small bowl. Drizzle glaze over top of cooled cake, allowing it to run down the sides. Serve immediately.

Note: The cake can be prepared up to 1 day in advance and kept at room temperature, loosely covered with plastic wrap.

Each serving contains:

466 calories | 118 calories from fat | 13 g fat | 8 g saturated fat | 83 mg cholesterol | 5 g protein | 79 g carbohydrates | 216 mg sodium

Variations:
- Substitute ground cinnamon for the Chinese five-spice powder.
- Substitute dried cranberries or chopped dried apricots for the raisins.

There isn't really an Aunt Jemima or a Jolly Green Giant, but there certainly was a Johnny Appleseed. Named John Chapman, he was born in Massachusetts in 1774. Unlike the artistic depictions of him propagating apples by tossing seeds out of his backpack, Chapman actually started nurseries in the Allegheny Valley in 1800 for European species of apple brought from England as seedlings. By the time of his death in 1845, he had established groves of apple trees as far west as Indiana.

Spiced Applesauce Cake

This is a large cake, which makes it great to bring to a party, and it freezes very well, too. It's spiced like an apple pie, and the cake has a light texture.

Yield: 12 servings | **Active time:** 20 minutes | **Start to finish:** 2½ hours

CAKE

½ pound (2 sticks) unsalted butter, softened

1½ cups firmly packed dark brown sugar

3 large eggs, at room temperature

1 teaspoon pure vanilla extract

1½ teaspoons apple pie spice

1½ teaspoons baking soda

½ teaspoon salt

3½ cups cake flour

2 cups unsweetened applesauce

¾ cup raisins

GLAZE

4 tablespoons unsalted butter

2 tablespoons molasses

½ cup confectioners' sugar

1. Preheat the oven to 350°F. Grease a 10-inch bundt pan.
2. Combine butter and brown sugar in a mixing bowl, and beat at medium speed with an electric mixer until blended. Increase the speed to high, and beat until light and fluffy. Beat in eggs, 1 at a time, beating well between each addition and scraping the sides of the mixing bowl as necessary. Beat in vanilla, apple pie spice, baking soda, and salt.
3. Reduce the speed to low, and add ⅓ of the flour, and then ⅓ of the applesauce. Repeat with remaining flour and applesauce. Stir in raisins, and scrape batter into the prepared pan.
4. Bake cake in the center of the oven for 50–60 minutes, or until a toothpick inserted into the center of the cake comes out clean. Cool cake on a rack for 10 minutes, then invert onto the rack to cool completely.

5. For glaze, combine butter and molasses in a small saucepan, and cook over low heat until butter melts. Whisk in confectioners' sugar, and drizzle glaze over the top of cake, allowing it to drip down over the sides.

Note: The cake can be made up to 2 days in advance—including the glaze—and kept at room temperature, lightly covered with plastic wrap.

Each serving contains:

512 calories | 188 calories from fat | 21 g fat | 13 g saturated fat | 104 mg cholesterol | 5 g protein | 78 g carbohydrates | 286 mg sodium

Variations:

- Substitute ½ cup chopped walnuts or pecans, toasted in a 350°F oven for 5–7 minutes or until browned, for ½ cup raisins.
- Substitute ground ginger for the apple pie spice.

Orange-Scented Cranberry and Apple Cobbler

I developed this recipe thinking about the cranberry-orange relish that my mother used to serve at Thanksgiving. It's a festive cobbler for all the fall holidays.

Yield: 8 servings | **Active time:** 20 minutes | **Start to finish:** 1 hour

1 juice orange
3 cups fresh cranberries, picked over and rinsed
½ cup dried cranberries
1½ cups granulated sugar, divided
1 cup cranberry juice cocktail
¼ cup Triple Sec or other orange-flavored liqueur
3 Golden Delicious or Granny Smith apples, peeled, cored, and cut into ½-inch slices
1 cup all-purpose flour
2 teaspoons baking powder
Pinch of salt
2 large eggs, lightly beaten
1 cup milk
3 tablespoons unsalted butter, melted
1 teaspoon pure vanilla extract
Sweetened whipped cream or vanilla ice cream (optional)

1. Preheat the oven to 375°F, and grease a 9 x 13-inch baking pan. Rinse orange, grate off 1 tablespoon zest, and squeeze out juice, straining out seeds. Set aside.

2. Combine fresh cranberries, dried cranberries, ½ cup granulated sugar, cranberry juice, liqueur, orange juice, and orange zest in a 2-quart saucepan. Bring to a boil over medium-high heat, reduce heat to medium, and cook, stirring occasionally, for 10 minutes, or until cranberries pop. Add apples, and cook, stirring occasionally, for an additional 10 minutes, or until apples begin to soften.

3. Combine flour, baking powder, and salt in a large mixing bowl, then add remaining 1 cup sugar, eggs, milk, butter, and vanilla. Whisk until well blended.

4. Pour apple mixture into the prepared baking pan, and scrape batter evenly over the top. Bake for 35–40 minutes, or until golden. Serve hot or at room temperature with sweetened whipped cream or ice cream on top, if using.

Note: The fruit mixture can be prepared up to 2 days in advance and refrigerated, tightly covered. Reheat it to a simmer, covered, over low heat, stirring occasionally.

Each serving contains:

398 calories | 57 calories from fat | 6 g fat | 3 g saturated fat | 66 mg cholesterol | 5 g protein | 81 g carbohydrates | 135 mg sodium

> There has been a glut of cranberries on the market for several years, but they're usually only available in season and few manufacturers sell them frozen. They're easy to freeze yourself, though. In fact, just toss the bags you find around the holidays right into the freezer. You can rinse them after they're thawed.

Banana Cake

This cake really delivers a banana flavor, and it's flecked with dots of brightly colored and brightly flavored dried apricot. It's also very moist, so no frosting is needed.

Yield: 8 servings | **Active time:** 10 minutes | **Start to finish:** 55 minutes

1¼ cups mashed very ripe bananas (about 3 bananas)
¾ cup firmly packed light brown sugar
¼ pound (1 stick) unsalted butter, melted
3 tablespoons whole milk
1 large egg, at room temperature
1½ teaspoons baking powder
½ teaspoon ground cinnamon
½ teaspoon salt
1½ cups all-purpose flour
¾ cup chopped dried apricots

1. Preheat the oven to 350°F. Grease and flour an 8 x 8-inch square cake pan.

2. Combine bananas, brown sugar, butter, milk, and egg in a mixing bowl, and whisk vigorously until smooth. Whisk in baking powder, cinnamon, and salt, and then briefly whisk in flour. Stir in dried apricots, scrape batter into the prepared pan, and smooth top with a rubber spatula.

3. Bake cake in the center of the oven for 25–30 minutes, or until a toothpick inserted into the center comes out clean. Cool cake in the pan on a rack for 15 minutes. Cut into 8 portions, and serve warm or at room temperature.

Note: The cake can be made up to 2 days in advance and kept at room temperature, lightly covered with plastic wrap.

Each serving contains:

348 calories | 115 calories from fat | 13 g fat | 8 g saturated fat | 57.5 mg cholesterol | 4 g protein | 57 g carbohydrates | 214.5 mg sodium

Variation:

- Substitute chopped walnuts or pecans, toasted in a 350°F oven for 5–7 minutes or until brown, for the dried apricots.

Never throw out a banana because it's black; that's when it has great flavor for baking. You don't have to take the time to mash it; just put it in the freezer right in the peel.

Pear and Gingerbread Upside-Down Cake

This variation of the theme of a cake with fruit on the bottom baked in a skillet is wonderful for fall and winter, when pears are in season and reasonably priced.

Yield: 8 servings | **Active time:** 20 minutes | **Start to finish:** 1½ hours

3 ripe pears
¾ cup (1½ sticks) unsalted butter, softened, divided
1¼ cups firmly packed light brown sugar, divided
2½ cups all-purpose flour
1½ teaspoons baking soda
1 teaspoon ground cinnamon
1 teaspoon ground ginger
¼ teaspoon ground cloves
¼ teaspoon salt
1 cup molasses
1 cup boiling water
1 large egg, lightly beaten
Vanilla ice cream (optional)

1. Preheat the oven to 350°F. Peel and core pears, and cut each into 8 wedges. Melt ¼ cup (½ stick) butter in a 10-inch cast-iron or other ovenproof skillet over medium heat. Reduce heat to low, and sprinkle ¾ cup brown sugar evenly over butter; then cook, without stirring, for 3 minutes. Not all of the sugar will dissolve. Remove the skillet from the heat and arrange pear slices close together on top of brown sugar.

2. Whisk together flour, baking soda, cinnamon, ginger, cloves, and salt in a mixing bowl. Whisk together molasses and boiling water in a small bowl. Combine remaining ½ cup (1 stick) butter, remaining ½ cup brown sugar, and egg in a large bowl. Beat with an electric mixer on medium speed for 2 minutes or until light and fluffy.

3. Reduce mixer speed to low, and add flour mixture in 3 batches, alternating with molasses mixture, beginning and ending with flour mixture. Beat until just combined. Gently spoon batter over pears, and spread evenly.

4. Bake cake for 40–45 minutes, or until golden brown and a cake tester inserted in the center comes out clean. Run a thin knife around the edge of the skillet. Wearing oven mitts, immediately invert a serving plate over the skillet and, holding the skillet and plate together firmly, invert them. Carefully lift off the skillet. If necessary, replace any fruit that might have stuck to the bottom of the skillet on top of the cake. Cool at least 15 minutes or to room temperature before serving, and serve with vanilla ice cream (if using).

Note: The cake can be baked up to 8 hours in advance and kept at room temperature.

Each serving contains:

579 calories | 155 calories from fat | 17 g fat | 10.5 g saturated fat | 69 mg cholesterol | 5 g protein | 104 g carbohydrates | 419 mg sodium

> Like bananas, pears ripen better off the tree than they do on it. If you're in a hurry to ripen pears, place them in a plastic bag with a few apples. The apples let off a natural gas that hastens ripening.

Pineapple Upside-Down Cake

The only state in the country that grows pineapples is Hawaii, and people all over the nation have thanked those growers for decades when making this classic American dessert.

Yield: 8 servings | **Active time:** 25 minutes | **Start to finish:** 1¼ hours

> ½ medium ripe pineapple, peeled, cored, and halved lengthwise
> ¾ cup (1½ sticks) unsalted butter, softened, divided
> ¾ cup firmly packed light brown sugar
> 6–12 maraschino cherry halves (optional)
> 1 ½ cups all-purpose flour
> 2 teaspoons baking powder
> ½ teaspoon ground cinnamon
> ¼ teaspoon salt
> 1 cup granulated sugar
> 2 large eggs
> 2 tablespoons whole milk
> 1 teaspoon pure vanilla extract
> ⅓ cup unsweetened pineapple juice
> 2 tablespoons rum

1. Preheat the oven to 350°F.
2. Cut pineapple into ½-inch slices. Melt 6 tablespoons butter in a 10-inch ovenproof skillet over medium-high heat. Add brown sugar, and cook for 2 minutes, stirring constantly. Arrange pineapple over sugar, overlapping slices slightly, and place cherry halves around them, if using. Set aside.
3. Combine flour, baking powder, cinnamon, and salt, and set aside. Combine remaining 6 tablespoons butter and granulated sugar in a mixing bowl and beat at medium speed with an electric mixer until light and fluffy. Beat in eggs, 1 at a time, beating well between each addition. Beat in milk and vanilla. Add ½ of the flour mixture at low speed until just blended. Add pineapple juice and rum, then second ½ of the flour mixture. Spoon batter over pineapple in skillet.
4. Bake cake for 45 minutes, or until a knife inserted in the center comes out clean. Remove cake from the oven, and place it on a cooling rack for 5 minutes. Invert a plate over the skillet, and then invert cake onto the plate; replace any pineapple from the pan that stuck. Serve warm or at room temperature.

Note: The cake can be made up to 1 day in advance and kept at room temperature, lightly covered.

Each serving contains:

465 calories | 170 calories from fat | 19 g fat | 11 g saturated fat | 99 mg cholesterol | 4.5 g protein | 69 g carbohydrates | 166 mg sodium

Variations:
- Substitute 4 ripe peaches, peeled, stoned, and sliced, for the pineapple, and substitute peach nectar for the pineapple juice.
- Substitute 1 pound fresh apricots, stoned and halved, for the pineapple, and substitute apricot nectar for the pineapple juice.

If you do not own an ovenproof skillet, cover the plastic handle of a skillet with a double layer of heavy-duty aluminum foil to protect it from melting in the oven.

Marian Burros' Plum Torte

Marian Burros is an old friend of mine who was a food writer for the *New York Times,* and to me it would not be fall if I didn't make her classic plum torte, one of the easiest and most delicious ways to enjoy this succulent fruit. A bonus is that since the torte freezes so well, you can relive the very short purple plum season during the cold days of winter.

Yield: 8 servings | **Active time:** 15 minutes | **Start to finish:** 1½ hours

> 12 purple Italian "prune" plums
> 1 cup granulated sugar, divided
> ¼ pound (1 stick) unsalted butter, softened
> 2 large eggs
> 1 teaspoon baking powder
> ¼ teaspoon salt
> 1 cup all-purpose flour
> 2 teaspoons lemon juice
> ¼–1 teaspoon ground cinnamon

1. Preheat the oven to 350°F. Grease and flour a 9-inch springform pan. Rinse plums, cut them in half, and discard stones. Set aside.
2. Reserve 2 tablespoons sugar. Combine remaining sugar and butter in a mixing bowl, and beat at medium speed with an electric mixer until combined. Increase the speed to high, and beat until light and fluffy. Beat in eggs, 1 at a time, beating well between each addition. Beat in baking powder and salt, and then mix in flour until just combined.
3. Spoon batter into the prepared pan, and arrange plum halves skin side up on top of batter. Sprinkle plums with lemon juice. Combine reserved sugar and cinnamon in a small cup, and sprinkle on top of plums.
4. Bake cake for 1 hour, and cool on a rack for 10 minutes. Remove sides of the springform pan, and cool for an additional 10 minutes.

Note: The cake can be made up to 1 day in advance and kept at room temperature, covered with plastic wrap. It can also be frozen for up to 3 months. Allow it to thaw at room temperature, and then reheat it, covered with foil, in a 300°F oven for 20 minutes, or until warm.

Each serving contains:

294 calories | 120 calories from fat | 13 g fat | 8 g saturated fat | 83 mg cholesterol | 3.5 g protein | 42 g carbohydrates | 125 mg sodium

Variations:
- Substitute 3 large red plums for the Italian plums; cut them into eighths, and arrange them skin side up on the batter.
- Substitute 6 ripe apricots, cut into quarters, for the Italian plums.

> Flour is always added to a batter last and is only beaten briefly, to keep the cake tender. Flour contains a protein, gluten, that becomes tough if it's overworked. That's why bread dough is kneaded for a long time, so the gluten will allow the yeast to expand, but cakes are mixed for a short period of time.

Biscuit-Topped Plum Cobbler

Plums are an underutilized fruit for desserts, and they are one of the succulent and juicy fruits that are available at a reasonable price for a good part of the year. For this cobbler they're topped with light and flaky biscuits.

Yield: 6 servings | **Active time:** 20 minutes | **Start to finish:** 1½ hours

FILLING

8 ripe plums, rinsed, stoned, and cut into ½-inch slices
½ cup granulated sugar
2 tablespoons cornstarch
1 teaspoon pure vanilla extract

BISCUITS

2 cups all-purpose flour
5 tablespoons granulated sugar, divided
1 tablespoon baking powder
½ teaspoon salt
½ teaspoon ground cinnamon, divided
¼ pound (1 stick) chilled unsalted butter, cut into ½-inch cubes
¾ cup plus 2 tablespoons heavy cream
1 large egg
Vanilla ice cream (optional)

1. Preheat the oven to 400°F, and grease a 9 x 13-inch baking pan.
2. Toss plums, sugar, cornstarch, and vanilla in a large bowl to coat. Transfer mixture to the prepared pan, and bake for 30 minutes, or until thick and bubbling at edges.
3. While plums bake, prepare biscuits. Combine flour, 3 tablespoons sugar, baking powder, salt, and ¼ teaspoon cinnamon in large bowl to blend. Add butter; rub in with fingertips until coarse meal forms. Whisk ¾ cup heavy cream and egg in a small bowl to blend. Stir cream mixture into flour mixture just until blended. Gently knead in bowl until dough comes together, about 5 turns.

4. Remove plums from the oven, and stir gently. Break off golf-ball-size pieces of dough and pat into patties ¾ inch thick. Arrange biscuits over hot plums. Brush dough with remaining 2 tablespoons cream. Mix remaining 2 tablespoons sugar and ¼ teaspoon cinnamon in small bowl, and sprinkle mixture over dough.
5. Bake cobbler for 30 minutes, or until fruit is bubbling, biscuits are browned, and a cake tester or toothpick inserted into the center of biscuits comes out clean. Serve hot or warm with vanilla ice cream, if using.

Each serving contains:

581 calories | 268 calories from fat | 30 g fat | 18 g saturated fat | 124 mg cholesterol | 7 g protein | 73.5 g carbohydrates | 352 mg sodium

Coconut Rum Cake

I'm always in favor of a one-bowl recipe, and this fits the definition. No creaming of butter and sugar, no folding anything. Just whisk it together and you're done. And the result is a moist and rich cake with great coconut flavor, all topped with cream cheese frosting.

Yield: 8 servings | **Active time:** 20 minutes | **Start to finish:** 3½ hours, including 2 hours for cake to cool

> 1½ cups sweetened coconut flakes
> 1¼ cups all-purpose flour
> 1½ teaspoons baking powder
> ¼ teaspoon salt
> 4 large eggs plus 3 large yolks
> 1½ cups granulated sugar
> 1½ teaspoons pure vanilla extract, divided
> ¾ cup (1½ sticks) unsalted butter, melted and cooled
> ½ cup well-stirred sweetened cream of coconut such as Coco López
> ½ cup dark rum
> 1 (8-ounce) package cream cheese, softened
> 3 cups confectioners' sugar
> 1 teaspoon grated lemon zest

1. Preheat the oven to 375°F with the rack in middle. Lightly grease a 9-inch round layer pan, and line the bottom with a round of parchment paper. Lightly grease the parchment paper, and then flour the inside of the pan, tapping out excess flour over the sink.

2. Bake coconut flakes on a baking sheet for 5–7 minutes, or until browned. Remove coconut from the oven, and set aside. Reduce the oven temperature to 350°F.

3. Whisk together flour, baking powder, and salt in a small bowl. Whisk together eggs, egg yolks, sugar, and 1 teaspoon vanilla in a large bowl, beating until mixture is thick and lemon-colored. Add ½ cup toasted coconut, flour mixture, and butter, and whisk until just combined. Pour batter into the prepared pan, and rap the pan on the counter to expel air bubbles.

4. Bake for 45 minutes, or until golden brown and cake starts to pull away from the side of the pan. Cool in the pan on a rack for 10 minutes. Invert cake onto the rack and discard parchment. Cool 10 minutes more.

5. Combine cream of coconut and rum in a small bowl, and stir well. Remove 3 tablespoons of mixture, and set aside. Using a meat fork, poke holes in the bottom of cake, and brush coconut rum mixture on the bottom. Allow it to soak in, and repeat. Turn cake over on the rack, and slice off the top so it is level. Spread remaining coconut rum mixture on top, and allow it to soak in. Allow cake to cool completely.

6. For icing, combine cream cheese, confectioners' sugar, remaining ½ teaspoon vanilla, lemon zest, and reserved coconut rum mixture in a food processor fitted with the steel blade. Process until smooth, and scrape into a bowl. Apply frosting to cake, and pat remaining 1 cup toasted coconut on the top.

Note: The cake can be baked and soaked with the coconut rum mixture up to 2 days in advance and kept at room temperature, tightly covered with plastic wrap. The cake can be frosted up to 1 day in advance and kept at room temperature, lightly covered.

Each serving contains:

807 calories | 309 calories from fat | 34 g fat | 21.5 g saturated fat | 264 mg cholesterol | 9 g protein | 109 g carbohydrates | 335 mg sodium

Ginger Cake

I like this cake far more than a classic gingerbread. It pairs the spicy flavor of ground ginger with the perky flavor of crystallized ginger. The cream cheese frosting is the perfect creamy accent.

Yield: 12 servings | **Active time:** 20 minutes | **Start to finish:** 4 hours

2¹/₂ cups all-purpose flour

2 teaspoons ground ginger

1 teaspoon baking soda

¹/₂ teaspoon salt

³/₄ cup (1¹/₂ sticks) unsalted butter, softened

1 cup granulated sugar

1 large egg, lightly beaten

2 tablespoons finely chopped crystallized ginger

¹/₂ cup unsulfured molasses

1 cup buttermilk

10 gingersnap cookies

1 recipe Cream Cheese Frosting (recipe on page 236)

1. Preheat the oven to 350°F. Grease and flour 2 (8-inch) round cake pans.
2. Combine flour, ground ginger, baking soda, and salt, and set aside. Combine butter and sugar in a large mixing bowl, and beat at medium-high speed with an electric mixer until light and fluffy. Add egg, crystallized ginger, and molasses and beat well. Add dry ingredients and buttermilk alternately, and beat at low speed until smooth.
3. Divide batter between the prepared pans and bake for 30–35 minutes, or until a cake tester or toothpick inserted in center of each layer comes out clean. Immediately invert the cake layers onto cooling racks and cool completely.
4. Break the gingersnap cookies into pieces, and finely chop them in a food processor fitted with the steel blade, using on-and-off pulsing. Alternately, place pieces in a heavy resealable plastic bag, and crush with the bottom of a heavy skillet.

5. To assemble cake, place overlapping sheets of wax paper on a cake plate. Split cake layers horizontally into 2 halves. Place 1 layer, top side down, on the paper and spread with ⅓ cup frosting. Place second layer on top of it and spread with ⅓ cup frosting. Top with remaining 2 layers with frosting in between them. Spread remaining frosting on top and sides of cake, and sprinkle cookie crumbs on top. Chill cake for at least 2 hours, or until the frosting has set.

Note: The cake can be made up to 1 day in advance and refrigerated, loosely covered with plastic wrap. Allow it to sit out for at least 2 hours before serving.

Each serving (including frosting) contains:

668 calories | 250 calories from fat | 28 g fat | 17 g saturated fat | 102 mg cholesterol | 7 g protein | 97.5 g carbohydrates | 424 mg sodium

> If you're in a hurry to begin a batter, you can grate the butter through the large holes of a box grater. But do not soften butter in a microwave oven. It will become too soft.

Flourless Chocolate Nut Torte

The batter for this luscious chocolate cake is created in a matter of minutes in a food processor. It's a dense and rich cake that is crunchy with nuts and topped with a candy-like ganache.

Yield: 8 servings | **Active time:** 15 minutes | **Start to finish:** 2¼ hours, including 1 hour for chilling

> 10 ounces bittersweet chocolate, chopped, divided
> 2 cups pecan or walnut halves, toasted in a 350°F oven for 5 minutes, divided
> 2 tablespoons plus ½ cup granulated sugar
> 1 cup (2 sticks) unsalted butter, softened, divided
> 3 large eggs, at room temperature
> 1 tablespoon rum

1. Preheat the oven to 375°F. Grease an 8-inch round cake pan, cut out a circle of waxed paper or parchment to fit the bottom, and grease the paper.

2. Melt 4 ounces chocolate in a microwave oven or over simmering water in a double boiler. Cool slightly. Reserve 12 nut halves and chop the remaining nuts with 2 tablespoons sugar in a food processor fitted with the steel blade, using on-and-off pulsing. Scrape nuts into a bowl. Beat ½ cup (1 stick) of butter and remaining ½ cup sugar in the food processor until light and fluffy. Add melted chocolate, then add eggs, 1 at a time, beating well between each addition, and scrape the sides of the work bowl with a rubber spatula. Add rum, then fold chocolate mixture into ground nuts.

3. Scrape batter into the prepared pan and bake for 25 minutes. The cake will be soft but will firm up as it cools. Remove cake from the oven and cool 20 minutes on a rack. Invert cake onto a plate, remove the paper, and cool completely.

4. To make glaze, combine remaining 6 ounces chocolate and remaining ½ cup (1 stick) butter in a small saucepan. Melt over low heat and beat until shiny and smooth. Place cake on a rack over a sheet of waxed paper. Pour the glaze onto the center of the cake, and rotate the rack at an angle so glaze runs down sides of the cake. Top with the nut halves, and allow to sit in a cool place until chocolate hardens.

Note: The cake can be prepared 1 day in advance and refrigerated. Allow it to reach room temperature before serving.

Each serving contains:

663 calories | 525 calories from fat | 58 g fat | 25 g saturated fat | 141 mg cholesterol | 7 g protein | 39 g carbohydrates | 30 mg sodium

Variations:
- Add 1 tablespoon instant espresso powder to the batter.
- Substitute Triple Sec or Grand Marnier for the rum, and add 2 teaspoons grated orange zest to the batter.
- Substitute blanched almonds for the pecans or walnuts, substitute amaretto for the rum, and add ½ teaspoon pure almond extract to the batter.

Chocolate has been found to contain catechins—some of the same antioxidants found in green tea. The catechins attack free radicals, which damage cells and are thought to lead to cancer and heart disease. So eating chocolate may help to prevent heart disease and cancer!

Oatmeal Cranberry Cookies

I know few people who do not adore homey, aromatic oatmeal cookies, and replacing raisins with tangy, colorful dried cranberries gives the cookies a New England touch.

Yield: 24 cookies | **Active time:** 15 minutes | **Start to finish:** 30 minutes

1 cup all-purpose flour
1 teaspoon ground cinnamon
½ teaspoon baking soda
Pinch of salt
6 tablespoons (¾ stick) unsalted butter, softened
½ cup granulated sugar
½ cup firmly packed dark brown sugar
2 large eggs, at room temperature
1 teaspoon pure vanilla extract
1¼ cups quick-cooking or old-fashioned oats (not instant)
1 cup dried cranberries
1 cup chopped walnuts, toasted in a 350°F oven for 5 minutes

1. Preheat the oven to 375°F, and grease 2 baking sheets.
2. Sift together flour, cinnamon, baking soda, and salt. Place butter, granulated sugar, and brown sugar in a large mixing bowl. Beat with an electric mixer on low speed to combine, then raise the speed to high and beat for 2 minutes, or until light and fluffy. Add eggs and vanilla and beat for 2 minutes more. Reduce the speed to low and add flour mixture until just blended. Stir in oats, cranberries, and walnuts.
3. Drop batter by rounded tablespoons onto the baking sheets, spacing them 2 inches apart. Bake for 12 minutes for chewy cookies and 15 minutes for crisp cookies. Move the cookies with a spatula to a cooling rack and cool completely.

Note: The cookies can be stored refrigerated for up to 1 week, tightly covered.

Each 1-cookie serving contains:

148 calories | 62 calories from fat | 7 g fat | 2 g saturated fat | 25 mg cholesterol | 2 g protein | 20 g carbohydrates | 34 mg sodium

Variation:

- Substitute chopped dried apricots or raisins for the dried cran-berries.

Brown sugar is granulated sugar mixed with molasses, and the darker the color, the more pronounced the molasses flavor. If a recipe calls for dark brown sugar, and you only have light brown sugar, add 2 tablespoons molasses per ½ cup sugar to replicate the taste.

Carrot Cookie Sandwiches

These cookies are a hand-holdable version of classic carrot cake, complete with cream cheese frosting creating the sandwiches.

Yield: 12 cookies | **Active time:** 15 minutes | **Start to finish:** 45 minutes, including 20 minutes for cooling

    1¼ cups all-purpose flour
    ½ teaspoon ground cinnamon
    ½ teaspoon ground ginger
    ½ teaspoon baking soda
    ¼ teaspoon salt
    10 tablespoons unsalted butter, divided
    ½ cup firmly packed light brown sugar
    ½ cup granulated sugar
    1 large egg, at room temperature
    ¾ teaspoon pure vanilla extract, divided
    1 cup firmly packed grated carrot
    ¼ cup sweetened coconut
    ¼ cup finely chopped fresh pineapple
    ¼ cup raisins
    ½ cup chopped walnuts, toasted in a 350°F oven for 5 minutes
    1 (3-ounce) package cream cheese, softened
    1 cup confectioners' sugar

1. Preheat the oven to 375°F, and grease 2 baking sheets.
2. Sift together flour, cinnamon, ginger, baking soda, and salt. Place 8 tablespoons butter, brown sugar, and granulated sugar in a large mixing bowl. Beat with an electric mixer on low speed to combine, then raise the speed to high and beat for 2 minutes, or until light and fluffy. Add egg and ½ teaspoon vanilla and beat for 2 minutes more. Reduce the speed to low and add flour mixture until just blended. Stir in carrot, coconut, pineapple, raisins, and walnuts.
3. Drop batter by rounded tablespoon measures onto the prepared baking sheets, spacing them 2 inches apart; you should have 24 cookies. Bake for 12–14 minutes, or until lightly browned. Cool cookies for 1 minute, then transfer cookies with a spatula to a cooling rack and cool completely.

4. While cookies cool, combine cream cheese, confectioners' sugar, remaining 2 tablespoons butter, and remaining ¼ teaspoon vanilla in a food processor fitted with the steel blade. Blend until smooth, and scrape mixture into a mixing bowl.
5. Create cookie sandwiches by spreading frosting on the flat side of 1 cookie and then topping with the flat side of a second cookie. Store at room temperature, tightly covered with plastic wrap.

Note: The cookies can be baked up to 2 days in advance and kept at room temperature, tightly covered. They can be filled up to 8 hours in advance.

Each 1-cookie-sandwich serving contains:

322 calories | 143 calories from fat | 16 g fat | 8 g saturated fat | 51 mg cholesterol | 3 g protein | 43 g carbohydrates | 150 mg sodium

Granola Cookies

All the healthy components of trail mix plus oatmeal make these almost guilt-free goodies to feed to children. They're also quick to make, which is an added bonus.

Yield: 36 cookies | **Active time:** 15 minutes | **Start to finish:** 30 minutes

> 1 cup (2 sticks) unsalted butter, softened
> 1 cup firmly packed light brown sugar
> $^3/_4$ cup granulated sugar
> 2 large eggs
> 1 teaspoon pure vanilla extract
> $^3/_4$ cup all-purpose flour
> $^1/_2$ cup whole wheat flour
> 1 teaspoon baking soda
> $^1/_2$ teaspoon baking powder
> $^1/_2$ teaspoon ground cinnamon
> $^1/_4$ teaspoon salt
> 2 cups old-fashioned oats
> $^1/_2$ cup unsweetened flaked coconut
> 2 cups trail mix, coarsely chopped

1. Preheat the oven to 350°F, and grease 2 baking sheets.
2. Combine butter, brown sugar, and granulated sugar in a mixing bowl, and beat at low speed with an electric mixer until combined. Increase the speed to medium-high, and beat until light and fluffy. Beat in eggs and vanilla. Beat in all-purpose flour, whole wheat flour, baking soda, baking powder, cinnamon, and salt at low speed. Stir in oats, coconut, and trail mix by hand.
3. Drop dough by heaping tablespoons onto prepared baking sheets, $1^1/_2$ inches apart. Bake cookies for 12–15 minutes, or until browned. Allow cookies to cool for 3 minutes on baking sheets, then transfer them with a spatula to racks to cool completely.

Note: The cookies can be baked up to 2 days in advance and kept at room temperature in an airtight container.

Each 1-cookie serving contains:

164 calories | 77 calories from fat | 8.5 g fat | 4 g saturated fat | 25 mg cholesterol | 3 g protein | 21 g carbohydrates | 83 mg sodium

Marble Fudge Brownies

I adore the combination of chocolate and cream cheese, and these brownies deliver both.

Yield: 12 brownies | **Active time:** 15 minutes | **Start to finish:** 1 hour

$\frac{1}{2}$ cup (1 stick) unsalted butter

4 ounces semisweet chocolate, chopped

3 large eggs, at room temperature, divided

1 cup granulated sugar, divided

$\frac{1}{2}$ cup all-purpose flour

Pinch of salt

1 (8-ounce) package cream cheese, softened

$\frac{1}{2}$ teaspoon pure vanilla extract

1. Preheat the oven to 350°F. Grease and flour a 9 x 9-inch square cake pan.
2. Melt butter and chocolate over low heat or in a microwave oven. Stir to combine, and set aside to cool for 5 minutes.
3. Combine 2 eggs and $\frac{3}{4}$ cup sugar in mixing bowl. Beat with an electric mixer on medium speed for 1 minute, or until well combined. Add cooled chocolate mixture, and beat for 1 minute. Add flour and salt and beat at low speed until just blended.
4. In another bowl, combine cream cheese, remaining $\frac{1}{4}$ cup sugar, remaining 1 egg, and vanilla. Beat with an electric mixer on medium speed for 2 minutes, or until light and fluffy. Spread chocolate batter into the prepared pan. Top with cream cheese batter and swirl layers together with a fork.
5. Bake for 35 minutes, or until the top is springy to the touch. Cool the brownies on a cooling rack, and then cut into 12 pieces.

Note: The brownies can be made up to 3 days in advance and kept at room temperature, tightly covered with plastic wrap.

Each 1-brownie serving contains:

276 calories | 156 calories from fat | 17 g fat | 11 g saturated fat | 95 mg cholesterol | 4 g protein | 27.5 g carbohydrates | 93 mg sodium

Variation:

- Add 1 tablespoon instant espresso powder to the batter.

Lemon Squares

I've been making these bars with a crisp cookie crust and creamy lemon topping since I was a child, and they remain at the top of my list. This is also a great last-minute recipe since most of us have a lemon or two in the house, along with basic baking ingredients.

Yield: 12 bars | **Active time:** 15 minutes | **Start to finish:** 1¼ hours

> 1 lemon
> ¼ cup bottled lemon juice, or as needed
> ½ cup (1 stick) unsalted butter, melted
> ¼ cup confectioners' sugar
> 1 cup plus 2 tablespoons all-purpose flour
> Pinch of salt
> 2 large eggs
> 1 cup granulated sugar

1. Preheat the oven to 350°F. Grate zest from lemon, and squeeze juice from fruit. Add enough bottled lemon juice to make ⅓ cup. Set aside.
2. Combine butter, confectioners' sugar, 1 cup flour, and salt in a mixing bowl, and mix thoroughly with a wooden spoon. Press mixture into an 8-inch square pan. Bake for 20 minutes, or until set and lightly brown. Remove crust from the oven, and set aside.
3. Combine eggs, granulated sugar, remaining 2 tablespoons flour, lemon juice, and lemon zest in a mixing bowl. Beat with an electric mixer on medium speed for 1 minute, or until well blended. Pour topping over crust and bake for 20 minutes, or until barely brown. The custard should still be soft. Cool the pan on a cooling rack, then cut into 12 pieces.

Note: The bars can be refrigerated for up to 1 week, tightly covered.

Each 1-bar serving contains:

200 calories | 78 calories from fat | 9 g fat | 5 g saturated fat | 56 mg cholesterol | 2.5 g protein | 30 g carbohydrates | 13 mg sodium

Variation:
- Substitute lime juice and lime zest for the lemon juice and lemon zest.

To get the maximum amount of juice from citrus fruits, roll them back and forth on a counter before squeezing, or prick the skin and microwave them on High power for 30 seconds.

Cream Cheese Frosting

I put cream cheese frosting on just about everything; it's my favorite, and it's so easy to make.

Yield: 3 cups, enough for a 2-layer cake to serve 12 | **Active time:** 10 minutes | **Start to finish:** 10 minutes

> 4 cups (1 pound) confectioners' sugar
> 2 (8-ounce) packages cream cheese, softened
> 4 tablespoons (1/2 stick) unsalted butter, softened
> 1 1/2 teaspoons pure vanilla extract

Combine confectioners' sugar, cream cheese, butter, and vanilla in a mixing bowl. Beat at low speed with an electric mixer until blended. Increase the speed to medium-high, and beat for 2 minutes, or until light and fluffy.

Note: The frosting can be prepared up to 2 days in advance and refrigerated, tightly covered. Allow it to reach room temperature and soften before using.

Each 1/4-cup serving contains:

313 calories | 134 calories from fat | 15 g fat | 10 g saturated fat | 53 mg cholesterol | 2.5 g protein | 41 g carbohydrates | 147 mg sodium

Variations:
- Decrease the amount of vanilla to 1/2 teaspoon and add 1 teaspoon almond extract.
- Decrease the amount of vanilla to 1/2 teaspoon, and add 3/4 teaspoon ground cinnamon.
- Decrease the amount of vanilla to 1/2 teaspoon and add 2 tablespoons frozen lemonade concentrate or orange juice concentrate, and 2 teaspoons grated lemon zest or orange zest.

Chapter 10:
Putting It All Together

Savvy menu planning is the first step to great cooking. It can be as simple as the choice between oatmeal or eggs for breakfast, and if the selection is eggs, how should they be prepared and what should accompany them. All menu plans are based on three interrelated factors: time; money; and ingredient availability, both in the home and in the supermarket.

In cooking, as in art, there are decisions that must be made taking color, texture, and form into account; in cooking, complementary flavors are added into the equation.

In every meal there is a "star," and the most important decision in menu planning is the selection of the stars; this is true for a multi-course meal as well as for a one-course family dinner that will include different foods on the same plate. The principle is that there is only one star on a plate, and the other foods are selected to glorify that star with complementary flavors and contrasting colors and textures.

Most entree plates contain some variety of protein, carbohydrate, and vegetable to achieve the time-honored concept of the "balanced meal." The vegetable can take the form of a tossed salad served on another plate either before, with, or after the entree; and the carbohydrate is traditionally potatoes, rice, grains, or pasta.

The choice has to be made as to which dish will be the most complex in terms of flavor and preparation—that's the starring dish—and then build the meal around it.

The star need not be the protein. If the protein is a simple grilled chicken or pork chop, then the star can be an elaborate potato gratin nestled next to stir-fried broccoli. If the star, however, is a complex casserole, then the carbohydrate should change to oven-roasted potatoes, since the sauce has elevated the protein to starring status.

Once the star has been chosen, then its color and texture determine those of the supporting players. Spicy should be balanced by mild, dark tones should be complemented by light, and soft should be contrasted with crunchy.

For a multi-course meal, the equation becomes extended to include not only the star of the entree, but which courses become stars for the meal. Some must be prominent, and others become subservient; it is the equivalent of the background and foreground of a painting. The background creates a depth of field and context for the elements placed in front of it.

An elaborate soup should be followed by a less complex entree, leading to a show-stopper dessert. Conversely, if the entree is the focus of the meal, then the starter should be a simple soup or salad. There should be rhythm to the progression of courses rather than keeping them in a straight line of complexity, even if the line is high and full of delicious flavors and complex recipes.

Choice of flavors in a multi-course meal becomes joined with complementary concepts. The courses should be balanced in terms of color, flavor, and texture in the same way that the entree plate is balanced. But additional factors are the spirit of the meal, from which cuisine or cuisines it is drawn, and the elegance of the table setting and occasion.

SUGGESTED MENUS

While compiling a menu becomes second nature when you know the dishes, knowing what foods are complementary is more difficult when you have a new cookbook in front of you. That's why I've selected some menus for you. You'll notice that desserts aren't part of the menus, and that's because I feel for these casual meals you can break away from the theme when it comes to a sweet ending.

A Picnic from Provence

Bean Bruschetta Provençale (recipe on page 50)

Tapenade (recipe on page 53)

French Pressed Tuna Sandwich (Pan Bagnat) (recipe on page 89)

Deviled Chicken (recipe on page 92)

Garlicky Potato Salad (recipe on page 142)

Garbanzo Bean Salad Provençale (recipe on page 148)

An Asian Picnic

Grilled Sesame Eggplant Finger Sushi (recipe on page 40)

Red Onion Pickles (recipe on page 133)

Thai Fish Salad (recipe on page 90)

Asian-Spiced Chicken Wings with Peanut Coconut Sauce (recipe on page 98)

Asian Beef Salad (recipe on page 112)

Jasmine Rice Salad (recipe on page 144)

A New American Picnic

Vegetarian California Rolls (recipe on page 41)

BLT Rolls (recipe on page 46)

Chilled Garlicky Cream of Tomato Soup (recipe on page 78)

Cobb Salad Wraps (recipe on page 76)

Jambalaya Salad (recipe on page 104)

Grilled Corn and Sausage Salad (recipe on page 118)

An Old-Fashioned American Picnic

Deviled Eggs (recipe on page 60)

Picnic Brisket with Herbed Mustard Sauce (recipe on page 110)

Buffalo Chicken Wraps (recipe on page 74)

Ham and Egg Salad Bread Roll (recipe on page 121)

Celery Seed Slaw (recipe on page 130)

Janet's Potato Salad (recipe on page 138)

A Southwestern Picnic
Southwestern Bruschetta (recipe on page 51)

Guacamole (recipe on page 57)

Gazpacho Salad (recipe on page 126)

Tortilla-Crusted Chicken (recipe on page 94)

Southwestern Chicken Wraps (recipe on page 72)

An Italian Picnic
Pollo Tonnato (recipe on page 107)

Italian Chicken and Bread Salad (recipe on page 106)

Caponata (recipe on page 124)

Gemelli with White Beans, Tomatoes, and Sage (recipe on page 149)

A Mediterranean Picnic
Gazpacho (recipe on page 79)

Moroccan Chicken Salad (recipe on page 108)

Tabbouleh (recipe on page 150)

Spanish Potato and Sausage Tortilla (recipe on page 120)

A Casual Asian Cocktail Party
Gingered Carrot Pickles (recipe on page 136)

Spicy Chinese Eggplant Dip (recipe on page 54)

Fish Satay with Thai Peanut Sauce (recipe on page 192)

Baked Fish Toast Rolls (recipe on page 194)

Chicken Teriyaki Rolls (recipe on page 44)

Vietnamese Spring Rolls (recipe on page 198)

An Elegant Holiday Cocktail Party

Miniature Cheese Puffs (recipe on page 180)

Curried Tomato Bruschetta (recipe on page 49)

Onion Pizza Niçoise (Pissaladière) (recipe on page 186)

Sauerkraut Balls with Mustard Sauce (recipe on page 190)

Dilled Swedish Meatballs (recipe on page 200)

An All-American Potluck Dinner

Cheddar Crackers (recipe on page 182)

Corn Fritters (recipe on page 188)

Chicken and Sausage Jambalaya (recipe on page 162)

Mac' and Cheese with Ham (recipe on page 176)

Baked Beans (recipe on page 146)

Sweet Potato Salad with Mustard Dressing (recipe on page 137)

A Mexican Potluck Dinner

Mexican Beef and Chile Dip (recipe on page 202)

Chicken and Cheese Enchiladas (recipe on page 160)

Tex-Mex Tamale Pie (recipe on page 170)

An Italian Potluck Dinner

Swiss Chard Bruschetta (recipe on page 52)

Minestrone (recipe on page 80)

Italian Pork (recipe on page 178)

Potato and Tomato Gratin (recipe on page 134)

Fennel Salad (recipe on page 123)

Appendix A:
Metric Conversion Tables

The scientifically precise calculations needed for baking are not necessary when cooking conventionally. The tables in this appendix are designed for general cooking. If making conversions for baking, grab your calculator and compute the exact figure.

CONVERTING OUNCES TO GRAMS

The numbers in the following table are approximate. To reach the exact quantity of grams, multiply the number of ounces by 28.35.

Ounces	Grams
1 ounce	30 grams
2 ounces	60 grams
3 ounces	85 grams
4 ounces	115 grams
5 ounces	140 grams
6 ounces	180 grams
7 ounces	200 grams
8 ounces	225 grams
9 ounces	250 grams
10 ounces	285 grams
11 ounces	300 grams
12 ounces	340 grams
13 ounces	370 grams
14 ounces	400 grams
15 ounces	425 grams
16 ounces	450 grams

CONVERTING QUARTS TO LITERS

The numbers in the following table are approximate. To reach the exact amount of liters, multiply the number of quarts by 0.95.

Quarts	Liter
1 cup (¼ quart)	¼ liter
1 pint (½ quart)	½ liter
1 quart	1 liter
2 quarts	2 liters
2½ quarts	2½ liters
3 quarts	2¾ liters
4 quarts	3¾ liters
5 quarts	4¾ liters
6 quarts	5½ liters
7 quarts	6½ liters
8 quarts	7½ liters

CONVERTING POUNDS TO GRAMS AND KILOGRAMS

The numbers in the following table are approximate. To reach the exact quantity of grams, multiply the number of pounds by 453.6.

Pounds	Grams; Kilograms
1 pound	450 grams
1½ pounds	675 grams
2 pounds	900 grams
2½ pounds	1,125 grams; 1¼ kilograms
3 pounds	1,350 grams
3½ pounds	1,500 grams; 1½ kilograms
4 pounds	1,800 grams
4½ pounds	2 kilograms
5 pounds	2¼ kilograms
5½ pounds	2½ kilograms
6 pounds	2¾ kilograms
6½ pounds	3 kilograms
7 pounds	3¼ kilograms
7½ pounds	3½ kilograms
8 pounds	3¾ kilograms

CONVERTING FAHRENHEIT TO CELSIUS

The numbers in the following table are approximate. To reach the exact temperature, subtract 32 from the Fahrenheit reading, multiply the number by 5, and then divide by 9.

Degrees Fahrenheit	Degrees Celsius
170°F	77°C
180°F	82°C
190°F	88°C
200°F	95°C
225°F	110°C
250°F	120°C
300°F	150°C
325°F	165°C
350°F	180°C
375°F	190°C
400°F	205°C
425°F	220°C
450°F	230°C
475°F	245°C
500°F	260°C

CONVERTING INCHES TO CENTIMETERS

The numbers in the following table are approximate. To reach the exact number of centimeters, multiply the number of inches by 2.54.

Inches	Centimeters
½ inch	1.5 centimeters
1 inch	2.5 centimeters
2 inches	5 centimeters
3 inches	8 centimeters
4 inches	10 centimeters
5 inches	13 centimeters
6 inches	15 centimeters
7 inches	18 centimeters
8 inches	20 centimeters
9 inches	23 centimeters
10 inches	25 centimeters
11 inches	28 centimeters
12 inches	30 centimeters

Appendix B:
Table of Weights and Measures of Common Ingredients

Food	Quantity	Yield
Apples	1 pound	2½–3 cups sliced
Avocado	1 pound	1 cup mashed
Bananas	1 medium	1 cup sliced
Bell peppers	1 pound	3–4 cups sliced
Blueberries	1 pound	3⅓ cups
Butter	¼ pound (1 stick)	8 tablespoons
Cabbage	1 pound	4 cups packed shredded
Carrots	1 pound	3 cups diced or sliced
Chocolate, morsels	12 ounces	2 cups
Chocolate, bulk	1 ounce	3 tablespoons grated
Cocoa powder	1 ounce	¼ cup
Coconut, flaked	7 ounces	2½ cups
Cream	½ pint (1 cup)	2 cups whipped
Cream cheese	8 ounces	1 cup
Flour	1 pound	4 cups
Lemons	1 medium	3 tablespoons juice
Lemons	1 medium	2 teaspoons zest
Milk	1 quart	4 cups
Molasses	12 ounces	1½ cups
Mushrooms	1 pound	5 cups sliced
Onions	1 medium	½ cup chopped
Peaches	1 pound	2 cups sliced
Peanuts	5 ounces	1 cup
Pecans	6 ounces	1½ cups
Pineapple	1 medium	3 cups diced
Potatoes	1 pound	3 cups sliced
Raisins	1 pound	3 cups
Rice	1 pound	2 to 2½ cups raw
Spinach	1 pound	¾ cup cooked
Squash, summer	1 pound	3½ cups sliced
Strawberries	1 pint	1½ cups sliced

Food	Quantity	Yield
Sugar, brown	1 pound	2$\frac{1}{4}$ cups, packed
Sugar, confectioners'	1 pound	4 cups
Sugar, granulated	1 pound	2$\frac{1}{4}$ cups
Tomatoes	1 pound	1$\frac{1}{2}$ cups pulp
Walnuts	4 ounces	1 cup

TABLE OF LIQUID MEASUREMENTS

Dash	=	less than $\frac{1}{8}$ teaspoon
3 teaspoons	=	1 tablespoon
2 tablespoons	=	1 ounce
8 tablespoons	=	$\frac{1}{2}$ cup
2 cups	=	1 pint
1 quart	=	2 pints
1 gallon	=	4 quarts

Index

Page references at main subject refer to general discussions on topic.